THE AUTHOR

Hilary Wainwright was born in Leeds in 1949, and educated at the Mount School, York, and St Anne's College, Oxford, where she studied Philosophy, Politics and Economics before doing postgraduate work at St Anthony's College (on the Labour left under the leadership of Nye Bevan). As a research fellow at Durham University, and then at the Open University, her work in association with shop stewards' committees and trades councils led to three books: *The Workers' Report on Vickers* (1978), with Huw Beynon; *State Intervention in Industry: A Worker's Inquiry* (1981), drafted with the Coventry, Liverpool, Newcastle and North Tyneside Trades Councils; and *The Lucas Plan: A New Trade Unionism in the Making?* (1982), with David Elliott.

Hilary Wainwright has been actively involved in the women's movement since the early 1970s and was a co-author, with Sheila Rowbotham and Lynne Segal, of *Beyond the Fragments: Feminism and the Making of Socialism* (1979), one of the most influential feminist and political works of the last decade. In 1982 she helped create the GLC Popular Planning Unit, and her time at the GLC led to a book of essays, *A Taste of Power: The Politics of Local Economics* (1987), edited with Maureen Mackintosh. She is a member of the Socialist Society and now works as a freelance writer and researcher.

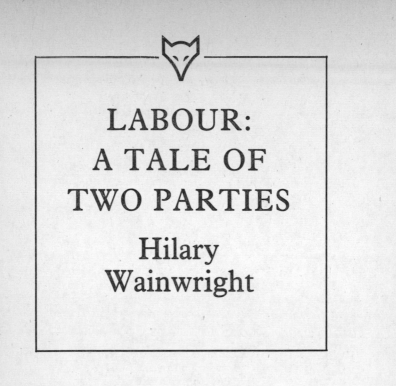

LABOUR:
A TALE OF
TWO PARTIES

Hilary
Wainwright

THE HOGARTH PRESS
LONDON

In memory of Lizzie Hollis:
fun-loving feminist, anti-apartheid campaigner,
miners' support organiser,
and a questioning member
of her local Labour party.

A TIGERSTRIPE BOOK
Published in 1987 by
The Hogarth Press
Chatto & Windus Ltd
30 Bedford Square
London WC1B 3RP

British Library Cataloguing in Publication Data
Wainwright, Hilary
Labour: A Tale of Two Parties
1. Labour Party *(Great Britain)*
I. Title
324.24107   JN1129.L32

ISBN 0 7012 0778 7

Photoset in Linotron Plantin by
Rowland Phototypesetting Ltd
Bury St Edmunds, Suffolk
Printed in Finland by
Werner Söderström Oy

Contents

Abbreviations

ACAS	Advisory, Conciliation and Arbitration Service
ACTT	Association of Cinematograph, Television and Audio Technicians
APEX	Association of Professional, Executive, Clerical and Computer Staff
ASCW	Association of Scientific Workers
ASLEF	Associated Society of Locomotive Engineers and Firemen
ASSET	Association of Supervisory Staffs, Executives and Technicians
ASTMS	Association of Scientific, Technical and Managerial Staffs
AUEW, AEU	Amalgamated Union of Engineering Workers, now the Amalgamated Engineering Union (AEU)
BUPA	British United Provident Association Ltd
CBI	Confederation of British Industry
CLP	Constituency Labour Party
CLPD	Campaign for Labour Party Democracy
CND	Campaign for Nuclear Disarmament
COHSE	Confederation of Health Service Employees
DEC	District Executive Committee
DLP	District Labour Party
EC	Executive Committee
EEC	European Economic Community
EETPU	Electrical, Electronic, Telecommunication and Plumbing Union
GLC	Greater London Council
GLEB	Greater London Enterprise Board

GMC, GC	General Management Committee (of a constituency Labour Party); changed formally to GC in 1980
GMBATU, GMB	General, Municipal, Boilermakers and Allied Trades Union now know as GMB
ICI	Imperial Chemical Industries
ILP	Independent Labour Party
IMF	International Monetary Fund
IMG	International Marxist Group
IS, SWP	International Socialists, now the Socialist Workers Party
IWC	Institute for Workers' Control
LCC	Labour Co-ordinating Committee
LDDC	London Docklands Development Corporation
LRC	Labour Representation Committee
MEP	Member of the European Parliament
MSC	Manpower Services Commission
NALGO	National and Local Government Officers Association
NATO	North Atlantic Treaty Organisation
NCB	National Coal Board
NCU	National Communications Union
NEC	National Executive Committee (of the Labour Party)
NHS	National Health Service
NOP	National Opinion Polls Ltd
NUJ	National Union of Journalists
NUM	National Union of Mineworkers
NUPE	National Union of Public Employees
PLP	Parliamentary Labour Party
PR	Proportional Representation
RVI	Royal Victoria Hospital, Newcastle
SCPS	Society of Civil and Public Servants
SDP	Social Democratic Party
SEAM	Save Easington Mines

SEC	Scottish Executive Committee
SLP	Scottish Labour Party
SNP	Scottish National Party
STUC	Scottish Trades Union Congress
TASS	Technical, Administrative and Supervisory Section (of the AUEW)
TGWU	Transport and General Workers' Union
TUC	Trades Union Congress
UCATT	Union of Construction Allied Trades and Technicians
UCS	Upper Clyde Shipbuilders
UCW	Union of Communication Workers
USDAW	Union of Shop, Distributive and Allied Workers
WAC	Womens' Action Committee

Introduction

Speaking personally

The Labour Party has always seemed to me to be a conservative party.

Labour was in government and Harold Wilson was Prime Minister when I first came to this conclusion. A nonconformist Liberal upbringing probably predisposed me in this direction: by the age of six, I was poking a loud-hailer out of the kitchen window and haranguing the respectable residents of Pudsey in Yorkshire with Liberal slogans: 'Do not vote for the party stooge', 'Do not vote for the slave machine'. By the late sixties, after a brief membership of the Young Liberals, I had come up against more than enough Liberal 'party stooges' and, in the Oxford Union, aspiring stooges, to realise that they were not unique to the 'other parties'. They were bred in large numbers by parliamentary politics itself.

At the same time, a series of different experiences inspired in me a belief in the possibility of more direct and effective forms of democracy than simply Parliament: campaigns in support of the liberation movements in Mozambique, Angola and Guinea, a visit to Yugoslavia, discussions with Czech dissidents and news of the action of students and workers in Paris. In different ways, these and other experiences illustrated forms of democracy through which people could have control over the institutions of daily life: their workplaces, schools and colleges, police and courts, local services and community provision. There was something beyond the Cold War choice of Cabinet versus Politburo.

So, like many thousands of students and young people in the late sixties and early seventies, I became a socialist of a militant and libertarian blend. The Labour Party then seemed to have little connection with our vision of socialism, beyond some rather blurred historical association. The few national Labour Party figures famous for their socialism – Fenner Brockway and (at that time) Michael Foot – seemed to me, from afar, like survivals of a bygone age: individuals beached on a party that was not the one they thought they had joined. To a revolutionary student from a middle-class background lacking a cultural Labour loyalty and unfamiliar with the intricacies of labour movement politics, there were no overt signs of the distinction which became familiar from 1974 to 1979 between the Labour Party and the actions of the Labour government.

Such a distinction anyway meant little to many party members themselves: the party had negligible leverage with the government. Party members dissociated themselves individually – and did so in large numbers – from a government that was supporting the United States' war in Vietnam, its napalm and its massacres, that was racist in its immigration policy, and made seamen striking for a decent wage the scapegoats for the economic crisis while it grovelled before the gnomes of international banking. By 1970, the headline 'Let It Bleed' in the revolutionary paper *Red Mole* seemed entirely appropriate: let the haemorrhaging Labour Party die, for the energy and intensity of the non-parliamentary movements – in the universities, on the streets and in the factories and public services – were bound to create a political force of their own.

This proved to be wishful thinking. Such a prediction grossly overestimated the political strength and independence of the movements. Similarly, it underestimated the continuing depth and complexity of Labour's historic roots, not to speak of capitalism! The industrial and social movements of the 1960s and seventies did breathe some new life into the Communist Party and even more into the various revolutionary groups influenced by Trotskyism, but they did not produce a credible electoral alternative to Labour – nor in most cases did they intend to.

At this time I joined one of the revolutionary groups, the International Marxist Group (my membership was to last for four years), partly in order to work politically with socialists beyond an increasingly parochial and self-centred student movement, and partly to learn about Marxism in both a theoretical and a practical way. My thoughts also turned towards trying to understand this thing, 'the Labour Party', which seemed to face you, impassively, at every turn. In particular I wanted to understand why the left wing was so weak. Was the left doomed by the very nature of the party, the unions and the limits of its own ideas always to be a hopeless minority? Or was there some way, not immediately apparent, by which they might turn the party into a party of radical socialist change?

To find some answers I chose for my graduate thesis, in 1971, to study the Labour left at its postwar peak, under the leadership of Nye Bevan. My aim was to see if its failure then shed any light on the possibilities for change in the future. Through this research, I witnessed, thanks to the archives, the overwhelming support for Bevan in the constituency parties, and how this power base was rendered marginal by the block vote of all the major unions. In this way I realised how crucial were the internal politics of the different unions in shaping the future of the Labour Party.

Fatal weaknesses in the politics of the Bevanite left itself also became clear to me.[1] For although changes *were* taking place in the unions in the fifties, subterraneanly, on the shop floor,[2] the Bevanites had little political inclination to build any direct association with shop-floor activists. The Labour left in the fifties and sixties on the whole accepted the prohibition on party involvement in the unions – other than through official channels controlled by the leadership. Bevan's reverence for the House of Commons, stemming from his belief in its power as 'the sword at the heart of private property',[3] meant that he and his followers saw little political significance in the growth of shop-floor power. Right-wing trade-union leaders such as Arthur Deakin of the T&GWU and Bill Cannon of the AEU could work hand in glove with the party leadership, with little fear of political challenge.[4] Where a minority of the Labour left did make common cause with the growing numbers of disaffected trade-union activists, for example with dockers, in the then right-wing T&GWU, they were swiftly disciplined by a party/union hierarchy working in ruthless concert.[5] More or less implicitly, the Labour left relied in many unions on the Communist Party to gain positions for the left and change the direction of the block vote.

Moreover, the Labour left in the fifties was on the defensive. It had not generated any new theoretical momentum which could take its ideas further than an extension of the programme of 1945. The policy initiative was with the leadership, with the exception of nuclear disarmament. The left concentrated its energies on trying to win positions on the National Executive, and, judging by the headlines of *Tribune* at the time, was quite ecstatic when it was successful ('For the Cause of Socialism Everywhere – Oh What a Beautiful Morning' was the front-page headline which reported the news in October 1956 that Bevan had won the election for treasurer).

My reading about this period and interviews with people who had been Bevanites consequently made me sceptical about the possibilities of the traditional, primarily parliamentary, left ever changing the Labour Party. And since their failures tended to discourage other socialists from joining or being active in the party, the best prospects for political change, it seemed to follow, lay outside.

The experience of the seventies, especially of Labour in government, only confirmed my doubts about change coming from within the Labour Party. During the first half of the decade, at least, the most creative and powerful political initiatives towards the kind of socialism in which I believed came from outside: from local and workplace trade unionism, from the women's liberation movement, from social and environmental campaigns in local communities and from a flowering of cultural alternatives.

As I became more involved in some of these movements, particularly the women's liberation movement and the local, Newcastle, trades council, the vanguard pretensions of the IMG and other Trotskyist groups came to seem increasingly arrogant and absurd. I still believed in the possibility of a political economy based on social ownership and popular democracy but I felt that the leadership of vanguard groups who proclaimed this goal did not give genuine credence to initiatives in this direction which they could not lead or even fully understand. In 1978, with Sheila Rowbotham and Lynne Segal, I wrote a book, *Beyond the Fragments*,[6] which argued the insights that feminism had for socialism. We saw the women's movement as an example of new ways of organising, independent of the Labour Party and suspicious of self-defined vanguards, which were also evident among trade unionists and community groups. We hoped that by writing about such politics, which are often undervalued and without political representation, we would give others confidence to do the same.

Many people did respond positively to the book, some more enthusiastically than we had ever expected. Some hoped that a political network could be created to connect 'the fragments'. But this proved to be unrealistic. Many of those who desired wider political connections and involvement joined the Labour Party and the others remained fragmented, though often creating wider alliances of their own.

At this time, from 1973 until 1979, I was working on Tyneside as a researcher with engineering industry shop stewards and local trades councils who were trying to resist the closure and redundancy plans of multi-plant and sometimes multinational engineering corporations. These groups of workers, with some political encouragement – notably from Tony Benn – produced imaginative plans and strategies for saving jobs, identifying new markets and meeting unmet social needs, the Lucas workers' 'alternative corporate plan' being the best known. A Labour government committed to industrial regeneration might be expected to have welcomed, and built on, these plans. But these socially minded shop stewards were rebuffed or diverted by a combination of ministerial hostility and reluctance amongst some trade-union leaders to allow any autonomy to groups of shop stewards' organisations.

These hierarchies, political and industrial, were reacting in a very similar way to the leaderships of the fifties. As organisations little had changed. Nonetheless, politically, both the party and the trade-union left had developed since the Bevanite period. The reverberations of the workplace militancy of the late fifties and sixties were being felt throughout the structures of the established unions such as those in the motor and engineering industries (mainly the T&GWU and the AUEW, the miners, the railway unions (the NUR and ASLEF) and the print unions (then NATSOPA). These unions joined newer unions such as the public-sector manual workers' union, NUPE, and the white-collar union ASTMS in supporting broadly left policies, such as nuclear disarmament, and radical forms of social ownership, within the party. But they were cautious about how they carried through these policies and, until the pay policies of 1978-79, they were loyal to the Labour government.

This new Labour left, born out of disillusion with the Wilson governments of the sixties and inspired by new kinds of militant action that trade unionists were taking to preserve jobs and communities, had a definite sense of the limits of parliamentary power. In this respect it moved in a different political direction from that of the Bevanites, and it was more open and enthusiastic about establishing contact with shop-floor leaders.

However, there were no party structures through which this relationship was possible. All kinds of *ad hoc* structures were used, often building on networks established in fighting 'In Place of Strife' – the legislation proposed in 1968 by Harold Wilson and Barbara Castle to constrain trade unions and curb shop-floor militancy – and then the Tories' 1972 Industrial Relations Act. The Institute for Workers' Control, based in Nottingham, was an important forum. For a time its conferences provided an unusual meeting-place for left politicians, industrial militants, socialist feminists and committed intellectuals. Many of these people were not members of the Labour Party – several had been expelled. They worked with the left inside the party as if they were in the same political organisation, but they had their own independent organisations and campaigns. Some were in the Communist Party or the International Socialists, others belonged to non-party groups and projects. These socialist gatherings were among many intimations of a socialist 'party' within the British labour movement, unable to break out.

This experience was reinforced when I went to work at the GLC in 1981. Here I had first-hand experience of the new breed of Labour politician. A group of them, led by Ken Livingstone, had embarked on a successful campaign to select GLC candidates who would be bound by a manifesto drawn up in 1980 by the London Labour Party. The economic policies in this manifesto committed them to local support for the kind of workers' initiatives on which Cabinet ministers had closed the door. In two minds, I went to help create a new Economic Policy Group. Unwilling to commit myself totally, I started off job-sharing with Mike Cooley, one of the architects of the Lucas workers' plan, who was also sceptical. It was not long before we went full-time.

There I was, an obstinate refusenik when it came to joining the Labour Party, working, eating, dreaming the Labour GLC – and not just because of the fat salary! It felt as if I had joined an open, campaigning socialist party without having to join the tight, conservative party that has its HQ in the Palace of Westminster. Ken Livingstone's Labour Party of course had its faults. The GLC often succumbed to the baronialism encouraged by the local government committee system with its vast bureaucratic empires; there was little Labour Party activity independent of the council and while the council appealed successfully for support from the mass of Londoners they did little to build a political relationship with their own lower-paid staff. On the other hand, they carried out most of their manifesto, and more. They persisted with ideas which were initially unpopular; on the whole, they did not bend towards the centre under pressure. They raised expectations and opened themselves to pressure from people outside the party, often outside the trade unions and far more radical than themselves.

Then came the miners' strike, through which I grew to know miners' and women's action groups in Durham, Nottingham and Yorkshire. Through them I came across Labour parties who were among the first people to support these communities, and to do so not by passing worthy resolutions calling on someone else to take action, but taking action – extraordinary, year-long action – themselves. Here was irrefutable evidence that there was something more to the Labour Party than an electoral machine tied to union head offices, and a pompous shadow cabinet much the same as cabinets and shadow cabinets before them.

This other hidden, but emerging, Labour Party does not have much of a voice, other than on local platforms. Nationally it has been told to keep quiet. As I write now, in a run-up to the general election it assumes that any break in its silence will be used against it. It is fragmented by regional differences that are both a source of its vitality and a cause of its invisibility. Its diverse political character does not fit in with the categories of either the Tory or the liberal press.

Moreover, looking at the left in the Labour Party is like looking at a reflection in a trick mirror. The institutions of the Labour Party are such that when the left is strong it appears very, very strong and when it is weak it appears tiny. This is one aspect of the change which has taken place over the last six years, since the defeat of Tony Benn's campaign for the Deputy Leadership, and not surprisingly, like someone seeing their reflection as half as tall as they thought they were, the left in the Labour Party has been somewhat disoriented.

In such circumstances an exaggerated image of weakness is internalised and creates what is in fact a self-fulfilling prophecy.

In September 1986, for this book, I set out to talk to a cross-section of the people who are part of this emerging party – in the constituencies, in the unions or in campaigning movements like CND. Also, with the help of some students, I carried out a short survey of some 60 randomly selected constituency delegates at the 1986 conference. I tried to find out the kind of politics they are creating, the difficulties they are facing; to discuss their strategies towards power, and to assess their chances of achieving it. I list at the back of the book the 100 or so people (excluding the 60 interviewed in the survey at conference) I talked to.

What I found was far from the media image of small groups of extremists plotting to subvert democratic processes. Instead, I found that a process of democratic renewal has been taking place. It has slowed down recently and is still uneven in its effects. But I found cases of rotten boroughs which had been taken for granted by their representatives, now transformed into campaigning parties having an open, working relationship with their MPs. I found town hall patriarchs old and new under persistent challenge from local parties. I found growing women's sections that were a focal point for political debate, and action by women quite new to party politics. I found black groups breaking down the monopoly of white people's power. I found CND activists dragging their local Labour Party into commitments that were thought to be electoral suicide, and then winning by a landslide in local elections. I found public-sector trade unions adopting a more political and campaigning stand and exerting pressure on the local Labour Party to do the same. I found left pressure groups in right-wing unions that had gained vigour and confidence from the campaign for democracy in the Labour Party. And I found a small minority of MPs fresh from local struggles for accountability trying hard to get the parliamentary Labour Party to organise on a democratic basis. I found abuses of this democratisation, for sure, and also mistakes which a hostile press escalated into disasters. But the dominant trend was a highly responsible and very determined attempt to reconstruct the Labour Party and to make sure, against the odds, that Labour governments will never again be like those of Harold Wilson and James Callaghan.

The reaction of the parliamentary leadership – first the Shadow Cabinet of Michael Foot and then that of Neil Kinnock – has been contradictory, especially in Neil Kinnock's case. They, or at least Walworth Road, the Party Headquarters, have taken on board some of the campaigning style of the new politics, but little of the content, in spite of the policies supported at party conference. At the same time, the parliamentary leadership has attempted to marginalise the very same left, or sections of it, who were responsible for this campaigning politics. From the moment the Gang of Four left to form the Social Democratic Party, in March 1981, the leadership's efforts have been concentrated on showing that nothing in the party's basic structure of power has changed: the parliamentary leadership was still in charge. And indeed, they have been highly successful in ensuring that nothing fundamental did change, at least nationally.

An atmosphere was created, from the moment of Tony Benn's campaign for the Deputy Leadership, in which the left was publicly defined as the enemy, not only by the press but also by the Shadow Cabinet itself. Moreover, each successive party leader, first Foot and then Kinnock, went a step further and set as his standard for good leadership his prowess in felling the left. In the 1983 general election and even more centrally in the build-up to the 1987 election the defeat of the left became an electoral strategy. The left was ill equipped to counter this onslaught. The potential which existed in the early eighties to build on the democratic reforms, the revival of many local parties, the growth of political debate in the unions, to establish a popular socialism was lost. The exceptions, such as the GLC, Sheffield and Manchester City Councils, where the left had a platform independent of the leadership, illustrate that the potential was real.

The weakening of the left was further achieved when the parliamentary leadership and the press alike blamed them for the 1983 election defeat. From then on, all that represented the left – the miners' strike, the Wapping dispute and local authority resistance to rate-capping included – was seen by the new leadership as an obstacle to electoral success. Consequently, a deep defensiveness set in throughout the party, even among those who had previously supported the democratic reforms. I analyse this process in Chapter 2, for it has put a dampener and sometimes a muzzle on the democratic momentum described in Chapters 1, 3, 4 and 5.

In all this, the leadership had a powerful source of conservatism on which to draw: the processes of parliamentary government, which pervade Her Majesty's Opposition as powerfully as Her Majesty's Government. This power – exercised through patronage, deference, the presssure for respectability – had an indirect effect in the constituencies, slowing down the process of reform. The strength of the reform movement has seemed to vary in inverse proportion to the closeness of the section of the party to the parliamentary process. For instance, mandatory reselection has on the whole turned out to be far less radical in its impact than those campaigning for it expected. On the other hand, women's sections and some parts of local government and the unions have taken the democratisation of politics far further than the initial campaign.

As I interviewed people, it began to feel as if I was encountering two different parties. Phrases such as 'It's as if we were in a different party' kept recurring from a wide spectrum of local activists, old and new.

Speaking historically

There have always been two distinct traditions in the Labour Party: the ameliorative, pragmatic tradition associated especially with the leadership of the trade unions and the Parliamentary Party; and on the other hand, the transformative, visionary tradition which in the past has only ever had majority support in the constituency parties – though this majority has been cyclical and unstable in its strength. From its origins the party has been an alliance of the two.

In other parts of Europe, these two traditions have been the basis, broadly, for two separate parties: Social Democratic and Communist. In Britain, by contrast, the Labour Party, until 1981, has united the majority of each tradition into one party. There are several reasons for this. First is the unique unity of British trade unionism, unparalled among European labour movements.

This unity has its roots in the early start of trade unionism in Britain, prior to the existence of any working-class party, prior even to manual workers' having the vote. Unions in Britain were therefore a product of workers combining for economic protection without the external impetus of a political party as in Italy, Germany and France.[7] The unions, through a single TUC, established the Labour Party as their political instrument; they continue to provide the vast bulk of its finance; and they have considerable power over its policy and organisation. The bedrock of the party's unity is consequently the unity of the trade unions and the dynamic of divisions within the party depend, ultimately, on political and industrial developments in the trade unions.

The second, more ideological, reason for the unusual political unity of the British labour movement is that in Britain the ameliorative and transformative traditions shared a common aim. This unifying purpose was to achieve parliamentary control over the existing British state and to use this control to improve the conditions of working people. For the ameliorators, this could be achieved through welfare provision, taxation, a degree of industrial planning and national economic management, within the continued framework of a capitalist economy. The transformers, on the other hand, had in mind a more thoroughgoing use of the state: to replace the private ownership of capital with the public ownership. But both traditions placed their faith in the existing state, the British nation-state, under the control of a Labour majority at Westminister.

How were such shared assumptions about the character of the state possible in Britain, when they were the subject of immense controversy elsewhere in Europe? Without attempting to provide a full explanation,[8] I would suggest that an underlying reason lies in the limited character of the British state's intervention in the economy. At a time, from the First World War onwards, and in some cases earlier, when German and Italian governments, for instance, were intervening directly in companies and banks to invest, to reorganise, to co-ordinate and to promote new technological developments, British governments limited their economic role to maintaining a balanced budget, supervising a foreign policy that protected trading and investment interests abroad, and ensuring the stability necessary for uninterrupted production at home. Successive British governments spent comparatively little money on industry, while other European countries spent considerable sums on guaranteed loans, industrial subsidies and public works. Only after the Second World War did British governments seriously begin to intervene, minimally, in the organisation of civilian industry.

The limited character of the British state's intervention in the economy does not mean that the state was weak. On the contrary, a central pillar of the British state, the Civil Service, had established from the 19th century onwards a long tradition of mandarin strength; a protection against the political consequences of the working-class franchise. This strength is itself part of the explanation of the limited nature of state intervention in the economy. The political impetus for this intervention has come mainly from Labour, and consequently the Civil Service has applied its strength to preventing or at least blunting such intervention, whether it was to modernise and improve industrial efficiency or advance socialism.

The importance of this for understanding the Labour Party was that it allowed for greater ambiguity in policy-making and debate concerning the state and the economy, and therefore concerning the nature of socialism. Throughout most of the Labour Party's history, that is until the aftermath of Wilson's 1964-70 government, a programme of state intervention was seen to be needed from a variety of ideological standpoints, to achieve any kind of domestic industrial efficiency. Such a programme could have different meanings for the two opposite wings of the party. There was always much debate and controversy between these groups, but in the end conference resolutions would be passed on nationalisation and state intervention, which those from the transforming tradition assumed meant the beginning of a complete socialisation of the economy but which those from the ameliorative tradition saw simply as necessary and limited steps to modernise the economy (Harold Wilson's speeches in the early sixties are exemplary in conveying both objectives at the same time).

An implication of this analysis is that as the state played a stronger, more active role in the management of capitalism (thanks mainly to the Labour Party), the transformative tradition would be thrown into turmoil, especially when the state, under a Labour government, lowered the relative living standards of working-class people and sought to restrain trade-union action.

The 1964–70 Labour government produced just such turmoil, which was exacerbated by the government of 1974–79. The tradition, in effect, split. One strand, symbolised by Michael Foot, reproduced by Neil Kinnock, remained loyal to the British state and the parliamentary structures of the Labour Party. For Foot especially, loyalty was to Parliament, which he saw as a uniquely democratic institution. The apparent democracy of Parliament for the political elite blinded him and his ilk to the lack of democracy in the state's rule over the population.

The other strand has two distinct origins. On the one hand there are those, from the old transformative tradition, who remained loyal to the goal of transformation and became disillusioned by the weakness of Parliament to influence the character of the state's role. Jo Richardson would be a notable example. On the other hand were a minority, most notably Tony Benn, who had been part of the modernising ameliorative tradition, assuming that this would bring benefits to working-class people. The experience of the Wilson government was a disillusionment for them too and led them to make a radical critique of the mandarin state, the strength of multinational capital, the feebleness of Parliament and the concentrated power of the Prime Minister.

Out of this combination has come a new transformative movement, allying with traditions entirely independent of Labourism – Marxism, feminism, syndicalism, pacifism and ecology. In practice, though too fluid and contradictory yet to produce a theory, this new tradition envisages a different kind of state as well as a different basis on which to organise production. Many of its initiatives move out from the locality in an international direction, although its parliamentary leadership has tended to remain determinedly national, and sometimes nationalistic, in their approach.

Not only is the new transformative tradition challenging the British state, it is also, in practice, challenging Labourism. Different aspects of Labourism will appear throughout this book, especially in Chapter 2, where I discuss the 1983 election and Labour's inability to change the terms of public debate. There I will discuss Labourism's optimism about the state and its sectionalism towards the economy. But the new tradition is also a challenge to Labourism's political values and its view of class.

The political values of Labourism stem from the combination of the values of trade unionism with those of parliamentary respectability. By 'the values of trade unionism' I mean the horizons, the priorities and the methods of the trade-union apparatus. This is not the same as, though it influences, local and shop-floor working-class culture. Such culture has many of the expansive, generous and potentially emancipatory qualities that historically have been absent from Labourism.

The political values of Labourism, generalising from the imperatives of trade-union organisation, tend to hold up political unity as paramount, at the expense of initiative and innovation, and to place loyalty before independence and critical debate. Rooted in the experience and circumstances of the male skilled and organised worker these values stress the common experiences and interests of the working class, at the expence of its diversity and its conflicting interests. Finally they stress the sectional character of working-class interests rather than its capacity to solve problems affecting society as a whole. In themselves, these values do not preclude a notion of transformation, but it is a transformation in which the working class has little active role. The working class, through the trade unions provides the money and the votes but the actual process of change is a matter for Parliament and the state.

The new tradition by contrast has emerged from circumstances, in the late sixties and seventies, in which a minority of working-class people were themselves, in practice, breaking out of Labourism. Through the experience of occupations and work-ins, demonstrations and strikes, new organisations and demands, this minority perceived the possibilities of a popular rather than purely parliamentary process of change.[9] For them initiative and innovation became as important as, and sometimes more important than, unity. Independence, autonomy and critical debate grew to qualify the value of loyalty. The different interests within the working class, of gender, race, region and work, asserted themselves with confidence, aspiring to redefine the common interests of class – a human pluralism against the monolithic tendencies of capital. And finally, trade-union organisations began to give a working-class base to campaigns that sought to present solutions to the problems of society: peace, the environment, the quality of services, the media and the state.

These developments were at the base of the unions and the party but they have had an influence on the apparatus of some of the unions, as we shall see in Chapter 5.

The new tradition has not, except for a small minority, found a new political home. Still, with increasing discomfort, it finds a niche within the Labour Party. This new politics tries to claim sections of the party as its own. It is trying to rebuild links with working-class activists on a more political, socialist rather than Labourist basis. These are some political resources on which to build. Moreover, the peculiarly disproportional electoral system of the British parliament has ensured that there is no alternative. However this subordinate position, in which the new left has to struggle for legitimacy without any platform of its own (except where it has gained local political control) has had serious disadvantages.

The new tradition is not engaged in 'the battle for the soul of Labour' in the same way as was the old. Its break from Labourism means that in a sense this tradition represents a new soul. The battle is for Labour's structure, that is, for power within the unions, the constituency parties' and the Parliamentary Party's power to reshape the structure or create a new one in accord with its distinct vision of transformation.

In the following chapters I explore the character of this new soul emerging out of the disintegration of Labourism. I argue that whether or not it can ever win the battle for Labour's structure – the outcome of this is not predictable – this radical left also needs its own, independent structures based outside as well as inside the Labour Party. It will need this independence if it is to develop its ideas, establish an active base in the unions and other non-parliamentary movements and win popular support. One purpose of this book is to show that the basis for this independence has in the last ten years or so been growing, but that it has now reached an impasse. It has been growing in local government, in political and social divisions within the unions, in the growth of women's sections and black organisations, in the peace movement and in the ideas of a socialist economy and state which these initiatives have helped to produce. I do not try to provide any kind of model or prescription for the independence that is urgently needed. But I do hope to encourage its self-confidence and to show that the political resources are available for it to flourish. I hope that by showing this I will encourage others to make the theoretical and political breakthroughs we need.

1 Reselection and the State

On July 23, 1975, a majority of the 48 delegates to the General Management Committee of the Newham North East Constituency Labour Party voted, in strict accordance with the party's rule book and under the watchful eye of the party's regional organiser, that their MP, Cabinet Minister Reg Prentice, be 'requested to retire at the next election'. All hell broke loose. The day before, the majority of the Parliamentary Labour Party had sent a letter to the constituency accusing the Newham party of betraying 'the principles of tolerance and free speech for which our movement has always fought' should it vote to sack Prentice. After the Newham decision, Harold Wilson threatened, at a meeting of the party's National Executive, that 'if this sort of thing continues, PLP will have to put up its own candidates'. And overnight those who wanted Prentice to go were described as 'extremists', ' bed-sit revolutionaries', 'members of the Trotskyist Militant', 'unrepresentative of the Labour voter' and 'enemies of democracy'. These descriptions, with the term 'hard left' added as a useful catch-all, have stuck for any group in the Labour Party which challenges established political (especially parliamentary) power. Who were the people they described in Newham North East?

John Wilson, the EETPU delegate to the Newham North East party, moved the resolution to deselect Reg Prentice. He would describe himself as 'just left of centre'. He was in his mid-thirties at the time and had been on the General Management Committee for several years. He was supported by a cross-section of the constituency party. They included old hands such as Claude Calcott, the 82-year-old party secretary (he had been secretary when Prentice was first selected), Harold Lugg, a retired milkman and party president, and Connie Clements, in her seventies, a strong defender of the younger people joining the party: 'Reg resents the young because they can argue and talk. This party will die if we don't encourage young people to join it and become active; it will die if this resolution is not passed,' she said at the special meeting called to consider John Wilson's resolution. Then there were younger members in their twenties and thirties. Some were local, like Michele Piggott and Lew Boyce – now the stationmaster at East Ham. Others were recent residents, like Denise Cohen, a social worker, and Hilary Jenkins, a teacher. And there were members in their forties and fifties, like Councillor Fred York, a delegate from the NUR Branch, and Owen Ashworth, a local teacher. No one lived in a bedsitter.

There were only four who were Young Socialist supporters of Militant among the twenty-nine who voted for Prentice's retirement, and none of them was in a leading position. There was no outside organisation conspiring to bring about Prentice's downfall: 'We'd all come to a similar assessment, with a heavy heart in many cases, for different reasons,' commented Alan Haworth, a vice-chair of the party who, ironically, worked – and still works – as clerk to the Parliamentary Labour Party. None were even members of the Campaign for Labour Party Democracy (CLPD) and, according to Haworth, they 'felt quite resentful when CLPD turned up with a banner', after the vote against Prentice. ' "What business is it of theirs?" we thought at the time. Though we've been involved since.'

Twenty-nine delegates supported Wilson's resolution. Nineteen delegates supported Prentice. Of these nineteen all but four were retired, and all had been in manual working-class jobs. Labour voters in Newham North East include a significant swathe of white-collar and professional workers, young unemployed and young manual workers. The twenty-nine were thus far more representative.

Anxiety about Prentice's public statements had been growing in the constituency for some time before John Wilson and his colleagues resorted to what is now termed 'deselection' ('deselection' and 'reselection' were not common currency at the time). It was particular statements he made against the unions and in favour of the EEC which worried constituency members, in particular because he never discussed his views with them. Wilson explains their view:

Prentice was behaving as if he could take the job for granted, as if it was his for life. He treated us with disdain. We don't expect an elected person to be a puppet but we do expect him to make his judgements after discussion with his constituency party. He was after all elected as a representative of the party.

Deselection *was* a last resort, and it was a decision arrived at in a most cautious manner.

In 1974, before the October general election, several trade-union delegates, from the T&GWU, EETPU and UCATT, had put a resolution to 'rescind the decision to adopt Reg Prentice for the forthcoming election'. It was defeated. Delegates were reluctant to 'rock the boat' in a run-up to the election. However, Prentice's attitude to the constituency party did not change, even though the vote confirming his re-adoption had been narrow. For instance, he refused even to talk to a trade-union delegation from his constituency who tried to lobby him about the three Shrewsbury building workers imprisoned for picketing activity under Heath's 1972 Industrial Relations Act.

In June 1975 the local party executive received the motion from John Wilson's branch proposing Prentice's retirement. The executive decided to set in motion the procedure in the Labour Party constitution for dealing with such a motion. A special meeting was convened and attended by the regional officer, Bill Jones. The decision was taken. Four months later, the Labour Party NEC ratified this by rejecting Prentice's appeal. Since then Reg Prentice has left the Labour Party, claiming it has been taken over by Marxists, has briefly flirted with the Liberals – they had no Cabinet positions to offer – and finally joined the Conservatives, becoming a member of Mrs Thatcher's government. Since his deselection, party membership has grown by around 25 per cent. And it has done well electorally: two notable successes were won, first in the GLC election and then in the 1978 borough elections. In the GLC election, Newham North East had one of the two highest swings to Labour – the other was in Ken Livingstone's seat in Paddington.[1] At the 78 local elections which were disastrous for the party in other parts of London, Labour gained six seats in Newham, including one previously held by a ratepayers' candidate who made much of the Prentice affair in an effort to retain her seat.

You might think this was a case of a local party exercising its proper duty to Labour voters in the area, and being vindicated.

It was controversial because of the Cabinet status of the MP, and difficult to go through with, because such conflict necessarily reflected badly for a time on the party. But it was party democracy nonetheless, and, as it turned out, proved healthy for the Newham party.

That was not the impression given at the time. The headlines spoke of 'ultra-leftists plotting to increase the number of pro-communist MPs'.[2] Few of the above facts about those who voted against Prentice are mentioned in any of the articles. All the newspaper stories concentrate on one person, Tony Kelly, high-lighting his separation from his wife and other supposedly damn-ing aspects of his background. Kelly was by no means the single driving force. In fact he was the only one which the press could smear. By association the media then smeared everyone else. Under the headline 'Hardline Marxist in charge at Newham'[3], the *Daily Telegraph* described Phil Bradbury as a member of Militant, which he was not, never has been and is certain that he never will be.

Pro-Labour or 'neutral' papers such as the *Daily Mirror* and the *Guardian* made assumptions based on hardly more facts than the other papers. The *Mirror*, for instance, asked: 'If the opponents of Mr Prentice are unrepresentative, who let them infiltrate?'[4] A good question. But the comment and conclusion goes on to assume that the 'if' is a fact. The *Guardian* made the same assumption: that it was those who voted *against* Prentice who were unrepresentative. In a leading article, the *Guardian* then pointed out the moribund character of many Labour parties which made them vulnerable to takeover, warned of the conse-quences of 'opting out of politics' and argued for the 'widest possible participation in the machinery of democratic life.'[5]

In fact, many of the people who supported the move to get rid of Prentice were the very model of the *Guardian*'s politically responsible citizen, 'campaigning to open the machinery of democratic life to a representative community'. Take Anita Pollock, for instance, whose face covered the front page of the *Evening Standard* as 'The Girl Out To Get Reg'. She is an Australian who was working as an editor in publishing at the time of the Prentice affair. She came from a 'right-wing country family' but became a socialist in Britain 'because it was such a divided country'. She decided not to join the Labour Party until she was 'settled in one area'. In 1971 she and her boyfriend Phil Bradbury bought a house in Newham. It took them several months to find the local Labour Party since it was not in the phone directory, but was, in fact, Claude Calcott's home.

'"Everybody knows that I'm the Labour Party", he said,' recalls Anita. 'We asked when the next meeting was. "Meeting?" he said, "we haven't had a ward meeting for three years." They called one specially for us. There we were with the three councillors for the area who didn't live in the ward, Claude and a sweet old woman who'd run the ward in the past. We were elected chair and secretary.'

Anita got hold of the address list of around fifty members and went to visit them, only to find that most of them were dead. She and Phil Bradbury then went round from door to door recruiting. Within several years they recruited 200 people of varying ages and backgrounds. Branch meetings have taken place regularly ever since, with an average attendance of twenty. Soon the councillors were from the area, and included the first Asian councillor on Newham Council. In other words, these two delegates who voted for Prentice to go were making Labour representative of local people for the first time indeed since the 1950s. The deselection of Reg Prentice was, it seems, a consequence not of the local party being moribund, but of its rising from the dead.

The reaction of the majority of the Parliamentary Labour Party was remarkably similar to that of Fleet Street, and was based on a remarkably similar absence of information. One hundred and seventy-nine MPs signed a letter to the Newham constituency party expressing their support for Prentice, and pleading with them not to remove him.[6] Gavin Strang, a junior minister at the time, described how 'it was just assumed that you would sign – especially if you were in the government – and that you accepted that the constituency party had been taken over or influenced by people without the party's best interests in mind'. Strang was rung up 'on the ministerial phone, which I thought was a bit off' by Bob Maclennan, then also a junior minister – he has since joined the SDP. 'He was taken aback that I wouldn't sign. "Everyone in the government has signed," he said.'

The general acceptance of the media interpretation of what was going on just five miles away in Newham is confirmed by

Alan Howarth, the Newham activist by night, clerk to the PLP by day. He clerked all the PLP subcommittees and was in constant contact with MPs. His position as a leading member of the offending party would be well known. Did any of those who signed the letter even casually ask him for his version of events? 'The only conversation which any MP had with me about it was a desultory one with Sir Frank Barlow who mentioned that he'd been in the same platoon as Prentice and had found him "a difficult chap". But that was it.'

What lay behind the solidarity which MPs showed towards their colleague? The MPs' letter mentioned three things. First, the work Mr Prentice had done for his constituency and his country. He 'is a distinguished Labour MP who served his constituency and his country for eighteen years'. Secondly, the letter called on the constituency to 'uphold the principles of tolerance and free speech for which our movement has always fought'. It concluded by saying that the removal of Mr Prentice 'would strike a grave blow at the unity of the party at this difficult time'. An interesting mixture of fellow feeling: 'you can't do a man out of a job he's had for eighteen years'; high principle: 'MPs must be able to exercise their independent judgement, don't make them party puppets'; and the somewhat more mundane protection of the party: 'don't rock the boat'.

The Reg Prentice affair was one of the most publicised early examples of a reform movement within the Labour Party, and it encouraged the movement for the introduction of mandatory reselection for all Labour Members of Parliament and for the election of the Labour leader by an electoral college made up of MPs, constituency Labour parties and trade unions.[7] Similarly the reaction to the 'deselection' of Reg Prentice by the Labour Party's parliamentary leadership and by the press became a pattern to be repeated with every advance of the movement for reform.

The purpose of this chapter is to try to explain why what at first appears as a modest set of reforms, such as reselection and the party's election of the leader – both common features of other European Socialist and Social Democratic parties – should provoke such blustering, self-righteous resistance, not only from the party leadership but, through the press, from the wider national political elite. Party members in Newham say now that, looking back, they had no idea at the time 'what we were taking on'. As Anita Pollock puts it: 'We thought it was a local issue, but in the end it seemed as if we had taken on the whole establishment.' Leaders of the wider reform movement remember the same amazement at the political earthquake which their reforms provoked: 'We knew we'd get a reaction from some members of the PLP but we never imagined it would be so widespread and so hard,' said Vladimir Dierer, the secretary of the Campaign for Labour Party Democracy. What in fact *had* they taken on?

I will start with the alarm expressed by the parliamentary leadership in their letter to Newham North East and their defence, as they claimed, of the principles of tolerance and free speech. A good way to discover whether professed principles are the real reasons for someone's behaviour is to find out whether they apply these principles to another, similar situation. The decision by a constituency party in Northumberland, one year before, not to readopt their MP, a backbencher called Eddie Milne, provides just such a situation.

Freedom, tolerance and the MP for Blyth

In November 1973 the Blyth Constituency Party voted by forty to thirty-six against the readoption of Eddie Milne. Milne had not held any higher office than PPS to Frank Soskice in the 1966 Labour government; he had been offered a job as a Whip, but turned it down believing it would curb his independence. But he had 'served his country and his constituency' as Member of Parliament for fourteen years. His constituents, at least, must have judged that he did so in a 'distinguished manner' because they re-elected him as an Independent Labour MP in the first 1974 general election with a majority over the Labour candidate of over 4,000. Such success for an independent candidate at a general election was remarkable, especially so when the party machine put every effort, including meetings addressed by Cabinet ministers, into winning the seat for the offical Labour candidate, Ivor Richard. At the second 1974 election Milne lost by only 44 votes. By 1976 his Independent Labour Party had won a majority of the seats on the Blyth Council.

Milne was an independent-minded MP and persistent in the

causes he pursued, mild-mannered and without any of Prentice's pomposity. He was on the left of the party, a firm supporter of state ownership and the planning of industry. He also had firm principles about how an MP should behave. In his autobiography, he quotes Edmund Burke as his guide on what an MP should be:

A strenuous resistance to every appearance of lawless power; a spirit of independence carried to some degree of enthusiasm; an inquisitive character to discover, and a bold one to display, every corruption and error of government; these are the qualities which recommend a man to a seat in the House of Commons.[8]

He found plenty of scope for an inquisitive and bold character in tracing and exposing the web of corruption spun by T. Dan Smith, Leader of Newcastle Council between 1966 and 1974, Andy Cunningham, Regional Secretary of the Northern Region of the General & Municipal Workers, and Chairman of the Regional Labour Party, and John Poulson, the Wakefield architect and consultant to the Bovis Construction company. In one way or another, just about every local authority in the north–east, and at least one in the south of England, was caught in this web even if they were not themselves all guilty of corruption. The national organisation of the Labour Party was also caught, since it had employed T. Dan Smith's company from 1964 as a public-relations consultant on a £35,000 contract for the party. Andrew Cunningham had been on the NEC of the Labour Party since 1965 and remained on it formally until October 1973, several months after his arrest.

Milne's suspicions that something was out of order were first aroused by a secret meeting held by Blyth councillors with T. Dan Smith and Crudens, the building company for whom T. Dan Smith was a public-relations consultant. Milne called for council meetings to be open to the press. Councillors resented his interference. Then, in 1971, came the trial of a leading member of Wandsworth's Labour Council on corruption charges which revealed more about the Poulson–Smith–Cunningham network. At this trial Smith had been charged with offering a bribe to the Chair of the Wandsworth Housing Committee, Councillor Sporle. Smith was acquitted but Sporle was jailed for accepting his bribe. Milne started calling for an inquiry by the Labour Party into the rumours of corruption in Labour councils in the north–east. He went to see Harold Wilson, one of T. Dan Smith's many friends in the leadership of the Labour Party, who promised to take action. Nothing happened. Rumours grew of the desire of the hierarchy of the regional party to get rid of Milne. Then came the Poulson bankruptcy hearings in 1972, where it was revealed that Poulson had paid Smith £155,000 over a period of eight years up to 1970. The call for an inquiry was supported by a narrow majority at the 1973 conference of the North East Labour Party. But still there was no action.

Meanwhile a by-election was called in Chester-le-Street, the home and part of the trade-union empire of 'backhandy Andy', as Andrew Cunningham was known in the north–east by that time. The *New Statesman* revealed how Cunningham maximised the number of G&MWU delegates by splitting branches in two, so that he could obtain the seat for his nominee, Giles Radice, the London-based head of the G&MWU research department. The article included a telling quote from a local miner, Ben Boomfield: 'Why can a man come in to Chester-le-Street, drop off the train and pick up forty-one votes? It's been fixed by bloody Cunningham. And what about this Poulson business? If it had been a local man I'd have put both my hands up, now I'm putting them both down against my principles and voting Liberal.'[9] Labour leaders Roy Hattersley, Bob Mellish, Michael Foot and Shirley Williams wrote what the *New Statesman*'s editor, Anthony Howard, remembers as an 'angry and intemperate' letter to the journal complaining of its lack of loyalty to the party for printing such an article. Eddie Milne, on the other hand, felt that party loyalty was not best served by loyalty to the Chester-le-Street party: he refused to join the campaign. The stench of corruption was too strong.

The antagonism grew between Milne and local councillors, supported by Milne's agent Peter Mortakis. Two inquiries took place, not into the rampant corruption in the north–east, but into why relations were so bad in the Blyth constituency. Each inquiry ended up with senior national party figures trying to get Milne to shake hands and make up. In the end Milne refused to work with Mortakis any more, knowing that Mortakis was out to get rid of him, with the backing of powerful individuals in the regional party. Finally, at a special meeting in November, Mortakis successfully led the party to turn down Milne's readoption as the parliamentary candidate at the next election. In effect Milne, like Prentice, was 'deselected'.

What was the response in Westminster? From Shirley Williams, Roy Hattersley, Michael Foot and others who claim to champion the independence of MPs? Total silence – and probably a good deal of relief among the northern group of MPs who had effectively excommunicated Milne. Did the Cabinet and MPs send a letter to the constituency chairman as they did to Newham, expressing a desire that the party should 'uphold the freedom and tolerance that the movement had fought for'? Not a word. As far as Emily Milne remembers (Eddie died of a heart attack in 1981), not one Labour MP offered any public support: 'Several had said privately that they would like to support him but they could not. There was one time when, after Ed was out of Parliament, he bumped into one MP in Central Station (Newcastle) who said: "It's not that I don't want to talk to you; it's just that I can't be seen talking to you".' The message that was being sent, not to the constituency this time but to the MP, was 'don't rock the boat, whatever your conscience says, and whatever your electorate wish.'[10]

Clearly, we need to go beyond defence of the principles of free speech and the MP's conscience to explain the parliamentary alarm at the deselection of Reg Prentice. The crucial difference between these two cases concerned the politics behind the deselection. In Newham, party members came to the conclusion that their MP no longer represented the policies and principles on which they campaigned for him to be elected. Moreover, he no longer listened to constituents who desired to lobby him on issues related to these principles. In other words, he was no longer the MP for whose election his party felt they could honestly campaign, and whatever the embarrassment to the national party, this had to be said. In Blyth, by contrast, it was the MP who was embarrassing the party machine. The decision not to adopt Eddie Milne had nothing to do with his representation of the policies on which he was elected or his work for his constituents; it had everything to do with his upsetting the powerful interests in the regional and national party machine. Neither the Newham party nor Eddie Milne were disloyal to the party's professed *policies*; on the contrary, both were trying to revive and reform it as a vehicle to carry them out. In different ways, however, they were challenging the party's *institutions* and the people who held power within them. The same is true of the later movement for constitutional reform. This movement was aimed at the central mechanisms of the party machine: the autonomy of the Parliamentary Party and the unaccountable power of the leader. For these reformers commitment to principles came before loyalty to the institutions and the public front of unity. No wonder they all caused such anger and venom; they infringed the essential values of Labourism.

Since most of the people concerned – the majority of the Newham party, Eddie Milne and his supporters and the founding members of the Campaign for Labour Party Democracy – themselves came from or were influenced by Labourism, it would be useful to summarise the strains within Labourism that led to such a challenge.

Its origins lie in the disillusion with Harold Wilson's government between 1964 and 1966 – the first Labour government for thirteen years. Within the Labour Party and among its supporters, the depth of disillusion was dramatic. Illusions had been high. Wilson's past associations with the left plus his confident, anti-establishment rhetoric had built up among Labour supporters the expectation that his government would make new socialist advances, building on the achievements of 1945–50. Instead, between 1966 and 1970, thousands left the party: when Harold Wilson came to office in 1964 there were sixty-six constituencies with a membership of over 2,000; when he left office in 1970 the number had fallen to twenty-two.[11] Party branches in effect closed down; trade unionists talked of contracting out; some of their leaders threatened to disaffiliate; constituency parties even debated – but rejected – proposals to disaffiliate from the national party. The party's electoral machine, which depends on the commitment of the party members, came almost to a standstill in some areas. 'People are just not willing to work,' complained the chairman of a London Labour party.[12] Lena Jeger, MP, drew out the implications in a pointed manner:

Obedient Ministers who tramp through lobbies strange to all they have ever said may preserve themselves from the Prime Minister's sacking. But they do not protect themselves from a sacking in their constituencies, a sacking which may well not be deliberate but may come just because nobody turns up to drive the loudspeaker van, nobody delivers the leaflets with the handsome photograph . . .[13]

It was only a matter of time, seven years to be exact, before a Cabinet minister, Reg Prentice, was literally sacked, as we have seen, by his constituency party. The implicit formula at the heart of the Labour Party – trade-union power plus the evangelical but powerless enthusiasm of constituency socialists equals Labour governments – was no longer adding up. 'In order to maintain the enthusiasm of party militants to do the organising work for which the Conservative Party pays a vast army of workers,' argued Richard Crossman, 'a constitution was needed which apparently created a full party democracy while excluding [these militants] from effective power.'[14] It was not long after the 1970 defeat that the dignified appearance of the Labour Party's constitution lost its awe and the 'party militants' took action to try to make it take account of those who were its daily organisers.

Rebellion

Those who stayed in the party throughout the sixties – and there were even a few masochists, including Ken Livingstone[15] and Jeremy Corbyn, now the MP for Islington, who joined at this time – concentrated, after the defeat of the Wilson government in 1970, on the development of policy, especially economic and industrial policy. They believed that the problem with the 1964–70 Wilson government, as far as economic policy was concerned, was not that they had a coherent socialist economic strategy which they betrayed, but that they had incoherent plans for capitalist restructuring, which capitalists could not believe in and which trade unionists could not trust. Those who stayed in the party sought to put this right with proposals for new kinds of social ownership and industrial democracy. Their aim was to get the party conference and thereby the party leadership committed to them. The conference, in 1973, was enthusiastic about the new economic programme. It was a programme which aimed to be interventionist where George Brown's 'National Plan' had been only indicative, to be negotiated with the unions where Wilson had sought to shackle them, to seek to control the City's institutions where Wilson had tried to placate them.[16]

This economic programme also included a detailed industrial policy which began to take account of the evident failings of the kind of state ownership – Morrison's model of a national corporation administered through a conventional hierarchy – introduced by the 1945 government. The 1973 policy contained a new and detailed stress on industrial democracy, to be based on the initiatives and ideas of workers themselves. Neither was this mere rhetoric. Between 1972 and 1975, Tony Benn and others, with help from organisations such as the Institute for Workers' Control, discussed with shop stewards, especially in shipbuilding, engineering and the motor industries, the details of the government support they would need to extend democratic control over production. Stewards' committees came up with extensive plans – the stewards at Swan Hunters on Tyneside called theirs 'Workers' Control with Management Participation' – based on learning the lessons of the coal and steel industries.[17]

I stress this part of the 1973 economic programme because one of the myths that became all-pervasive in the early eighties was that the left, associated with Tony Benn, were unthinking, dogmatic nationalisers whose policies had no popular appeal. I will return to this theme in Chapter 2 when I discuss the 1983 Manifesto and the evidence that although support for nationalisation has fallen significantly, support for government action to achieve industrial democracy has increased.

The reformers, led by Tony Benn and Stuart Holland, had the high ground as far as economic policy was concerned. The party establishment was silenced by the economic disaster of the 1964-70 government. The best tactic for them was meekly to don the new clothes, at least in public. The new plans, contained in the 1973 Party Programme, were launched in an atmosphere of euphoric unity. However, when it got down to detail, the unity proved precarious. Harold Wilson flatly asserted that no government of his would carry out the 1973 Programme's commitment to bring twenty-five top private companies into public ownership. The fact that it had been passed at conference was for him irrelevant. This statement opened up the first shots in a continuing struggle to make the Parliamentary Labour Party accountable.

Motions began to appear on conference agendas calling for the reselection of MPs and the election of the leader by the conference. Until 1977 these motions had no major trade-union support. The experience of the IMF cuts, and the behaviour of Denis Healey, who spoke to the conference more like a delegate from the IMF than from the Labour Party, changed that. As a delegate from the Battersea Labour Party put it: 'The IMF cuts sent seismic shudders throughout the party.' The shudders turned the trickle of resolutions into a tide, a tide that increasingly swept the block vote with it. For many unions, especially those representing the lower paid, Callaghan's 5 per cent pay policy in 1978/9 and the consequent 'Winter of Discontent' was the watershed. Tom Sawyer, now Deputy General Secretary of NUPE, and at the time leading the strikes by hospital and local authority workers in the north-east, describes its impact: 'From that moment we decided we had to get more involved in the party. We could not let the parliamentary leadership become so arrogant and out of touch ever again.' The T&GWU had already given its support in 1977, spurred in particular by the problems they had had with one of their panel of MPs: Reg Prentice.

Deeper, economic, pressures bearing on workers in the public- and private-sector jobs throughout the seventies underlay the political militancy of unions like the T&GWU and NUPE. In the public sector, cuts in spending by Labour and Conservative governments alike meant managements constantly seeking to reduce labour costs. The result was a steady spread of organisation and militancy among manual and white-collar workers. In the private sector too, pressures for increased productivity provoked the growth of shop-floor resistance. By the late seventies and early eighties, however, multi-plant, multinational management, working in favourable political conditions, was outmanoeuvring and defeating this shop-floor strength. For some of the industrial unions their greater involvement with the Labour Party was in part a reflection of the limits, and frequently the defeat, of their industrial power.

This combination of powerful trade-union pressures and a well-organised campaign in the constituencies meant that by 1981 mandatory reselection of MPs and the election of the leader by an electoral college of trade unions, constituencies and MPs were part of the Labour Party constitution.[18]

Hopes

In retrospect, the wide alliance of party and trade-union activists had two general aims. First they hoped that with these reforms, constituency parties and trade unions would exert both a check and a spur to a Labour government of a sort that Parliament could never provide. Instead of playing at being 19th-century parliamentarians without any of their power, Labour MPs would now have to recognise the power and demands of the party that they represented. As Chris Mullin, a journalist on *Tribune* at the time of the reforms – and later its editor – put it:

All the pressure on you as an MP is to look up to the fount of power: the Prime Minister, and do what he would like you to do. The object of reselection and other mechanisms, however humble, was to cause MPs to look down to the base, to the people who put him there.

The reformers also hoped that the changes would help to reinvigorate the party and make it once more a party that socialists would feel was worth joining. Speeches in favour of the reforms stressed, in the words of one delegate, the 'inability to recruit young people to the party and to recruit people in the new towns . . . to even vote Labour.' He went on to explain:

Part of the reason is that people need to feel involved. It is no longer good enough to offer constituency workers the jobs of addressing envelopes. They need to be involved in a political party and that means that they need to be involved in the selection of the party leader. (Chris Palmer, Newham North East, 1979)

The following year another delegate expressed the same anxiety about the collapse in the party's credibility and placed her hope in the reforms:

Mr Chairman, I believe that the proposals for constitutional reform will give a new lease of life to the party. Too many of my friends have left the party in disgust. Too many of my friends have given up moving resolutions because they have no effect. (Christine Healey, Eccles, 1980)

For a few years Christine Healey proved right: constitutional change in the party did draw in recruits. 'I felt I wouldn't just be banging my head against a brick wall,' said Billy Haynes, a postman from Merseyside, who became active in the party in 1980. There were many like him, especially among women and young people. Parties which in the sixties and seventies were in varying stages of decline began once more to grow. For instance, the annual reports of the Brixton party show that it declined from 1,212 members in 1965 to 292 in 1970; in the late seventies and early eighties an approximate calculation of membership of the same wards (boundary changes have altered the constituency) picked up again, reaching around 900 by 1983. Widnes shows a similar pattern: it sank from 2,900 in 1960 to 2,300 in 1970. In the late seventies it began slowly to grow again to over 3,000 by 1980.[19] Nothing spectacular, but at least signs of recovery.

The reforms had practical benefits outside the party too, for Labour supporters and constituents more generally. Before mandatory reselection many MPs lived and had an office only in London, going to the constituency for surgeries and, less regularly, for the party's General Management Committee. Since reselection, the expectations of constituencies and the behaviour of many MPs has changed: 'It's far more the normal thing now to have an office in the constituency, to employ someone there and to live in the constituency,' commented Gavin Strang, Member for Edinburgh East. 'Reselection,' he added, 'has turned MPs into better campaigners for the local party.' Increases in salaries and secretarial allowances have of course made this easier, but perhaps reselection has been a spur to the pay demands of Labour MPs!

Several deselections have themselves, on almost everybody's judgement, been of benefit to the constituents. Since mandatory reselection only twelve MPs have been deselected. Another twenty or so retired early or joined the SDP because they assumed they would be deselected. At least half of both these groups were, by the standards of those on both the left and right, plain incompetent. (It is remarkable how MPs opposing mandatory reselection will say of a Member, Neville Sandelson for instance, whose threatened deselection they turned into a *cause célèbre*:[20] 'I expect the SDP would like us to take him back, he was so useless.' It seems a little arrogant to assume the constituency parties should put up with such a representative.)

Other deselections fall into two categories: MPs who though widely respected, including by their constituency parties, were just not thought to be as good an MP for the constituency as another candidate. This applied to several politicians on the left or centre left such as Ernie Roberts and Norman Atkinson, who were replaced by the black candidates Diane Abbott and Bernie Grant respectively, and Frank Hooley, who was replaced by a local candidate. The number of deselections or likely deselections based primarily on the political disagreements between the constituency and the MP was in fact very small: Harold Lever in Manchester is one of the few examples. He retired quite contentedly, it seems, to the House of Lords.

Reselection, then, generally improved the relation between CLPs and their MPs, but so far it has not significantly altered the relations of power between the party outside Parliament and the PLP. Given this outcome of mandatory reselection, the hostility – it would not be inaccurate, in many cases, to call it hatred – towards the left, who had pressed the constitutional reforms, is at first puzzling. Although policy issues, especially defence, enter into the argument, it is not policy alone that lies at the root of the hostility. There have always been periods of animosity between the left and the right. But the challenge to the power of the Parliamentary Party and, through the Deputy Leadership campaign, to the parliamentary leadership, has turned more or less fraternal rows over policies – few sisters were involved – into bitter estrangement.

The sense of two hostile camps, especially in Parliament, was reinforced by the 1983 election disaster, for which the right and the centre blamed the left. The leadership became locked in a 'mindset' which saw the defeat of the left as a precondition of political success. This has continued, and been professionalised, under the Kinnock leadership. But the reaction to the constitutional reforms is fundamental. The initial response, illustrated by the contrast between the Reg Prentice case and that of Eddie Milne, was partly a matter of defending the party machine. To government ministers the action of the Newham party seemed so 'disloyal' that there must be some conspiracy at work; 'ordinary party members just do not behave like that' was the implication. Soon it became clear, in the support at conference for mandatory reselection – a majority in 1980 – that most party members would be willing to behave exactly like that in similar circumstances. Yet still the hostility to constitutional reform continued. Clearly something deeper lay behind the opposition of the right than loyalty to the unity of the party and its institutions. The constitutional changes challenged the *content* of

Labour's institutions. In particular, the reforms began to question Labour's relation to Parliament.

To understand this, it is necessary to understand the legacy
of Labour's history to its present-day institutions.

The historical legacy

The historical legacy of the Labour Party's first eighty years
(treating the formation of the Labour Representation Committee
in 1906 as its foundation) is contradictory, but in the end parliamentarian values can be seen to predominate over any wider
notion of popular democracy.[21]

From its foundation the Labour Party's organisation, in particular its links with the unions, has contained an implicit challenge to the Burkean notion that only the individual MP alone
with his conscience can ultimately determine how best to represent his constituents. The Labour Representation Committee
and the Labour Party, which followed after, were founded to
represent in Parliament the interests of the working class, a force
already organised, at least in part, outside Parliament. Clearly
this aim implied some spirit of accountability more defined than
the MP's judgement of his or her constituents' interests. It
also went beyond the notion of guidance by a party, like the
Conservative and Liberal Parties, established to mobilise voters
and to bring some discipline to bear on Members of Parliament
elected on the basis of party policies. It involved an ambiguously
defined, constantly redefined, idea of accountability to forms of
democracy – trade-union organisations in particular, but also
socialist clubs and women's labour organisations – established
independent of Parliament, yet desiring political representation.

On the other hand, the leaders of the LRC and then the Labour
Party assumed that the needs of labour could be represented
adequately within the existing parliamentary institutions. In
spite of its extra-parliamentary basis, it would, chameleon-like,
become in Parliament a proper Parliamentary Party.

Most trade-union leaders, from the party's origins up to and
including the present time, have seen no contradiction in this
parliamentarianism. The extra-parliamentary character of the
party was in their view purely and non-politically a trade-union
one: few trade-union leaders have accepted the potentially politi-

cal character of a workers' industrial organisation and its potential to play a leading role in the planning and control of production. They have desired simply to be represented within the existing political system in their corporate trade-union capacity.

To achieve this representation and eventually to be in government, Labour's leaders tended to play down non-parliamentary connections, almost as if they had something to hide. Since the Second World War, and the growth of trade-union bargaining power, the search for respectability and acceptance has taken a new twist as Labour leaders turned their trade-union base to an advantage as a claim to govern. Only a Labour government – was, and sometimes still is, their argument – can bring the trade unions into the state and in doing so contain their demands. At all times (except, briefly and rhetorically, in the aftermath of the Russian Revolution) Labour leaders have taken for granted the given, inherited framework of parliamentary representation and the existing state.

One aspect of this framework is the unwritten rule that *in theory* MPs are not accountable to anyone outside Parliament other than, as they see fit, their constituents. I stress 'in theory', because the beauty, for some, of Britain's unwritten constitution is that theory and practice can contradict each other, but outsiders to the unwritten rules lose out because there are no agreed rules to argue over or agitate to change. Thus MPs have always represented interests other than those of their constituents (undoubtedly they will have squared the interest concerned with their conscience). They have often been paid for doing so (though only since 1974 have they had to declare such payment), and in all sorts of ways they are accountable to these interests whether through the club, the boardroom or some more formal arrangement. It was precisely *because* this was going on and every other interest but labour's was being thus felt, that the LRC and the Labour Party were formed: to have MPs who would be accountable to labour.

The party's constitution provided for a general framework of accountability of MPs through the PLP to party conference, but there was always considerable room for flexibility, and the accountability of MPs to their constituency was never defined. The balance of power between conference and the parliamentary leadership varies.[22] Two factors affect it profoundly: one is the success, and therefore authority, of the parliamentary leadership in government. Thus in the early to mid-fifties the parliamentary leadership had exceptional authority stemming from what were seen as their achievements between 1945 and 1950. By contrast, the authority of the parliamentary leadership in 1970–73 and again in 1979–81 was at rock bottom. The second fundamental factor in a party based on the trade unions is the industrial strength and political confidence and independence of the unions themselves. The early seventies were a period not just of strong but of confident, mobile, innovative trade unionism: developing new kinds of resistance through occupations and work-ins, spreading direct forms of workplace organisation through national and international shop stewards' organisations, and finally taking on the Conservative government. This militancy and its lasting legacy lay behind the shifting balance of power against the Parliamentary Party throughout the seventies.

I say 'against' the Parliamentary Party, because although trends in the trade union seep eventually through the union–party channels into conference and the block vote, they do not so easily, if at all, reach the majority of the Parliamentary Party. The PLP has inherited, and enveloped itself in, many layers of protective clothing. It is extremely loath to undress.

Reflected glamour

For an MP, parliamentarian values have a certain personal attraction. They set the MP apart, giving him or her a certain untouchable quality; it is almost as if in swearing the Royal oath they gain a little of the reflected glamour of royalty.[23] They gain (or gained, for this is one respect in which reselection has made a difference), a little deference beyond that of any other profession, and certainly beyond the electorate's assessment of their practical worth (MPs always rate low in surveys of people's assessments of the social value of different professions.) For MPs of long standing, high status or, simply, great vanity, to be *required* to submit themselves for reselection before ward and trade-union delegates is all rather demeaning. This is a very strong, perhaps not fully conscious, motive behind the passion with which many MPs resisted the idea of reselection.

Sweated labour

A more material explanation for the emotional strength of the opposition is the assumption, especially among M Ps for safe seats, that they had a job for life. Joe Ashton is the self-appointed shop steward for male Labour M Ps facing a threat to their job security – though a strong minority have walked out of his shop – so I will let him put his case. He does it regularly. He put it like this at the 1978 conference:

I have four minutes to try to save 300 jobs – because that is what you are talking about. There are 300 M Ps who work in a non-union factory. There are no shop stewards . . . We do not come under the Employment Protection Act. There is no unfair dismissal we can appeal to. There is no redundancy pay . . .

A lot of them are not here today. In fact eight died in the past year, some of them because they went to work when they were sick, working crazy hours to try to keep this party alive. All we are saying . . . is that before you sack a man you give him the right to a defence.

M Ps are people, we have got wives, we have got kids, we have mortgages the same as you have. If you cut us, we bleed. [By this time tears were beginning to roll down delegates' cheeks.] We cannot win. If we vote for the 5 per cent we get kicked up the backside by the constituency and the unions. And if we do not vote for it and bring down the government we get kicked up the backside by the electorate and lose our jobs that way.

Not many M Ps will be quite so explicit. However, Ashton's views represent a strong conservative pressure, especially among the older trade-union-sponsored M Ps in 'safe' seats. In a more democratic culture someone would only consider being an MP if they were prepared to face the possibility of not being reselected by the constituency party, just as in theory they are prepared now for election defeat.[24]

Patronage

A stronger, more pervasive pressure in which politics and self-interest intertwine is the pressure of patronage. M Ps resisting the principle and now the practice of mandatory reselection usually justify their stand in terms of the principle of their independent judgement. They warn against constituency parties turning M Ps into 'honourable midgets, right honourable marionettes', to use a phrase of Michael Foot's. The experience of the last fifteen years or so, however, is that an MP's constituency party is generally more sympathetic to MPs who vote according to their political conscience, so long as they have consulted with the party first, than are the Whips and the parliamentary leadership.

So the issue is not a straightforward one of political independence versus accountability to the constituency, but rather, a different version of the one that Joe Ashton used in his defence of MPs' job security. Using his example – a good one – the dilemma is this: If MPs voted for the 5 per cent, they were in danger of trouble from their constituencies and the unions. If they had done as their constituencies might have preferred and voted against or abstained on the 5 per cent they might have forced the government to change its policy and saved it from what proved to be a disastrous mistake, but they would have been out of favour with the leadership and less likely to be offered one of the 150 jobs that the leader has at his disposal. In other words, mandatory reselection potentially weakens the pressure of patronage because it subjects the ambitious MP to a counter-pressure.

'Unrepresentative activists'

As support for mandatory reselection gathered momentum, a strong rallying point for those who opposed it was the argument that General Management Committees (GMCs) were unrepresentative. This was argued most loudly by the Campaign for Labour Victory (CLV), an organisation of MPs, councillors and activists supporting the right wing of the party. (The majority of its members later helped to form the SDP.) Once it became clear, in 1980, that mandatory reselection was likely to become part of the constitution, the proposal was floated on the right, for one person, one vote for all party members through a postal ballot. (Some supporters of reselection too argued for 'one person, one vote', though not on the basis of a postal ballot.)

It was not until the 1982 conference that supporters of CLV's successor, Solidarity,[25] put forward a formal proposal that reselection would be based on 'one person, one vote' (with a postal ballot). The left, almost unanimously, opposed this proposal at that time because it would delay the introduction of reselection, and because they believed that reselection should proceed on the basis of the existing structures of the party. The selection of MPs, the choice of conference delegates, important decisions of policy were made by delegates to the GMC, normally after discussion and sometimes votes in their party or trade-union branch. This procedure, argued the left, eventually with the support of a majority in the party, should at least initially be the basis of reselection. Many on the left, for instance the Campaign for Labour Party Democracy, went further than this and argued that, as a matter of principle, the reselection decision should rest with delegates to the GMC, since it was to them that the MP was accountable month by month. The fundamental principle for CLPD is that accountability and reselection must go together.

There are two separate questions here: first, whether or not GMCs are representative, and secondly, the democratic and practical arguments for and against 'one person, one vote'. It would be quite possible to find that GMCs are in general representative of the party membership – as seems to be the case – and yet support 'one person, one vote' at a general meeting on the grounds that the greater the involvement of party members in such important decisions, the better for the democracy, the level of political debate and awareness, and the recruitment to the party.

There is considerable evidence that GMCs are on the whole representative of party members. GMCs are made up of delegates from the party branches which make up a constituency and from the union branches which are affiliated to the local party. They meet once a month. First, a comprehensive study of the Barnsley CLP by J. A. Tidball[26] shows, contrary to the assumptions of CLV, a wide political agreement between members regardless of their degree of activism. This agreement centred on support for the constitutional reforms, greater social ownership and withdrawal from the EEC. There were disagreements, but these cut across the passive member/activist dimension. Tidball's study, carried out in May 1981, supports the conclusions of an earlier study, in 1976, of constituency parties by Richard Rose: 'Activists are neither forces for extremism nor are they placid followers of whatever policy the leadership wishes them to follow.'[27] Further evidence of the representative character of GMC comes from recent battles over reselection, for instance, the conflict in 1983-85 over the reselection of Peter Shore. In Shore's constituency, Bethnal Green and Stepney, the left – London Labour Briefing – organised a determined campaign to deselect him. Several delegates on the GMC were critical of their campaign, believing it could damage the party. Not all of them were politically sympathetic to Shore. One of them, John Rentoul, describes how he was 'pretty suspicious of him and reluctant to be supporting his reselection'. Rentoul was sympathetic to many of Briefing's policies, but he did not believe that their candidate was a credible alternative to Shore. 'I came to the conclusion,' he says, 'that the deselection of Peter Shore would be a media disaster for the Labour Party. So I decided to grit my teeth and, for the good of the party, organise for Shore's reselection.'

All the party branches were holding preselection meetings at which votes were to be taken to guide, though not formally to mandate, the delegate to the GMC. Rentoul and his colleagues organised mainly in the branches. Shore's own office lobbied the trade unions. The result was an overwhelming vote, 60 out of 90, for Shore at the GMC, with Shore leading among both party and union delegates. Rentoul was surprised at the extent of the majority: 'I had overestimated Briefing's organisation,' he said. He also drew an important conclusion from the experience: 'There are real democratic procedures in the Labour Party. The left cannot just fix things.'

The campaign to support Shore showed that if the supporters of right or centre MPs campaigned for their candidate and took the democracy of the existing procedures seriously – for example branch debates and votes – these procedures could work in their favour.

But the campaign in the branches and wards of Bethnal Green and Stepney was unusual. It was more common, when a member of the parliamentary leadership was in any danger from reselection, for his supporters to rely quite cynically on increasing the number of trade-union delegates. Some of this happened in Bethnal Green and Stepney: Rentoul describes how. 'A whole load of EETPU affiliations arrived quite late in the day. Maybe half a dozen, perhaps only four or five, but still quite a significant block.' (One sixth of Shore's majority). However, the bulk of Shore's support came from party branches.

In Bristol, where in 1981 Michael Cox was competing with Tony Benn for a safe seat as a result of the boundary changes, there was well-organised mobilisation of trade-union delegates by supporters of Cox, solely for the purpose of voting at selection conferences. On November 23, 1981, John Golding, then an MP and political officer of the Post Office Engineers' Union, convened a meeting of trade-union officials, 'to discuss local involvement of trade unions in the affairs of the CLPs'.[28] Six people attended; one was a T&GWU official who wrote a report on the first half of the meeting, including Golding's opening remarks. According to this report:

Golding outlined a plan to obtain increased representation by TU branches on CLP management committees, and particularly those constituencies where the difference between right and left representation was marginal and/or where there is likely to be a contested parliamentary candidate selection in the event of boundary changes, 'such as between Michael Cox and Tony Benn', expressing the need to protect Michael Cox's back against the far left . . .

Golding went on to say that . . . TU representatives could be offered the inducement of not actually becoming actively involved in the CLPs but simply getting themselves registered as a trade-union delegate and only attending the annual meeting of the GMC or selection conference as necessary.

Reports of this kind cast doubt on the claims that the unrepresentative character of GMCs was a real reason for parliamentary alarm. Golding's approach indicates that this was not the problem for the right; the problem was that the representatives were likely to vote the wrong way. The right could not dissolve the GMC but they could it seems ensure that new representatives were elected.[29]

Another hint that 'unrepresentativeness' was not the real cause for concern is found in the remarkable equanimity with which MPs associated with the CLV and the proposal for one person one vote have tolerated some of the smallest, worst-attended GMCs in the country. These include Mike Thomas's old constituency, Newcastle East; Roy Jenkins's old constituency, Stechford in Birmingham; and Tom Ellis's constituency in Liverpool. It is perhaps not surprising that when such MPs became avid supporters of an extended franchise for reselecting the MP, their proposals should be regarded with suspicion.

Many on the left have reacted to the factionalism of CLV by treating 'one person, one vote' as the property of the right. There are a number of exceptions, Eric Heffer being the most notable. He believes that: 'Sooner or later we have to get one person, one vote. I think that's a really sensible thing to do. It's not going to be too popular with some people, but I think it's the right thing to do.'[30] The problem is to devise a form of individual membership involvement which takes account of trade-union affiliations and avoids absentee politics encouraged by a postal ballot. But this is a different question to the accusation of 'unrepresentative GMCs'. On this latter question the conclusion I draw from the analysis of GMCs and the right's use of trade-union delegations is that, like the appeals to 'tolerance and freedom' from those who remained silent over Eddie Milne, the appeal by such people against unrepresentative GMCs is not a convincing explanation of their hostility to constitutional reforms.

The wider challenge

Inherited values, reflected glamour, job security and job promotion all help explain why mandatory reselection caused so much anger and bitterness among Labour MPs, and led them to turn on the left that campaigned for it, thus provoking further animosity from the left. But they do not provide an adequate explanation for the high priority and persistent hostility given to the issue by the press, and (both reflecting and reinforcing press coverage) by the parliamentary Labour leadership. To understand this it is necessary to explore the potential of reselection, the precedent it has established and the further changes that it implies. The establishment, including the Labour establishment, was reacting not primarily to a personal threat (Peter Shore was the only member of the Shadow Cabinet who was at all personally vulnerable from reselection though there were unsubstantiated press rumours about Gerald Kaufman) but to an institutional and ideological challenge.

The achievements of reselection so far do not reveal its potential. Many things weakened its momentum, not least the pressure it came under: the 1983 election; the decline in trade-union pressure; and finally, a version of the left's own parliamentarianism: once we have got the right man or woman into the job, we can relax. As a result there are numerous broken links in the chain of accountability of which reselection was intended to be part. An understanding of these will indicate the kind of challenge reselection could potentially represent, in combination with further reforms.

The chain of accountability: broken links

Earlier in this chapter I quoted Chris Mullin's hope that reselection will be a pressure on the normally upwardly mobile MP to 'look down or over his or her shoulders at the people who put them there'. There are some signs that this is happening. But then what? Most MPs are capable of looking both ways at once. They can keep a good relation with their GMCs with regular reports, visits to the constituency, speeches of the sort the constituency wants, involvement in local campaigns, picket lines and so on, and at the same time follow the leadership's line in the PLP and in the lobby. They can moan about it to their GMCs: 'What can I do? I raised it at the PLP meeting, but nothing happened.' In other words, reselection can improve the relationship between the MP and his or her constituency party without significantly checking the power of the party leader or Prime Minister. Reselection could thus merely add to the appearance of democracy, without changing the reality of Prime Ministerial government.

One reason for this has been the response of the constituency parties themselves. Bob Clay, who became MP for Sunderland North at the 1983 election, described a problem which has been raised by several left-wing MPs and members of the Campaign for Labour Party Democracy:

I'm quite sure that there are a lot of exceptions round the country, but it still amazes me that constituency Labour parties take so little interest in what their Members of Parliament are doing.

The best way I can put it succinctly and practically is this: if I ceased to be an MP and went back to being on the management committee where there was a Labour MP, I would – not out of malice, but out of genuine interest – be asking how he or she voted on this, that and the other. I would ask whether such and such a question was raised at the PLP on Wednesday morning, and who said what. I wouldn't be satisfied if the MP said 'Oh, the PLP has closed meetings, it's secret, blah, blah.' Then I would be asking what else they'd been doing. Had they spent the whole week at the House of Commons? There was a demonstration on Cruise, did you go on it? What speeches have you made, what questions have you asked?

On my GMC there are very few occasions when I'm questioned. There are very few examples of where my GMC has actually shared the kind of choices that MPs have to make.

Yet, as Clay adds: 'If we are going to have real accountability, and if there's any point in MPs really playing a part in changing society towards socialism, then GMCs have got to be sharing all the time with MPs what they're doing.'

Reg Race, MP for Haringey between 1979–1983, makes a similar observation: 'CLPs are still extremely trusting and deferential. MPs can get away with a lot.'

This could change in conditions when Labour is in government or in a strategic parliamentary position. There would be more at stake. But it does not sound as if many constituency parties have been getting into practice. Clay admits that, as an MP, he knows what to ask. But after all the pressure for reselection, one would have thought that constituency activists would have their questions at the ready. Deference still remains, however; also, there is a culture gap: 'MPs coming out of their world to share the thoughts of party members, and party members coming out of their world to share the thoughts of MPs. There is a real gap,' says Clay, 'particularly if you're a long way from London.'

There is also a more fundamental problem: the habit of leaving the responsibilities to someone else. The left works hard in the build-up to reselection, gets its socialist MP and then leaves the MP to get on with it. Clay again:

People say to me, if you ever do anything wrong, we'll let you know, but in the meantime, just get on with it. But I'm not interested in simply being a Labour MP because it's a job or career. So the more I get cut off from the live contact, the less am I involved in building a different kind of relationship between Parliament and society – even if it's socialism in one constituency! – and then there's no point as far as I'm concerned.

The parliamentary Labour farce

The other side of the problem, the inside break in the chain of accountability, is the character of the Parliamentary Party: above all, its almost total absence of democratic organisation and, behind this, the leader's patronage.

Much has been written about the PLP's position within the party's power structure and the permanent tensions and shifting balance between the parliamentary leadership and the party conference. The PLP's internal structure is more mysterious. The majority of MPs prefer it that way. Until two years ago, it did not even distribute its minutes to its own members, let alone have regular formal voting. The PLP dislikes the idea that a minority of MPs report its proceedings back to their CLPs. Willie McKelvey, MP for Kilmarnock and Loudon, was one of those who pressed for the minimal formalities. He wanted a lot more. He wanted the attendance and votes of each MP at PLP meetings to be recorded as part of the process of keeping CLPs informed. Only with this kind of information and formality could reselection have any real influence on the behaviour of the PLP. He and Ernie Ross, MP for Dundee West, entered Parliament in 1979 fresh from battles to achieve accountability in the Dundee Council (which put two Labour councillors in jail for corruption). He described to me his first PLP meeting:

It was a shambolic affair. Mainly Jim Callaghan pontificating. Only around sixty or so there at the most. Ernie and I looked at each other, not quite being able to believe it. We thought that at least it would be organised to the level of the trade-union branch. We tried to excuse it: 'Well, this is just the first meeting, maybe it's a sort of inaugural meeting and the next one will get down to things.'

But the second one was just as bad. We were appalled, truly appalled. There was no discussion about policy. So we just got up and let loose. Ernie went in hard and I followed up softer. We said, 'You'd better reform the PLP yourselves or it'll be reformed from the outside.' Some of the people who've now joined the SDP virtually spat at us. We got some sympathy. But many on the left had come to accept it. They felt we were young – in parliamentary terms – and inexperienced. And the Whips, they don't like anyone to get organised.

At times it was laughable. Early on I asked for the minutes. (They were kept, you know, but not distributed, just typed out and kept in a book.) They said I'd have to ask the chairman. I asked the chairman and he pondered long and hard. 'You can look at them in the Whip's office,' he said, 'you can read and digest them.' They were astonished that we wanted to see them. So I went into the office and sat and copied them.

Another ridiculous thing was resolutions. If you put in a resolution to be discussed, you'd find it wasn't on the table. 'The shadow cabinet are looking at it,' we'd be told. It would have completely disappeared by the next meeting: 'up the lumb [chimney],' we'd say.

Here was a clear clash of expectations and political cultures. McKelvey and Ross's experiences of democratic institutions in the labour movement outside Parliament led them to expect a more organised, more transparent, more accountable and in a sense more powerful organisation. As an ex-AUEW convenor and district and divisional committee member McKelvey was used to clear relations of accountability and regular elections to any position of privilege from branch doorkeeper to chair, and he and Ross wanted to help *do* something.

They were also accustomed to discipline that was the outcome of democratic debate and decision-making. Similarly, as leaders of a Labour group and district Labour party that had been through a democratic revolution, they were used to minuted meetings; recorded votes on important matters; elections to all senior council positions (the Labour group was in power, almost permanently); a close working relationship between the party and the group, with the non-voting attendance of party officers at group meetings.

In other words, their experience had been of relationships in which elected representatives, from the leader downwards, were accountable to party members and to the people whose support the party seeks to win. The reselection of councillors or the annual election of stewards in the AUEW was part of this process, and as a consequence it has a direct bearing on decision-making at the top. In Parliament there is no such structured process, just an inner circle consisting of the Leader, his office and a core of the Shadow Cabinet on which pressure can occasionally be exerted by a variety of guerrilla tactics, by individuals and groups who have little desire for a parliamentary career.

The inner circle

In opposition
When the Labour Party is in opposition, part of the inner circle, the Shadow Cabinet, is elected by the PLP. But that does not

mean that the decisions of the Shadow Cabinet are matters for debate and final decision at the PLP's weekly meetings. Indeed, votes are not normally taken in the Shadow Cabinet; it is a consensual body whose main purpose is to help the Leader round out policy and co-ordinate its implementation. PLP meetings are purely consultative, a sounding board for the Leader and the Whips, an occasion for the left to harmlessly let off steam.

The only time when a PLP meeting becomes a more serious affair is when MPs threaten a large-scale revolt in the lobbies. But in opposition such a threat is on the whole empty. There are also 'subject groups' which meet regularly, but they too are consultative. The important policy-making bodies are the MPs and the sympathetic experts whom front-bench spokespeople group around themselves. Each senior front-bench spokesperson receives funds for researchers and assistants through the state money that is available for opposition parties. In the case of the Labour Party these funds are distributed by the Leader. In opposition, then, there is no decision-making mechanism whereby back-bench MPs can have a real say in their party's parliamentary work. It is no wonder that patronage is such a powerful influence: it provides the only chance of being anywhere near the parliamentary action, or even the semblance of it. For these reasons, the link between the constituency party and the work of the Parliamentary Party in opposition is extremely tenuous, without further reform of the Parliamentary Party and an elimination of the Leader's powers of patronage.

The contrast between the action of the vast majority of constituency parties and the prevarications of the PLP during the miners' strike illustrates well the lack of influence of the CLPs on the PLP. A minority of MPs in the Campaign Group and the Tribune Group pressed for action: a debate at least. Yes, the Shadow Cabinet would say, but leave the timing to us. It seemed the time would never come; and nothing could be done through the PLP to hasten it. The Campaign Group found that the only way they could draw attention to the forgotten issues of the strike and achieve a debate was to take direct action in the Chamber. On November 21 1984, after the government announced that it would increase the amount which strikers were 'deemed' to receive in strike pay (with a consequent cut in their social security), members of the Campaign Group stood on the floor of the House until the Speaker agreed to a debate. Members of the Tribune Group resorted to similar tactics in 1971 over the Industrial Relations Bill.

In government

When Labour is in government, the formal mechanisms are no better. In many ways they are worse, because Cabinet ministers have in effect been transported into another sphere altogether. They hardly have to spare a glance downwards from their departmental fastnesses to the Parliamentary Party below because their future lies above, in the hands of the Prime Minister, whose judgement is likely to depend on the inner politics of the Cabinet, the minister's performance in the House, the competence of the department and only occasionally on the minister's standing in the Parliamentary Party, let alone the party more widely. A liaison committee exists to link the two spheres, consisting of six MPs elected each session from and by Labour backbenchers, one Labour peer and six ministers nominated by the Prime Minister; it is chaired by the Chairman of the parliamentary Party who is elected annually by the MPs. However, this does not provide MPs with any means of checking and controlling government policy; it is rather a means of ensuring the smooth progress of government business through the two Houses.

The only power of backbenchers is their vote. It is only when they threaten to use this against government policy that they are listened to. The impact of mandatory reselection on the way that MPs vote has not yet been put to the test. Much will depend on the ability and cohesion of independent groupings of MPs which develop their own strategy and tactics towards the Parliamentary Party and the support that needs to be won for outside movements and campaigns.

The state in Parliament

The fundamental problem facing any attempt to challenge the power of the parliamentary leadership is the weight of the state's presence on Parliament. This is what distinguishes it in kind from local government. This authority of the state is implicit in the obligations or oaths that Members sign. Councillors, committee chairs and council leaders are bound by a 'fiduciary duty to the ratepayer', an obligation to spend ratepayers' money for the benefit of the ratepayer, that is, the public. MPs, ministers and Prime Ministers are bound by an oath to the Crown. There is no oath or statement of obligation to the people.

Does this really matter? Surely oaths are just empty rituals, sworn one day, forgotten about the next. It's true, they may not have an obvious material effect. If you ask an MP 'How has your political behaviour been affected by the oath you swore to the Queen a few years ago?' he is unlikely to tell you anything very interesting. The significance of these oaths is symbolic, a clue to what is and is not acceptable, what changes can be taken on board and what will cause one almighty row. In other words, they give you an idea of when you are about to knock into the constitutional equivalent of Parliament's balls! The crown in effect stands for the moral authority of the British state.[31]

The significance of these oaths is that, in between elections, moral authority lies within Parliament, and that means not simply in the laws it makes or agrees to, but in the process by which it does so. To suggest it lies anywhere else is in effect a challenge to the authority of the state. That is what the unsuspecting delegates to the Newham Labour Party did, without realising quite what they were doing. In this way too, mandatory reselection and non-parliamentary election of the Labour leader, not to speak of proposals for the election of the Cabinet and party control over policy, confronted the long tradition of British rule from above.

The trade unions and the state

Week after week therefore, during 1980 and 1981, *The Times* – which was still at that time the 'representative' paper of the ruling class – attacked the reforms not merely as an internal party affair but as matters of importance to the state. The underlying fear was not of constituency 'extremists', though these were frequently the objects of abuse. The most important cause of their concern was the increased influence which these reforms would give to the trade unions, that is, to the organised working class. And at that time, the late seventies and early eighties, 'trade unions' conjured up not the meek, subservient Len Murray at the TUC, but memories of striking miners, able to cause the downfall of a Conservative government, shop stewards leading occupations of the property of their employers and municipal workers refusing to collect the garbage and bury the dead. To *Times* leader writers, Conservative MPs and to the leadership of those who split from the Labour Party to form the SDP, the idea that these people should have a significant say in electing a future Prime Minister was a challenge to the constitution. It certainly upset the customary role that the Labour Party had been relied on to play within this constitution.

Peregrine Worsthorne, contemplating predictions of the demise of the old Labour Party, writes that '. . . much of the stability of this country depended on the Labour Party which, in some ways, was just as powerful a force for continuity and tradition as the Tory Party.'[32] How is it that the party formed by the organised working class could be revered in such terms by an arch-Conservative? Egon Wertheimer, a German political journalist observing the Labour Party in 1929, provides at least one clue. He notes an apparently inexplicable disparity in the years 1924 to 1926 between the policy of the trade unions and the policy of the party in Parliament. On the one hand, the trade unions were becoming increasingly militant, finally responding to the employers' lock-out in 1926 with a general strike. On the international scene they were pursuing a united front with revolutionary Russia. By contrast, the party in Parliament 'conducted a purely defensive policy, refused all extreme measures of socialisation and made the greatest possible concessions to national political traditions'. Internationally, it formed a strong anti-Communist front. The explanation for this disparity, and the consequent fact that the militant policies of the trade unions had no national parliamentary voice, lay, according to Wertheimer, in the following peculiar state of affairs in British politics. This is such that:

the party organisation does not represent the decisive factor in the Parliamentary Party. On the contrary, in practice the Parliamentary Labour Party controls the party organisation . . .

After an election the Parliamentary Party detaches itself from connection with the party organisation to an extent almost unthinkable from a Continental standpoint, and becomes an independent organism known characteristically as the Parliamentary Labour Party, which is not a function of the party nor its expression of political power, but a party in itself.

In comparison with the German Social Democratic Party, the Labour Party is still a mere voting machine.[33]

After the defeat of the General Strike, the unions themselves, at least the majority of them, became moderate in their policies. The tension between the Parliamentary Party and the party outside, most notably the unions, relaxed, though it never completely disappeared.

By the late sixties and seventies, however, the renewed strength and confidence which built up in the unions during the postwar boom produced once again, as we have seen, a disparity between the party organisation and the trade unions on the one hand, and the Parliamentary Party on the other. The stakes in this disparity were even higher than in 1924–26 because by 1980 Labour had three times in the previous fifteen years been a majority government, and was expected to return to government at the next election. Moreover, the unions in the late seventies and early eighties had retained much of their strength.[34]

The unions' concern, or rather the concern of their active members, in supporting the constitutional reforms was to make it impossible for the Parliamentary Party to act as 'a party in itself'. Yet it was precisely this ability of the PLP, though attached to the unions, to operate autonomously from them which made the Labour Party such a force for stability.

The unions' assertion of their potential power within the party made Labour unreliable as a 'force for continuity and tradition'. For though trade-union leaders tend themselves to be traditionalists, in just about every sense of that word, they are ultimately in the hands of their members. They are not able to guarantee that their members will make the kind of decisions that preserve continuity and tradition, especially at times of economic instability.

This momentary assertion by the unions of political power beyond what is considered their proper subordinate place in the party they had created struck at the heart of the 'old Labour Party'. It posed a problem for the leaders of Labourism accustomed to a trade-union movement which, in general, leaves them to get on with their parliamentary business. If they dissociated themselves from the unions, they would have little chance of a future in the party's leadership. If they were loyal to the unions they would have to assume that the constitutional reforms were a temporary disturbance, sit it out and blame something else for the upset. David Owen and the rest of the Gang did the first. Jim Callaghan, Denis Healey, Peter Shore and Roy Hattersley did the latter.

In their efforts to show that the Labour Party was unchanged, the Labourist leaders who stayed with Labour blamed alien 'factions' for the upset. If, for one minute, they acknowledged the role of the unions, they would have played into the hands either of Owen, who condemned the unions, or Benn, who supported them. An interview in which Brian Walden questions Jim Callaghan on the reason why the party moved to the left in the seventies and early eighties illustrates this wilful amnesia. Walden asked simply for Callaghan's explanation for the shift to the left. Callaghan replied that he did not know why there was such a turn to the left: 'I cannot trace the activities of these groups. I do not follow these factions burrowing away.'[35]

Thus 'factions' – none of which in fact played any significant role in the movement for the constitutional reforms, and which were not mentioned by Walden[36] – became the scapegoats for, and a means of minimising the role of the unions in a potentially profound political challenge, not only to the constitution of the party but also to the British state.

Democracy in and against the state

The constitutional reforms were not and are not anti-Parliament; they are anti-parliamentarian. That is, they challenge the view that Parliament, and the state in Parliament, is the sole source of moral political authority. The reforms attempted to extend constitutional legitimacy to forms of political democracy outside Parliament as well. In this sense they are 'republican' in spirit, they seek to treat people as potential citizens with sovereign rights.

The democratic left that campaigned for these reforms wants Parliament to become a democratic national assembly. A Parliament which takes final decisions on the government of the country yet is flanked by an elected judiciary to preside over the enactment of its laws. What the left questions is the idea that

Parliament is an exclusive sovereign which once elected decides, like a private club, its own rules and decision-making processes.

The left's questioning of Parliament's claim to such total sovereignty arises not so much from an abstract belief in extra-parliamentary democracy – their ideas on this are still untheorised and pragmatic. Rather it arises from long observation that even (or perhaps especially) under a Labour government, Parliament's decision-making, in particular the government's role in it, is already in fact based on non-parliamentary processes. Here they observe the power of the Civil Service (well beyond its advisory brief), of the defence establishment and NATO, the security services, the CBI and the financial institutions of the City. The left's initial desire was to protect and to stiffen the resistance of a democratically elected Labour government against these unaccountable pressures, by allying it to the pressures and initiatives of the people who elected it. For this the radical left turned to the only instrument at hand, ill-equipped though it is in its present form: the party. And through it they strengthened the one lever they have over Parliament, weak though it may be: the selection of their MP.

In several local authorities the left has gone further in creating a formal non-parliamentary element in council decision-making and execution, outside the institutions of the Labour Party. This has been possible, partly because reselection was already an established – though in the past underused – procedure of local councillors. It was also because, at first, the power of the state was less heavily present in the council chamber. Less was at stake. But local experiences can at least illustrate the logic of a popular, rather than purely parliamentary democracy. Chapter 3 describes the detail of these experiences in Manchester, Sheffield and London. But the essential points illustrate the potential of the left's challenge to Parliament's all-encompassing sovereignty.

In these three towns,[37] to varying degrees, the Labour Party and other socialists working with it have based some council decisions on a sharing of power with other, popular forms of democracy. In Manchester the council is increasingly sharing the power to run local services with neighbourhood groups; at the GLC the Women's Committee shared its power to allocate resources to women's needs with women's organisations across London; at the GLC and Sheffield a good part of the councils' employment policies were based on workplace trade unionism. Increasingly these forms of democracy have a formal power within the council's decision-making and execution. As we shall see, they certainly strengthen the council's position in relation to hostile institutions: property developers, multinationals, government quangos, entrenched local-government officers – the council equivalent of the City, the defence establishment and over-powerful sections of the Civil Service, respectively. As with the left's view of Parliament, the council has the final decision on overall policy.

These local experiences will best illustrate the potential logic of the Labour Party's constitutional reforms: they open up the prospect of popular democratic institutions having a formal power in the making and execution of legislation.

Imagine representatives of CND along with shop stewards and technicians from the shipyards making Trident in Barrow, working as members of an 'Arms Conversion Council' in the Ministries of Defence and Industry, preparing detailed plans for putting the resources and skills of the nuclear arms industry to useful purposes. Or think of women from Greenham, with other leaders of CND and sympathetic technicians being given the power and resources to monitor the withdrawal of Cruise missiles. Or workplace and community representatives with local authorities drawing up investment plans for the Department of Industry and the Treasury for areas of economic collapse like London's Docklands, parts of the north-east and Merseyside. And you begin to see why, when the peace movement is strong and the nightmare of trade-union strength could once again come true, the idea of giving power to the Labour Party Conference and to constituency Labour parties – in the establishment's eyes all part of the same dreadful group of people – sets the alarm bells clanging.

Reselection and the state

Except in relation to local government, few on the left explicitly *have* thought out these connections.[38] There is a tendency on the Labour left to postpone all questions of the state 'until we have control of the party'. But it did not take a huge leap of imagination to see the link between constitutional reforms in the party and challenges to the conventional operation of the state itself. Tony Benn's activity in the Department of Industry from 1974 until he was sacked in July 1975 provided evidence that even if the left do not make the connections, the right, the City and the mandarins do.

Much has been written about Benn's work at the Department of Industry and the reactions of the City, the CBI, the Treasury and Harold Wilson.[39] But a personal minute he wrote to all Industry ministers when he became Secretary of State sets out the principles behind his and their activities. He describes 'our twin role' as 'spokesmen, representatives, champions and educators as well as mere managers within a Labour government team'. The Prime Minister had also sent round a memo listing the obligations on ministers as managers.[40]

Benn is quite explicit about ministers' loyalty and accountability to the Labour Party and movement:

Our debt to the party
We are also members of the Labour Party and the labour movement owing loyalty to its policies and the people in it upon whose efforts we relied for our electoral strength . . .

Loyalty and accountability
That loyalty extends to those we represent in Parliament, to those to whom we are accountable as Labour candidates and to the Labour government . . .

He goes on to describe ministers' 'twin role':

There is a distinction between the broad exercise of our political role and our official ministerial acts or statements. The movement and the government has everything to gain by seeing that that difference is widely understood.

By 'our political role' he meant involvement in the policy-making of the party outside Parliament 'contributing our views as to what we think should be done next, even if that means reviewing past government decisions'. This is necessary, he adds, 'if we are to mobilise the energy of the movement to work enthusiastically for the policies we have jointly discussed and agreed. This means we must keep it fully informed about the progress of our work.'

There are two ways in which Tony Benn here extends political authority beyond Parliament. One is through the idea of accountability, 'to the party and to the movement'. The other is through the idea of active involvement in government: his aim is for 'the movement to work enthusiastically for the policies we have jointly discussed and agreed'. During his brief period as Minister for Industry he began to develop these ideas in practice: preparing government Green Papers for 'meetings with trade-union officials, local authorities, local employer associations, shop stewards and gatherings of working management whose support is essential if our policies are to succeed'; encouraging shop-stewards' organisations to draw up production plans that would save jobs and meet local needs to be backed by the government in negotiations with management.[41]

After one year Benn was removed from the Department of Industry. Joe Haines, Harold Wilson's press secretary at the time, gives the background: 'The whispers from the Treasury's contacts grew stronger. Only if Tony Benn was sacked, it was said, would the confidence of British industry be restored.'[42] What 'the Treasury's contacts' feared was not state interference: the private sector could deal with this. Such policies had already been emasculated in Cabinet and anyway the major companies knew how to negotiate with the DOI. What was more alarming was that they would not, if Benn had his way, be negotiating with the civil servants in the manner to which they were accustomed, in confidence and to sympathetic ears. Benn, a Cabinet minister, was seeing shop-floor representatives independently; he was going round the country encouraging workers in their demands, buiding confidence, raising expectations, giving out information. In a sense it was as much Benn's democracy – of a radical kind – as his socialism, in the conventional sense of state intervention, which caused the panic and loss of confidence.

The secrets behind Prime Ministerial power

It should be clear that reselection and the election of the Leader do not automatically challenge the character of the state. That depends, among other things, on the strength of mass movements for change. But the establishment's responses to these reforms and to Tony Benn's activities – mirrored in the responses of the Labour leadership – had the hysterical, frequently paranoic quality they did because these ideas touched on the secret that lies beneath Prime Ministerial government:[43] the closed, class-based character of the British state. Once Prime Ministerial government is challenged from outside Parliament as well as inside, this will expose the character of the state: its secrecy, its subservience to unaccountable financial and industrial powers ('the bailiffs', in Wilson's famous description of the financial pressures on the tenancy of his elected government[44]), and its domination by the Atlantic Alliance. Parliament has protected this state well. The constitutional reforms of the Labour Party, modest though they were, and the behaviour of their well-placed champion, cautious though he was, introduced an unacceptable degree of instability into this protection. Parliamentarians, inside Parliament and outside, united to block what they regarded as the thin edge of what was for them a very dangerous wedge.

The explanation for the outcry over Reg Prentice's deselection – an outcry which grew louder and louder with each advance towards constitutional reform – has moved a long way from the defence of 'freedom and toleration' called for by the 179 Labour MPs. The exploration in this chapter demonstrates that to differing degrees these parliamentarians were not defending principles. They were defending the mystique of their position, their job security, the hope of patronage, the exclusivity of the parliamentary club and the sovereignty of the state in Parliament. They were defending their right to exclusive rule. No wonder party members in Newham felt as if, unprepared, they had disturbed a hornets' nest.

The wider Campaign for Labour Party Democracy was also in crucial ways unprepared for the repercussions of constitutional reforms. These astute and determined campaigners operated on the assumption that the Labour Party was electorally secure. This was not a conscious assumption: it was just taken for granted. This meant that their focus was exclusively on the inside job of winning power, using every procedural lever and mobilising every pocket of inside support they could find.

The logic of their demands and their desire to democratise government affected the majority of the population: the 71 per cent who felt that they had no say in what the government does and the 66 per cent who felt that MPs generally lose touch with people pretty quickly.[45] But the Labour Party's reform movement was not geared up to speak to these people. Except briefly during Tony Benn's campaign for the Deputy Leadership, it had created no platform from which to speak 'to the nation', or at least to the majority of working-class people; to provide the socialist equivalent of an alternative to the lectures delivered by Roy Jenkins in preparing the way for the SDP.

This is a constant dilemma for the Labour left, reflected at every level of its activities: to achieve anything within the party, especially power as distinct from paper policies, it has to spend an inordinate amount of energy taking its proposals through the sometimes blocked and convoluted procedures of the labour movement. This easily becomes an all-engrossing task. The labour movement can appear to be a whole world in itself. Meantime it has no independent access to the public. Its message comes out often only through the attacks made on it by the leadership – like sending prison letters through a revengeful censor.

2 The Devil's Mark:
Verdict on 1983

When it was proposed that Labour parties should regularly reselect MPs in 1980, a Gallup Poll found that 83 per cent of would-be Labour voters supported the idea.[1] Since that time, the demonisation of the new left has gone so far that the idea of their constitutional reforms being electorally popular is hardly believable. There are other survey results which cast doubt on the notion that the ideas of the radical left have no popular base. In 1983 74 per cent of working-class voters (defined by the pollsters as manual working class – 34 per cent of the population) agreed that 'the government should give workers more say in running the place where they work'. This was an increase of 11 per cent from 1974.[2]

I do not normally pore over survey data, but this figure on industrial democracy is an important statistic because of another one which has become a regular and influential reference point in public political debate and policy-making: the statistic that only 23 per cent of working-class voters agree that 'more industries should be nationalised'.[3] The conclusion from this latter statistic is that Labour's traditional supporters have moved to the right. But attitudes towards industrial democracy indicate that the situation – and the definition of left and right – is altogether more complicated.

On other issues, too, the left's policies struck a significant chord. For instance on the distribution of wealth: in 1983 61 per cent agreed that 'income and wealth should be redistributed towards ordinary people'; on Northern Ireland, 58 per cent of voters in 1983 supported the reunification of Ireland and 59 per cent supported the complete withdrawal of British troops from Ulster; on American nuclear missiles, over 55 per cent of Alliance and Labour supporters felt the siting of these missiles in Britain made Britain less safe.[4]

By 1983, however, the Labour Party as a whole, whatever that whole is, had become mightily unpopular, even with its own traditional supporters. Its meagre 28 per cent of the poll meant that it had lost a quarter of the votes it had in 1979, already a low vote by comparison with the 1960s. More fundamentally, it lost the old certainty that dissatisfaction with the Conservative Party meant automatic votes for Labour. And the most commonly accepted verdict for this, inside and outside the Labour Party, put the blame on the left.

This verdict placed the devil's mark on the left. It poisoned the changes it had helped to bring about in the recent past and it then worked to isolate its activities over the following years. It set the terms of Neil Kinnock's leadership: 'It was important for the long-term success of his leadership,' says Kinnock's admiring biographer, 'to set out his stall as an opponent of the far left.'[5] Indeed almost all the major events of Kinnock's leadership have been in this role: the expulsion of members and suspected members of Militant, the disassociation from the NUM leadership, the imposition of a candidate at Knowsley North, the attempts, only slightly more subtle, to influence the choice of candidate at Greenwich, the echoing of Norman Tebbit's attacks on 'loony left' councils, the attempts to suppress black sections and their spokespeople. The attacks on Militant were seen as so important electorally that when Kinnock launched his famous attack at the 1985 conference on Militant and Liverpool City Council, Denis Healey believed that, 'We shall look back on this day as the moment when Labour won the next election.'[6] The reason Healey could think this was because the attack on Militant had a significance far beyond the small sect which in most areas it is. Militant had by this time, through a combination of their own grandiose claims and the party leadership's desire for a visible, definable scapegoat, become the symbolic surrogate for the left.[7] By 1987 some Labour MPs were reported to be positively relishing the prospect of a renewed attack on the left – this time it was black sections – as a means of pulling Labour up in the opinion polls.[8]

Michael Foot and the centre right leadership around him had initiated this process. For them it was *ad hoc*, a product of more or less uncontrolled panic at the signs of the SDP's likely electoral success. Neil Kinnock's leadership was a professional re-run of the strategy followed instinctively under Foot; the strategy that led to the 1983 defeat. The defeat of Labour in 1983 and the verdict on this defeat is vital to the understanding of the recent divisions within the party, including the build-up to and aftermath of the 1987 election.

In arriving at their fateful verdict on 1983, Labour leaders blamed the reforms that had taken place in their own party. Denis Healey was the most vituperative (in public). He took a wide and all-encompassing sweep and damned the whole period of constitutional change: 'In that period,' he said, 'the party itself acquired a highly unfavourable public image, based on disunity, extremism, crankiness and general unfitness to govern.'[9] Others were more specific. Some blamed the Manifesto, 'the longest suicide note in history', Gerald Kaufman called it.[10] Many put the emphasis on the divisions in the party and implied that it was the left that was the divisive force. This was the view of the Communist Party historian, Eric Hobsbawm, whose analysis has been very influential. He accused the left of 'engaging in a civil war rather than in fighting the right (the Conservatives).'[11] There was a lot of criticism of the organisation of Walworth Road, which was seen as, in part, the fault of officials associated with the left, in particular Jim Mortimer, the General Secretary appointed in 1982. And some of the criticism of Michael Foot's leadership included accusations that he conceded too much to the left.

A section of the left itself, led by the Labour Left Co-ordinating Committee (LCC), agreed that it shared some responsibility for the defeat, though they pointed to the long-term decline of Labour's popularity, associated especially with the record of Labour governments. They saw the problem as the 'stalemate in the party between right and left'. This meant that 'As each was manoeuvring for power the right and the left became more concerned with NEC elections than general elections. The arguments about Militant came to dominate the agenda of party discussion. Policy became frozen as no one dared to rethink left or right mythology.' They assumed, quite rightly, that it was only the left that would make concessions. They were reflecting a loyalty to the party which has always, for good or ill, been more characteristic of the left than the right, or at least the more ideological sections of the right.[12] They were also reflecting the internal crisis, the weakness of policy and organisation within the left following Benn's campaign for the Deputy Leadership.

On this basis a significant section of the left made their truce, or rather, as Nigel Williamson, the editor of *Tribune* from 1984 to 1987, put it: 'We threw in the towel.' Many leading members of the LCC were also optimistic about the new leader, Neil Kinnock, elected in 1983. They expected that in exchange for their loyalty he would listen to their ideas about policy and campaigns – most of which was party policy.

The loyalty of the left

Since the left is frequently cast as the doubting Thomas, if not Judas, it is worth exploring its real loyalty. It has two distinct roots. First is the belief that in a fundamental sense the party is *their* party. The party's primarily trade-union origins do not alter this but reinforce it, because whatever the character of the parliamentary leadership, the bond with the unions anchors the party in the working class. To be disloyal to the party – whether by leaving it or by undermining its chances of becoming a government – would be to be disloyal to the working class. This latter view would be shared, though in a less ideological form, by the more Labourist right like Hattersley, Healey and by all accounts, had he lived, Anthony Crosland.[13] They did not join the SDP for 'tribal' or simply egalitarian reasons; they had some commitment to the working class. This view of loyalty runs particularly deep on the left, making the left ultimately most responsive to the call for unity. A more tactical, and controversial, source of loyalty is dependence: 'the left needs the right to win,' as Nigel Williamson put it. By winning he meant winning elections. This lack of confidence within the left helps to explain a crucial feature of the left's history in the early eighties: the left's disintegration, nationally, after Benn's losing campaign for the Deputy Leadership. Behind this lay the absence of any strategy or organisation capable of winning a popular base for socialism independent of the electoral politics of the party leadership. I will return to the case for such independence in the conclusions to this book.

Accepting the terms of public debate

I want to ask a question which, in my view, arises from Labour's defeat and has continued to arise throughout Neil Kinnock's leadership. The problem in 1983 was not 'just' that Labour lost, it was also that Labour was unable, and has continued to be unable, to change or even positively influence the terms of public debate. Why is this so? A subsidiary question follows: under what conditions could it once more challenge, rather than echo, the terms set by the Conservative Party and its powerful allies?

The conventional verdict against the left rules out these questions. It accepts uncritically the existing terms of debate. It accepts the received wisdom as to the terms of the electoral race, to which the party must adapt or lose. And if it loses, then that is the fault of those who did not adapt.

The 'terms of public debate' are not the same as 'public opinion'. To challenge the former does not mean that I think we should ignore the latter.[14] On the contrary, it means to fight for opinions in a creative fashion. For 'public opinion' contains cross-cutting currents – as the statistics at the beginning of this chapter illustrate. Their varying strengths depend in part on the clarity and confidence with which aspirations are articulated in the wider political culture. Perhaps because Labour's version of the consensus, a corporatist consensus, had for so long dominated *both* the terms of public debate and the main trends in public opinion, the party leadership confused the two. So that when public opinion moves away from the party their instinctive response is to follow it, rather than to challenge the ideas and interpretation of events that have led it to move. The result is that, increasingly, policy priorities are the result of new polling rather than new thinking.[15]

This is not to argue that opinion polls are inherently reactionary. Surveys and polls are important to help identify, listen and give political expression to those quieter, suppressed or confused voices within public opinion which potentially share the party's objectives. An understanding of the trends in public opinon is an essential aid rather than an alternative to challenging the terms of public debate.

People have different ways of trying to understand the mobile and contradictory trends in public opinion, independently of the officially defined consensus. For my part, I was influenced particularly by a study of the 1983 election which goes beyond a study of voting patterns to consider political and social attitudes and how they have changed over the last six elections.

It is called *How Britain Votes*, by Anthony Heath, Peter Jowell and John Curtice.[16] I draw on their very thorough analysis to ground my exploration of why the party leadership had so little influence on the terms of public debate, in the reality of how people voted in 1983, what their opinons were on central issues and how these had changed since previous elections.

The longest suicide note in history?

First consider the 1983 Manifesto. Many on the left, most publicly Tony Benn, shared with the Manifesto's critics a belief in its importance for the election result. For Benn its importance was positive. In a notorious article in the *Guardian* a few weeks after the election, he highlighted the distinctively socialist character of the Manifesto.[17] He then argued that in spite of the opposition of the parliamentary leadership, 'the 1983 Labour Manifesto commanded the loyalty of millions of voters and a democratic bridgehead has been established from which further advances in public understanding and support can be made.' For Benn the election defeat had a silver lining: eight and a half million votes for socialism. It is true that most of the Manifesto's specific policies were more radical than those of any manifesto in the last twenty years, and it is true that front-bench spokesmen were openly hostile –[18] but Benn's attempt to see the bright side of Labour's eight and a half million votes gave the impression that as far as he was concerned, the election had gone according to plan. Ironically, his statement simply provided the incriminating evidence for the left's responsibility for defeat. No doubt he had meant to give a lead and lift people out of despondency. But his claims for the Manifesto were treated rather like those of an over-confident burglar returning to the scene of a crime to claim further loot. They were seen as proving his guilt beyond doubt.

How Britain Votes assesses the role of the Manifesto by analysing the results of several surveys of attitudes towards the issues that dominated the election. From these they calculate what the result would have been if people had voted according to the positions of each party on these important issues. They conclude that if detailed policy stances were decisive, then 'Labour would not in fact have gone down to defeat at all'. They then present the responses to their survey on each of the issues which dominated the election campaign, and show that on none of them were the Conservatives, exclusively, in the lead. On unemployment and inflation, Labour were in the lead followed by the Alliance; on taxation and government spending, it was the Alliance which came first with Labour second, and on defence, the Conservatives tied first with the Alliance.

Their data suggest therefore that voting choices are not made on the basis of a conscious weighing of alternative policies. Rather, they argue, 'electoral choice is based on a much broader, more "synoptic" evaluation of parties . . . into which may come all such factors as ideology, policies, record in office, putative ability to implement a programme, leadership, and unity of purpose, but none of these are paramount.' So the Manifesto was neither a suicide note nor a charter which rallied the faithful. But the *way* it was written and presented did affect the factors which influenced people's vote. An examination of its formulation and its presentation provides vital clues to the fact that the left were not as close to the scene of the crime as their enemies (and some of them) seemed to think.

Programme-making

The fundamental ideas behind the Manifesto came from an extensive process of discussion in the party and the unions; or rather, as extensive a discussion as ever has taken place in the postwar Labour Party. I add this qualification because even at the height of the reform movement, membership involvement in policy development was minimal. Of course, constituency parties debated broad resolutions, but any deeper or more practical considerations tended to come about not through formal party discussion, but through local involvement in a movement such as CND, women's liberation and anti-racist, anti-fascist organisations like the Anti-Nazi League, or in the course of specific struggles, for example over redundancies and new technology, problems of health and safety, or the privatisation of services.[19] Moreover, the channels by which detailed policy discussions at the *base* of the party can feed up to the top have always been circuitous – or non-existent. In the seventies they were improved, but only through informal, rather *ad hoc* arrangements. These were dependent on the NEC members in particular policy areas, who encouraged the committees to co-opt party members involved in campaigning movements and who arranged occasional consultative conferences and schools. It was a failing of the left that when they did have control of the NEC (between 1974 and 1980) they did not radically refashion the policy-making process and its relationship to radical movements and initiatives independent of the party.

Bearing these qualifications in mind, the policy debate in the NEC's subcommittees from 1970 onwards was remarkably thorough in its range and its detail. A particularly strong thread of policy development on economic policy and on defence ran from the debate opened by the Wilson *débâcle* of 1966–70, through the alternative policies which the party constantly put forward during the 1974–79 government, to the bitter post mortem on why these policies were never carried out, which in turn set off the momentum for constitutional reform.

Throughout the three years from 1979 leading up to the constitutional reforms of 1981, policy *development* was not the priority of the organised left. The priority was to gain the power to get them implemented. So as far as policy processes within the party were concerned, the emphasis was on consolidation, and winnning support from the unions. However, a fresh intellectual impetus came, all too briefly, from new members attracted by the refashioned Labour Party that seemed to be emerging out of the encrusted shell. This was a period, as the last chapter illustrated, when large numbers of people joined the party bringing with them the expertise and ideas gained from involvement in movements and pressure groups outside. By 1980/81 they were knocking on the doors of the party's policy-making. They provided the impetus behind the successful discussion journal, *New Socialist*[20] – a project entirely novel to the Labour Party.

But fresh political and intellectual energy did not get much further. For in 1982, at the very same conference which agreed the NEC's draft programme – the product of ten years' debate and experience – the right and 'moderate' wing of the trade-union leadership made a dramatic and effective push for seats on the NEC. The left consequently lost its dominant position. Furthermore, it had no adequate structures of its own to develop ideas and to maintain anything more than casual connections with organisations outside the party.

The barons get back on top

In 1981, the trade-union right was able to exploit a leadership vacuum in the trade-union left caused by the departure of Jack Jones and the loss to the right of the AUEW. It began to use its potential control over the party's leadership. Cajoled by John Golding, then an MP, now General Secretary of the National Communications Union – 'my role was to get them to turn up, to give them a conscience if they didn't, to badger them' – the right-wing trade-union leaders, drawing on the loyalty of others, got themselves sufficiently organised by the 1982 conference to replace three of the holders of the trade-union places who voted with the left, and three of the left-voting members of the women's section – whose five positions are in the gift of the (male-dominated) block vote. They also successfully mobilised the block votes to ensure that Eric Varley replaced the left-winger Norman Atkinson as Treasurer. Then the right used their new strength to undermine the left's dominance in the NEC's policy committees.

At first sight, the rapid shift in the position of the trade-union majority seems strange. It had moved, over the past eighteen months, from support (albeit in many cases reluctant) for the constitutional reforms to support for a determined effort to push back the influence of the left, who had led that very movement for reform. This looks especially odd if, like me and indeed most trade-union members, you are unfamiliar with the backroom, or bar-room, bargains that form as important a part of Labour Party conferences as the debates in the conference hall. Part of the explanation lies in precisely this: the closed negotiations, the bartering – 'we had to support Betty Boothroyd in order to get our choice on', as one left-wing trade-union leader put it – which determines who fills the seventeen trade-union-controlled places on the 32-strong NEC. Unlike the decisions on whether or not to support the constitutional reforms and some of the decisions over the Deputy Leadership, these negotiations are almost immune from membership pressure. There is no campaign or open competition, the individuals are not usually known outside their own union, and are often rather grey figures within it. Moreover, the system of election inevitably encourages bargaining between union leaderships in which general secretaries play a key role.

There are signs of change however; the pressure for democratisation in the party and the unions is reaching even this redoubt of baronial power. Since 1981 the way each union cast its block vote has been a matter of record, which opens the negotiations to some scrutiny and debate. In addition, the make-up of many delegations has itself become more democratic in many unions, involving a greater proportion of lay delegates in place of full-time officials. General secretaries can no longer treat the block vote as their own, as Sid Weighell, the past General Secretary of the railwaymen (NUR) found to his cost when, in 1984, he went against the decision of his delegation and voted for a right-winger rather than Eric Clarke of the NUM. Two months later a special conference of the NUR voted to appoint a new general secretary.

Greater membership participation in these elections would not necessarily have meant dramatically different decisions. The experience of wider membership involvement in decisions over the constitutional reforms and the Deputy Leadership demonstrates that whether the leadership is left or right, the membership cannot be counted on to follow. For instance on the constitutional reforms, the members of the miners' union (under Joe Gormley), the construction workers' union and the Union of Communication Workers all overturned their leadership's negative recommendations. In the vote between Benn and Healey for the Deputy Leadership, consultation – albeit uneven – of the membership in two cases, NUPE and the T&GWU, indicated majority support for Healey where the leadership would have favoured Benn and in one case, ASTMS, voted for Benn after the leadership had recommended for Healey.

In the past when its supporters were in the leadership of powerful unions like the T&GWU and the AUEW, the left itself has benefited from the trade-union bartering. This was the case in the late 1970s, and helped the press create the false impression of an all-powerful left dominating the labour movement outside Parliament. Jack Jones in particular played a decisive role in ensuring a left majority on the NEC. 'He really knew how to make the machinery work' observed Jim Mortimer, who as chair of ACAS and closely involved with the leadership of the trade unions and the party had seen him at work. The left's strength in the trade unions and women's sections was also a product of the right and centre's lack of interest in the party's internal affairs. 'We just dealt with the [Labour] government. *The government* was the important thing; we hardly gave a thought to the party,' commented David Warburton, now the National Officer in the G&MBATU responsible for its liaison with the party. In other words the advances of the left were due in part to the indifference of the right, which nonetheless remained in place.

Throughout that period the right and centre put a low priority on the NEC; for them it was the TUC where the glittering prizes were to be won. Seats on the NEC were simply a matter of Buggins's turn, and more often than not Buggins was not much interested in the NEC's proceedings. From 1981 however, with the shift to the right in the AUEW and the weak leadership in the T&GWU (partly due to Moss Evans being ill, but also because of a certain complacency on the left of the T&GWU after having controlled the leadership for over a decade), the Bugginses had to start attending more regularly and at least vote the right way, even if they did not say very much.

In this way the left lost control over the process of turning the 1982 Conference Programme into a manifesto and building a campaign around it. The result was that the right were the final editors of a manifesto which represented everything with which they most disagreed.

Policy as power struggle

The new trade-union overseers of the party's policy process on the NEC did not use their power to alter the 1982 policies. Members of the Shadow Cabinet were not always so restrained. Denis Healey successfully deleted the party's commitment to scrapping Polaris and substituted instead the proposal that Polaris 'be included in the nuclear disarmament negotiations in which Britain must take part'. Beyond this, neither the NEC majority nor that of the Shadow Cabinet had their hearts or minds in the policy. Since they disagreed with most of its proposals they could hardly be expected to be creative in drawing out its underlying themes and principles.

The joint PLP–NEC committee on the Manifesto was the battlefield of a peculiar kind of power struggle. It was not a struggle over present power. In 1981, it saw a struggle to be in the best position for the exercise of anticipated future power: power under what everyone, left and right, assumed would be the coming Labour government. The Shadow Cabinet were like a fortified castle. Secure in the assumption that once they were in government, the sniper fire from the left would be merely background noise, they and their trade-union allies cared little for the detail of the Manifesto. Then, after the Falklands in 1982, as it became increasingly clear that they would not make it to government, the tacticians among them decided that any-way, as John Golding put it, 'if we weren't going to win, we may as well lose on left-wing policies'.

The left's behaviour, too, was dominated more by the inner power struggle than anything else. But they really believed in the Manifesto. For them, it was a matter of what written positions would put them in the strongest vantage point from which to breach the Shadow Cabinet's defences and hold the government to party positions. Audrey Wise illustrates this:

My main aim was to get in a commitment to encourage and support workers' plans; for others it was the commitments on women, for others on defence and so on.

It just was not the sort of group where you could discuss the overall themes and vision we wanted to get over.

She added that she

would have been quite happy with a manifesto which said that we intended to redistribute power and wealth in favour of working people, if we were going to have a government we could trust.

No new vision could possibly survive the manoeuvres of the Manifesto Committee – even assuming the Manifesto contained the ingredients for it. But the Campaign Committee was even worse. It was set up in the autumn of 1982 and was dominated by right-wing trade-union leaders and Shadow Cabinet ministers; for most of them, their only experience of campaigns was in campaigns for themselves. Few of the left were members of the committee. Its minutes were secret even from the rest of the NEC, and so, it seems, were its campaigns. No contact was made with any of the organisations who could make the ideas live: CND on defence, shop stewards' combined committees and public-sector trade unionists on industrial democracy,[21] women's groups on economic and social policy, or the new

Labour councils attempting to democratise local government. (During the election campaign itself, Ken Livingstone was actually banned from entering Walworth Road, such was the level of nervousness about the left. The ban was only lifted when Vincent Hanna of *Newsnight*, who had wanted to film a discussion with Ken Livingstone and others in Labour's HQ, threatened to reveal the ban that night on television.)

Engaging latent support: convincing the unconvinced

How important was all this in explaining the defection of Labour voters? My argument will be that the lack of a clear vision integrating and highlighting the details of the Manifesto, and the lack of a wholehearted campaign to make that vision live, meant that potential ideological support was never mobilised. The unconvinced remained unconvinced.

The electoral popularity of the left depends on far deeper changes and movements in society than ever an election campaign, or a primarily parliamentary party, can achieve. But the analyses of *How Britain Votes* and the history of the GLC's popular support provide evidence for concluding that a campaign marked by conviction, carried through by a party committed to the ideas of the 1983 Manifesto, could have been more successful than the defensive, divided, and demoralised party that faced the electorate in 1983. Although the focus of this chapter is on the underlying reasons for Labour's defeat in 1983, I hope through this to understand the choices facing the left in the new political situation that was first revealed by this defeat.

The 1983 election saw the emergence of a fully-fledged three-party system. *How Britain Votes* turned out to be a study of the constituencies of each of the three parties in these new circumstances. Political commentators have drawn mainly on the information it provides about the character of the Alliance's constituency. The question of whether there is such a constituency and if so what its character is obviously provokes particular curiosity. However, the book's opinion surveys and analysis of voting patterns in 1983 also provide strong evidence through which to explore an argument about the Labour Party in a three-party system. The argument is that in such a system a radical left-wing party with a united, persuasive leadership is more likely to be successful than either a centrist trade-union party on the defensive or the divided party which in fact faced the electorate.

In this context the most significant findings of *How Britain Votes* are those which the authors analyse in order to identify the importance of ideology in explaining the defections from Labour. They identify the size of Labour's 'ideological heartland' in terms of people's responses to different political questions since 1966. They then show any changes in the proportion of these people who have voted Labour between 1966 and 1983.

With this information they answer two questions: first, how far is the decline in Labour's vote associated with a decline in the size of the heartland? Second, how far is the decline associated with a decline in the percentage of this heartland who actually vote Labour?

The way they identify these 'heartlands' is to build a two-dimensional diagram based on the state intervention-free enterprise spectrum and the liberal-illiberal one. This provides a far more useful, and realistic, way of identifying ideological positions than applying a left–right label to single-issue answers. Heath and his co-authors take as indicators nationalisation versus free enterprise and spending on services versus cutting taxes, or abolishing and retaining the death penalty (their indicators are limited by the questions asked in previous years).

Thus Heath *et al* see voting changes at the 'extremes', or, in their terms, 'ideological heartlands' of British politics as being possibly as important as voting movements at the centre. This at any rate is one of the arguments that they explore.

In their model the Labour heartland would then consist of people who support proposals for further nationalisation and public spending. The 'natural' Conservatives would be those who support further privatisation and tax cuts. In 1983 a new constituency was added – that of the Alliance – which seemed to be concentrated among people who were closer to Labour in their views on public spending but midway between the two parties on attitudes towards free enterprise.

The first major finding in relation to 1983 was that since 1966 there had been a very slight decline (1 per cent) in the percentage of people who held views traditionally associated with Labour's heartland, and closest to its 1983 Manifesto. But this was nowhere near large enough to explain the extent of the electoral defection from Labour (10 per cent).

The second major finding concerns the size of the Labour vote and the relevance of ideology. They show that Labour has been losing votes *even within its ideological heartland, ever since 1966.* Labour had lost ground since 1966 among its natural allies, whereas the Tories had gained ground amongst theirs. This simplified table illustrates their findings:

Percentage of the heartland vote

	1966	1974	1979	1983
Labour	89	75	79	72
Conservative	73	71	87	81

Heath, Jowell and Curtice also add that:

These short-run changes in support, in given concentrations of ideological view, decisively refute the conventional wisdom that elections are won and lost in the centre ground. They are won and lost in the heartlands as well. It would be quite wrong in our view to attribute Mr Foot's defeat in 1983 solely to changes in the party programme or to the shift of the electorate to the right . . . Whatever it was that caused these fluctuations in Labour's popularity affected those voters who remained in Labour's ideological heartland as well as those who had abandoned it.[22]

They conclude that other factors making up the overall image of the party, in particular the lack of coherence and a unity of purpose reflected in Michael Foot's leadership, were the crucial explanations for the decline of electoral support especially in Labour's ideological heartlands.

Heath *et al* conclude that the results of their surveys show the importance of parties in shaping people's perceptions of their latent interest. They back this up with data, in class and ideological terms, on the increase in Conservative votes in 1983 compared to 1964. In other words they show how important 'good' (or to put it more neutrally, confident) leadership and apparent unity of purpose was in explaining the ability of the Conservatives to mobilise their natural and potential allies.

They break their sample into five categories based on economic interests and employment conditions: salariat, routine non-manual, petty bourgeoisie (self-employed, small employers), foremen and technicians, and working class (skilled and unskilled manual workers). They explore both changes in the shape of this economic class structure and changes in the relationship between class and voting patterns. The study comes to two important conclusions which go against the conventional wisdom that class is no longer the basis of politics. First, they show that though the shape of the class structure – using their notions of class – has changed, class interests, or rather people's perceptions of them, remain and play a central role in voters' choices. But this role is not determined only sociologically or economically. Ideology, and therefore political leadership, 'can help to shape subjective awareness of class interests and to translate these into class values'.

Class Composition of the Electorate: 1964 and 1983

	1964	1983
Salariat	18	27
Routine non-manual	18	24
Petty bourgeoisie	7	8
Foremen and technicians	10	7
Working class	47	34

There has been a particularly dramatic shift to the right on the issue of privatisation amongst the petty bourgeoisie and the salariat. There is some small shift amongst the other three groups, but here the changes are qualified by evidence of shifts to the left on government intervention for job creation, income distribution and industrial democracy.[23] It is relevant here that in fact the 1983 Manifesto and the 1982 Programme on which it was based contained very few proposals for increased nationalisation. What new proposals there were consisted mainly of recommending public stakes in industries already supplying the public sectors such as pharmaceuticals, health equipment and building materials in addition to 'public assets hived off by the Tories'.[24] Heath *et al* conclude from their study of class and ideology that 'the shift to the right could perhaps be described as a successful attempt by the Conservatives to articulate the latent interests of their natural supporters' (the petty bourgeoisie and salariat).

Is there any evidence that an equivalent success could be achieved by Labour among *its* natural supporters? In order to 'articulate the latent interests' of such groups, Labour would need (and, I would argue, has already begun in some sections of the party) to take account positively of important facts about its 'natural' supporters. First, it must pay attention to changes in its historic core of natural support: the skilled and unskilled manual working class has declined. But contrary to some analyses, this 7 per cent decline since 1964 is not a sufficient or even primary explanation of the decline, which amounted to a 16 per cent drop in the vote over the same period.[25] A further source of potential support, the number of routine non-manual workers, has grown.

Second, the social composition and therefore the interests of both these categories of workers have changed. Women are more likely to be in employment (though under conditions influenced by their gender), and black workers now make up a significantly greater proportion of both groups. They, like women, are in an economically and politically subordinate position within class categories.[26]

A third factor which affects potential support – or lack of it – is that the association of latent class interests with Labour has been deeply eroded by the experience of recent Labour governments, and the record of those councils and state institutions connected with Labour in the public mind. The nature of this disaffection and its intensity, of course, varies: between workers in the public sector and the private sector, between council-house tenants and homeowners, between the generations with their quite different historical memories and expectations and between people with a range of distinct experiences of the state: as client, patient, or victim. Any attempt to articulate the latent interests of these diverse groups will have to convince them that Labour can transform its own bureaucratic mentality and their powerlessness into a capacity to influence positively the decisions that affect their lives.

This cannot be achieved primarily through electioneering. It involves building a conscious vested interest in democratic control in every area of society, in the economy as well as the polity.

A tall order. One purpose of this book is to demonstrate that there are groups of socialists inside and outside the party who are doing just this. Although their socialism requires a lot more power than can be achieved by electoral success alone, winning a popular majority has to be one of their aims. The voting and attitude studies of Heath *et al* have demonstrated that with a three-party system, electoral success is achieved as much, if not more, through extending and mobilising the ideological heartlands as through courting the centre. There is at least one case where such a political strategy has been put to the test of public opinion: the Greater London Council.[27]

The left's potential popularity

The GLC's policies and image fused strong class and collectivist commitments with radical democratic ones. Its class aims included cheap transport, municipal enterprise, campaigns against privatisation, public ownership of land, the improvement of parks and their wildlife, expansion of the public sector, political and material support for working-class organisations. These were allied with democratic commitments: to open up public-sector decision-making, to discriminate positively in favour of black people, women and the disabled, to back the rights of gay men and lesbians, and to provide for the diversity of people's needs and desires in the arts, leisure and the environment. Although the GLC was a part of local rather than national government, it, or rather its leadership, took over a part of the national stage, appearing at times as the real opposition to Thatcher. They made a continuing stand in favour of British troops coming out of Ireland, nuclear disarmament and support for the Palestinians. What was the response of Labour's two groups of potentially 'natural supporters'? Did they feel that the GLC expressed their latent interests?

At first they most definitely did not. In August 1981 one opinion poll showed that the majority of Londoners believed that Livingstone's leadership was 'bad' or 'appalling';[28] and Labour came third in people's voting intentions. Another opinion poll around the same time found that 47 per cent believed

Livingstone was doing a bad job, and only 20 per cent a good job.[29] However by April 1983 Livingstone's poll ratings were higher than Michael Foot's. This might not be saying much but by December 1983 Labour was doing 12 per cent better in London than nationally, and this was before the GLC's advertising campaign which began in March 1984. The opinion polls conducted by Harris after this campaign had begun are interesting too because they indicate positive support for the new GLC's policies as well as its existence.[30] Moreover these polls indicated higher Labour support in the GLC area than nationally amongst the traditional working-class voter as well as amongst women and ethnic minorities. They also indicate higher support amongst the social classes ABCI, the 'yuppies' as they are sometimes called. Harris pollsters concluded, 'You do not have to water down your policies in order to be popular but they do need to be explained in a calm and rational way.' The GLC's popular base was a result of political confidence and the courage and openness that often goes with it; political unity on a set of radical commitments (preceded by divisions and splits) and a lot of money. None would have been sufficient on their own.

The structure and the soul

The Labour leadership in 1983 did have money, from Trade Unions for Labour Victory – though not very much. With this it could afford a pollster and an advertising agency. The only problem was that it was not able to agree a message to advertise. Much was said at the time to explain this, with mocking descriptions of chaos at Walworth Road, as if a strong dose of professionalism in organisation and in presentation would do the trick. The advertising agency did try. Its 'market' research said that people wanted a positive lead. There is not much that advertisers can do about this except pretend. So the slogan which they came up with was 'Think positive – Vote Labour'. But the problems in the election campaign were not administrative. They were deeply political: the product of a yawning gap in the party, a gap between its controlling structures and its motivating soul – the ideas, principles and vision that lead people to work and vote for the party.

As we saw in Chapter 1, a new political soul had been emerging among party and trade-union activists in reaction to the failures of Labourism. But the right and centre had regained control over the structure. They then acquiesced to, and in some cases actively promoted, the leadership of Michael Foot and the old left as the only way to protect their position from the new left. The result was incoherence, a total inability to influence the public debate and consequently a thumbs-down from the electorate.

This incoherence needs exploring. For it has continued since 1983, albeit glossed over by smart public relations.

Labourism

When Nye Bevan referred to the conflict between the left and right in the Labour Party as 'the struggle for the soul of Labour', he meant by 'soul' the ideology and interests of Labourism. The reason why Labourism has always been the object of the struggle between left and right within the British Labour Party is that Labourism is not a fully-fledged ideology, in the sense of having a distinct view of the state, the economy, and the international order. It is a powerful but sectional theme: the political protection of workers' living standards. As I argued in the introduction to this book, Labourism is essentially an extension of trade-union aims, from industrial bargaining to legislation and political bargaining, 'in the direct interest of labour'.[31] Depending on the economic and political circumstances, it has been able to advance, or hope to advance, under either of the two banners competing to be at the head of the labour movement: the ameliorative banner of the centre and right or the transformative banner of the Tribunite left.

The old transformative tradition has always been in an uneasy position. It claims to speak for labour, yet British Labourism, with its sectional trade-union origins, has always inclined towards the pragmatists of the right. Labourism is essentially an ideology of decent and dignified subordination.

Its complaint against capitalism is that labour receives little of the wealth that it creates; Labourism's rationale is to bargain, politically as well as industrially, for more. Consequently it is hostile to capitalists but presumes the continued existence of capitalism. Clause Four of the party's constitution, expressing the commitment to social ownership, has always been seen by trade-union leaders more as an identity mark. Harold Wilson, who opposed Hugh Gaitskell's attempt to delete Clause Four after the 1959 defeat, later explained that he did not think one should remove Genesis from the Bible even if you knew that it had taken more than seven days to create the world. It was sufficiently vague to act simply as an enabling clause: there would be certain industries, such as the coal industry, where an infrastructure was in such a state of collapse that 'common ownership', or nationalisation, as it was later called, was a necessary step from a Labourist, never mind a socialist point of view. Certainly modern trade-union leaders, who declare their allegiance to Labourism, have scant belief in Clause Four. 'Utter rubbish, bloody rubbish,' declares John Golding, one of the frankest of exponents of modern Labourism. Labourism is not interested in moving towards a different way of organising the economy.

The Social Contract of the 1974–79 government illustrated this feature of Labourism most starkly. In 1974, after the three-day week and the success of the miners' strike, the balance of power was unusually favourable for a radical move towards a socialist economy. 'For a brief moment, the establishment was crushed,' recalls Frances Morrell, from her first days working with Tony Benn at the Department of Industry; 'we could have carried our most radical policies through, with the political will and trade-union support. Once the establishment realised that Labour was not going to take advantage, that's when their resistance began.'[32] Morrell is describing a situation where workers' trade-union power had gone as far as it could in terms of the redistribution of profits; but Labourism, being a political reflection of this power, could not take it any further. In its economic struggles over the previous decade, the trade unions had not prepared, with a few scattered exceptions,[33] any vision of a different kind of economy. Neither had the party. Efforts had been made, but they never became sufficiently rooted to persist against concerted opposition.[34] An economic stalemate of the sort that existed between the unions and the employers throughout the seventies cannot last long in the present competitive world capitalist economy. The Labour government was unwilling and unable to turn trade-union power into a power for economic transformation. It consequently ended up preparing the way for monetarism and the defeat of trade-union power.

Labourism's sectional aspirations tend to take for granted, and work within existing, capitalist definitions of efficiency and viability. It has not the conceptual tools to generate alternative ways of being competitive, or socially governed definitions of efficiency and viability. In response to the present economic and technological restructuring it can only be impassive – pretending the world has not really changed – or capitulate. As a result, in 1983 and since, Labour has faced a situation where the majority of people consider unemployment the most important issue and favour government intervention to reduce it, but do not believe that Labour can provide the answer.

Similarly with the state: so long as Labour is in the legislative driving seat and believing that it is driving hard on labour's behalf, the existing state apparatus is a perfectly good vehicle. Labourism contains no image of a different kind of state. Instead its representatives pride themselves on their ability to run the present one. John Golding, who worked as a junior minister in the Department of Employment during the 1974–79 government, again expressed clearly the narrow but hard-headed approach of Labourism along with its illusion of its own mastery: 'I found out what needed to be done, on training for instance, by talking to careers officers and to kids – I don't need any theorists to advise me, I despise theorists. And then I would tell the civil servants what they had to do. They try and tell us, but I would have none of that.'

A further limit to Labourism concerns its definition of those on whose behalf it bargains or administrates. Traditionally, it has seen the worker it represents as first and foremost British and as the male wage earner and his family. John Golding again: 'I'm a class politician. I'd prefer to have a straightforward Labour Party, without these trendy socialists, always bringing up women and blacks.'[35] British Labourism gained its particular meaning and logic when Britain was still an imperial power. Its overriding commitment to the living standards and conditions of British workers means that at its core is British nationalism.[36] It has always required from its political leader the championship of Britain as a major power. Socialists who have challenged this notion have rarely had political influence within Labour. On the old Labour left this feature of Labourism has encouraged a fervent moral imperialism. It was this that lay behind Labour's most disastrous failure to challenge the terms of public debate: over the Falklands.

Labour's moral imperialism, expressed at the same time most eloquently and most ridiculously by Michael Foot, harmonised completely with Thatcher's desire to be the Prime Minister who put the 'Great' back into Britain: who appeared before the British people as the Churchill of the 1980s. Foot set the stage for Thatcher's star performance. He beckoned her on by accusing her of 'betraying' the islanders and claiming that she now needed to prove 'by deeds' that she would come to their protection. From the moment that public doubts and disquiet were snuffed at birth by the fabricated consensus of Parliament's 'unanimous' support for the task force, the Labour Party's defence policy was doomed. In the public's eyes nuclear disarmament meant taking the 'Great' out of Britain, just as they were being beguiled into thinking it could be put back in. During the election campaign a year after the Falklands, Jim Callaghan seemed responsible, by his carefully planned and publicised rebuttal of Labour's defence policy. But Foot's presumption that the British government should 'uphold the rights of our country *throughout the world*' and be 'a defender of people's freedom *throughout the world*, particularly those who look to us for special protection, as do the people in the Falkland Islands [added emphasis]',[37] prepared the way for the principle of Callaghan's stand.

The Labourist left, as well as the right, have assumed Britain's role as a 'world leader' in all their international campaigns. In the early years of CND (1957–63) they presumed that this greatness could be deployed 'by example' to bring about world peace. It is a stance which is not only an arrogant fantasy but is also, in the end, self-imploding. For when the last remaining symbols of Britain's role as a major power are its nuclear weapons – Polaris and Trident – the claim to be a world leader, even if for the goal of peace, becomes very difficult to sustain if they are abandoned. If Britain gives up her weapons, she gives up the only basis on which she remains a world power. The only way to be a consistent unilateralist therefore is to give up pretensions of moral leadership and follow a policy of non-alignment. It is not surprising that Nye Bevan, like Foot an ardent exponent of moral imperialism, should in the end refuse to 'go naked into the negotiating chamber'. Similarly Michael Foot, when chairing the PLP/NEC committee to draw up the 1983 Manifesto, although he stood by every other part of the 1982 Party Programme, could not prevent Denis Healey from insisting that Polaris should be kept to contribute to disarmament negotiations.

Michael Foot: the illusion of soul

Michael Foot's leadership epitomised the separation of the structure from the soul. On the one hand he symbolised, more than anyone else, the continuities and promise of the old transformative tradition: left Labourism. The idea of his leadership held out the hope of the Labourism of the left moving from its position of opposition into power:

There he stands, Member for Ebbw Vale, bone of our old bone, blood of our very blood, in his white hair and his cheekbones, his humanity, his generosity, his literacy and his stick, the only legitimate heir in the apostolic succession.[38]

Gwyn Williams, the Welsh socialist historian, puts it well and in doing so explains why socialists with a few exceptions,[39] everywhere (those over 30, at least), inside the Labour Party and outside, felt some elation at the news of his election. It was not that they thought he would lead the party to socialism, but that he would rebuild the labour movement's confidence and lead popular disaffection with the government. I have to admit that I shared those feelings: I can remember exactly where I was and what I was doing when I heard the news that Michael Foot had become Leader of the Labour Party – and it was the news rather than what I was doing that made the moment memorable. Looking back I blush at my naïvety, but the memory of the news is so vivid that it must have seemed to offer hope: hope at least of a change in the political atmosphere, a renewal of people's confidence to resist. His promise to lead a nationwide movement against unemployment gave grounds for such optimism. Many party members went further and welcomed Foot's victory as an unexpected fruit, and confirmation, of the left's advance since 1979. *Tribune*, for instance, wrote that his victory demonstrated how the majority of MPs not only accepted the constitutional changes but recognised that these changes provide 'the groundwork on which a revived labour movement can sweep to power'.[40]

Michael Foot: loyal to the structure

This really *was* naïve, for Foot was in fact totally dependent on the structure and, in practice, entirely uncritical of its character. While he was Leader he behaved as if preservation of the party in its historic form was his main task – so much so that while for Nye Bevan in the 1950s the struggle was for 'the soul of the Labour Party', for Michael Foot the battle was for its institutions, its parliamentary institutions. It was for this struggle that he submitted to the pressures to become Leader: 'only you, Michael, can save the party,'[41] they all said. It was for this that he depended on an alliance of trade-union leaders with whom, on every major issue of policy and philosophy, he would totally disagree.

John Golding, at that time both an MP and a trade-union representative on the NEC, puts it like this: 'Michael Foot remained pure for some time, believing in rational argument. But he suffered defeat after defeat. I soon stopped that. I created an alliance of loyalists in the trade unions and that way gave him the support he needed.' Golding is a multilateralist who says quite proudly that he 'never reads books – got better things to do'. Moreover, discussing the position of the left in the party he says that he 'would prefer a party for labour without the middle-class socialists'. One of the aims Foot *did* share with Golding, flowing from their common loyalty to the party machine, was to minimise the effects of the constitutional reforms. Within a month of becoming leader Foot was meeting trade-union general secretaries to ensure that the constitutional changes in the election of the Leader would not produce any actual change. The general secretaries committed their block votes to the status quo, represented by Michael Foot and Denis Healey (overconfidently, as it turned out: several of them had their recommendation for Denis Healey overturned by their conferences).

The view from the Westminster bunker

In spring 1981, in spite of these assurances, the old structure was in an extremely shaky state. An electoral college had been agreed in which the trade unions had the greatest say, the SDP had been formed and was doing well in the opinion polls, and Tony Benn had declared his candidacy for the Deputy Leadership. A besieged, bunker mentality took over the Shadow Cabinet and Foot in particular. On the one hand he was besieged by MPs threatening to join the SDP if Militant, which increasingly became an easy surrogate for the left in general, was not dealt with. On the other hand he was besieged by the press taunting him for being too soft on the left, mocking his weakness as a caretaker Leader. And the two sides of the siege were in regular if informal contact. Foot was susceptible to this pressure.

Most of the Shadow Cabinet, including Foot himself, were, more or less explicitly, as unhappy as the 'Gang of Four' with the constitutional reforms. They were in no mood to put up a confident defence of the refashioned, or seemingly refashioned, party. The Shadow Cabinet felt positively threatened and, for a brief period in 1980/81, even beleaguered. 'They felt completely marginalised,' commented one of their political aides; 'after all, momentous changes had taken place without them . . . For some,' he added, 'the main concern was to watch their own backs.' In general they were so consumed with anger at what had taken place, their mind's eye was so fixed on the memories of recent party conferences – the hostile looks, the accusing fingers pointed in their direction, the shouts of glee at every advance towards reselection – that they could not imagine that the view from Westminster was not the view of every sane and 'ordinary' voter. The suggestion that a significant proportion of the electorate might consider the reforms to be positive and attractive, and that these changes could even be turned into an electoral bonus, was repellent.

The indications are, however, that the view outside the threatened bunker at Westminster was, initially, more positive. In August 1980, the *Observer* reported its opinion poll in which, as I quoted at the beginning of the chapter, a large majority of Labour voters agreed with the proposal for the reselection of MPs at least every five years.

The left on the defensive

The problem between 1981 and 1983 on the question of 'selling' the party reforms was not just the leadership. To make the changes in the party seem relevant and attractive, the reformers themselves, the left, needed to develop and explain the significance that changes in the Labour Party could have for the reform of other national political institutions – the power of the Prime Minister and of the Civil Service, the secrecy of government, the weakness of Parliament as a democratic force. But by late 1981, many of the left were also retreating into a bunker, from which to exchange sniper fire with the leadership. Apart from the speeches and writings of Tony Benn, which ranged confidently over all these matters, and the work of intellectuals such as Raymond Williams, Ralph Miliband and Tom Nairn on the periphery of or outside the party, these issues were never properly addressed, let alone publicly explained. The Campaign for Labour Party Democracy saw these wider constitutional issues as matters for debate, as Vladimir Dierer, the Secretary of CLPD, put it, only 'after we have won control of the party'.

From the point of view of building alliances with the party around immediately winnable reforms, CLPD's narrow focus was extremely effective. The problem was the one with which I concluded the previous chapter: there was no independent platform where wider issues could be debated and from which the left could present its own profile. Every organisation on the left of the Labour Party was sucked inwards by the maelstrom of the internal power struggle. None had built the independence and the self-discipline to devote their energy to longer-term strategy and a distinct public appeal. Many of the reasons for this lie deep in the traditions of the British left. But in 1981 the tentative trends towards taking up these wider constitutional issues in a confident public manner were reversed by the way that Michael Foot's leadership very quickly threw the left on to the defensive.

Pestilential nuisances

The Shadow Cabinet view that the nature of Labour's internal reforms was calamitous meant that Foot had little option but to concede to the demands of MPs threatening to join the SDP. Their blackmail was 'control/expel the people who are trying to deselect us/divide the party or we go'. For Foot, concessions to their demands must have seemed the only way of closing the floodgates. Throughout 1981 Westminster was rife with rumours of thirty or forty MPs being ready to go if Foot did not exert his authority, or worse, if Benn became Deputy Leader. Foot's mind was fixed on keeping them, in stopping the leaks, in holding things together. Whoever disturbed this precarious exercise must be dealt with, controlled, or challenged. Militant; Peter Tatchell, the radical community activist and would-be parliamentary candidate; Ken Livingstone, the outspoken leader of the London left; anyone seeking to deselect any Labour MP anywhere . . . they all blurred in his mind into one great 'pestilential nuisance'.

However, the problem was that by attacking these people and thereby feeding the appetite of the hostile press Foot was promoting hostility which would in the end devour him and the Labour Party itself. Labour's increasingly indiscriminate attacks on the left, under Foot and then under Kinnock, accorded and continue to accord perfectly with an offensive coming from an entirely different direction: from the Thatcher government itself.

Thatcher's purposes were quite distinct. She and other ardent monetarists used the label 'socialist' to discredit any democratic or public institution that came between her government and market forces: local authorities, nationalised industries, educational institutions, the BBC and many others, depending on the particular direction in which she was lashing out at the time. Insofar as any such institution was acting autonomously and potentially against government wishes, then it must be overrun by 'socialists'. 'Socialism' became a term of abuse rather than pride or at least respectability.

Increasingly the standard by which the Labour leadership let itself be judged, and judged itself, was its toughness towards the left. The more it attacked, the more the press taunted it to go further; the further they went and the longer the chase lasted the more that Labour complied with the image their detractors tried to paint, an image of a party overrun by sinister 'left-wing' forces. In December 1981 this vicious spiral encircled the constituency of Bermondsey.

Bermondsey

Bermondsey was a constituency party rather like that of Newham North East, described in Chapter 1. Membership was down to

400; in its heyday in the thirties it had been around 3,000.[12] Attendance at ward meetings was never much more than six councillors or party officers. The organisation was stagnant, a fact indicated by the average age of the Labour Group on Southwark Council being over 60. Moreover, whatever its achievements in the past, it was no longer competent. In fact, in 1978 they could not even manage to have the manifesto ready in time for the local elections – it was three weeks late. The party was dominated by a right-wing rump whose members included John O'Grady, the leader of the council, and Bob Mellish, the MP. They did not encourage new members, so for many years nothing really changed. However, by 1978 a combination of local anger at the incompetence of the council, especially over housing, and disillusion with the Labour government, produced a rebellion. A group from all wards in the constituency, long-standing members and new, left and centre, started to come together to plan a challenge to the old regime. The policies of the council were a powerful unifying force: the last straw was the council's decision to spend up to £30 million on a new town hall complete with a boudoir for the mayoress – this at a time when council-house tenants were facing large rent rises. Tenants' groups, local unions and pressure groups such as the North Southwark Development Group began organising protests on this and other council policies. The new caucus made common cause with these campaigns; in wards where it was influential it tried to rebuild the party, producing local newsletters and supporting local campaigns.

One issue which came increasingly to the fore was the use of Southwark's derelict, but increasingly valuable dockland. In 1980 the government set up the London Docklands Development Corporation (LDDC), a non-elected organisation which it made responsible for land and property development with an £80m annual budget. The government took away all land-use planning powers from the docklands borough councils, and gave it to the LDDC, along with the power to vest (i.e., take over) land including areas earmarked by the local council for rented housing. Chaired by Nigel Broackes, also the Chairman of Trafalgar House, the LDDC had an aggressively commerical approach to Docklands; it was the government's showcase of monetarism in practice. In early 1981, when Labour councillors from other parts of Docklands as well as Labour front-bench spokespeople, not to mention local people, were still fighting a long battle against the formation of the LDDC, Bob Mellish accepted an offer from Nigel Broackes to become Vice-Chairman of the LDDC – with a salary of £16,000 once he had resigned from Parliament.

This might seem a strange thing for a Labour MP to do. However, if we take a brief look at the history of Bob Mellish it is not as odd as it appears.[43] He had enjoyed close relations with the private sector before, and had been linked with a property developer, Oliver Cutts, who operated in Bermondsey and the surrounding districts in the early 1960s. Cutts received an MBE but was later stripped of his honour as a result of criminal activities. Further questions raised by Duncan Campbell in the *New Statesman*, and repeated elsewhere, concerned Mellish's encouragement to local authorities to use the controversial industrialised building methods, designed by John Poulson and promoted by T. Dan Smith, while he was at the Ministry of Housing and Local Government between 1964 and 1967 and responsible for government policy towards housing in London and the New Towns. At one point, in 1962, Mellish himself ventured into private business, setting up a company, Personal Relations Ltd, with a Tory MP, Paul Williams. The intention was to act as 'industrial peacemakers'. But Mellish resigned from the project after protests from the Sunderland Labour Party (where Paul Williams held the seat for the Conservatives).

This was the man who in November 1981 succeeded in persuading Michael Foot to repudiate the new candidate, Peter Tatchell, selected by Bermondsey Constituency Party to replace him at the next general election (as a result of accepting the LDDC offer, Mellish had already said he would not seek re-election). Mellish threatened to resign there and then and cause an embarrassing by-election. A year later, after a second selection process had confirmed Peter Tatchell as the candidate, he did exactly that.

Tatchell had recently become secretary of the constituency party – the reformers had won all the party's officerships in 1980. He was a young Australian who had come to live in England to avoid being called up to fight in Vietnam and had then worked as a social worker, becoming active in community politics in Rotherhithe, Bermondsey. Right-wing MPs wanted a leftie's head brought to them on a ceremonial platter before they would drop their threat to join the SDP. Tatchell had written an article calling for extra-parliamentary action – of an entirely symbolic character: a march against unemployment led by Labour MPs followed by a tent city of the unemployed, encamped outside Westminster. This appeared in *London Labour Briefing*, the paper of an organisation which was seen by several on the Shadow Cabinet as almost as sinister as Militant. Tatchell had been part of a 'takeover' of a colleague's constituency. So Tatchell's head would do.

The rest of the story is well known. Mellish resigned, and a by-election was called. Foot, after initially attacking Tatchell publicly, and then trying to persuade him to resign, eventually accepted him as the candidate, after the local party refused to select anyone else. An anti-red and gay-baiting press campaign, the ground for which had been prepared by the internal campaign against Tatchell, ensured that Labour lost their 11,756 majority and the Liberals gained the seat by 9,319.

The story indicates the deep divisions over the character and direction of the party. It expresses the intensity of the conflict between a new socialist party struggling, sometimes clumsily, to be born, and the old Labourist machine with all the grim strength of the parliamentary and trade-union leadership behind it.

Livingstone

Other similar conflicts studded Foot's brief leadership. A less dramatic dispute, where the party machine was defeated, occurred over the leadership of the newly elected GLC in May 1981. The leader of the GLC Labour group before the election was Andrew MacIntosh, a conventional and unimaginative market researcher. Throughout the election campaign it was public knowledge – in fact the object of an extremely hostile campaign by the *Evening Standard* – that the leader of the left, Ken Livingstone, would challenge MacIntosh for the leadership after the GLC election.

Michael Foot worked hard to stop Livingstone. Foot had never met Livingstone and probably knew little of his politics except that he was associated with *London Labour Briefing*, whose name was frequently quoted by the press and by Labour leaders as one of the organisations that must be purged. In fact *Briefing* was nothing like Militant either in its political ideas or its ways of organising. On the contrary, one of the motives of those establishing *Briefing* was the desire to strengthen a non-sectarian left: a left concerned to achieve things here and now, for instance in local government. Such details were of no interest to Foot. He accepted the categories of the media because in many ways it was the press and, through them, the would-be supporters of the SDP, that he was seeking to convince.

When the GLC Labour Group met after their narrow victory – three seats – to elect their leader, the chairman, George Page, had in his hand a letter from Michael Foot. It conveyed, or rather intended to convey, his support for MacIntosh and his hope that the Group would re-elect MacIntosh to lead the new administration. The letter was never read out. Page, a traditionalist, on the right of the party, was a stickler for procedure. The election of officers was first on the agenda and that was how the meeting should proceed. No letter from the Leader of the Party could alter that. Moreover, many of the older working-class councillors found MacIntosh aloof and rather snobbish.

So Livingstone was elected. But Foot and the parliamentary leadership remained hostile, right up to and during the election campaign. Even when, three years later, the Conservative Manifesto contained a commitment to abolishing the GLC, the front bench would not issue a joint protest. The spokesman, Gerald Kaufman, was equivocal in response to questions on *Newsnight* about whether he was for or against retaining the GLC. Such was the overriding importance of defending the old party and dispersing and discouraging the new. Given the support for the GLC, Kaufman showed he was willing to surrender clearly expressed public support to avoid risking the party's status quo by giving credence to the left.

Unity, loyalty and Labour governments

Why did Michael Foot, the socialist rebel, himself expelled from the party in the fifties, end up in 1981–83 the instrument of an attempt to suppress a new generation of rebels and to reverse a process, however messy, of regenerating the party towards the left? I ask this question not in order to embark on a potted political biography, but because the attempt to answer helps to explain the incoherence that lay behind the 1983 defeat. It reveals important differences between the old left, whose political education came through Labour's splits and disarray in the thirties, and the new left, whose view of the party was formed by the experience of Labour governments of the sixties and seventies. For Foot's behaviour was no simple matter of a betrayal of the ideals of his youth.

Among the elements in Foot's socialism the most powerful has always been his commitment to the unity of the Labour Party and labour movement, based on his loyalty to them and the nation's institutions, especially Parliament. His tolerance of different views on the left, his belief in argument and debate, even his role in the first wave of CND during the 1950s, were all framed by his fidelity to Westminster and to the unity of the Labour Party.

For him the disunity of the party and damage to the sovereignty of the House of Commons were one and the same. In 1968, asked in an interview to describe his formative political experience, he replied:

The plight of the Labour Party in the thirites. People sometimes forget how deep was the disaster which the Labour Party suffered in 1931. The outward sign of it was the drop in the Labour Party membership in the House of Commons . . . but even more spectacular was the collapse in union membership . . . So I think that all that has a decisive influence on what I thought afterwards. When the labour movement in this country is scattered, very serious events follow – the standard of living goes down.[44]

Moreover, he shared Nye Bevan's belief that 'maintaining the unity of the party is the responsibility of the left'. He was guided by his advice: 'Never (to) underestimate the yearning for unity.' This appears to have been the maxim he applied in 1970 when he became the peacemaker between Harold Wilson and the left-wing trade-union leaders. The advocate of dissent became the symbol of loyalty. After 1974, when Labour again formed governments under Harold Wilson and then Jim Callaghan, Foot was their most steadfast supporter. According to Joel Barnett, who was number two at the Treasury, his support for both Prime Ministers was notable: 'Michael's position was unique. He was tremendously loyal to both Harold Wilson and Jim Callaghan and the government could never have survived so long without him.' In exchange he had influence, if very limited. Joel Barnett again: '. . . if Michael felt very strongly on a subject, both Prime Ministers would be ready to make concessions to him. That would not include concessions on the central economic strategy . . . It was precisely because Michael was on the losing side on the big issues that the Prime Minister must have felt it reasonable to give way to him on lesser issues.'

It was because the left saw Foot as a prisoner of the right and, if sentimentally, believed that he too saw himself in this way, that the left saw his elevation to the leadership as a breakthrough. In fact Foot himself does not write as if he lost on the big issues. Commenting on both the Wilson and the Callaghan administrations, he agreed:

We carried through, sometimes only by one or two votes, a series of socialist measures, manifesto commitments, more ambitious and consistent than anything the previous Labour Government had attempted. Moreover, the programme executed with such determination covered a whole range of policies – industrial relations, public ownership, the rescue of many industries large and small, the extension of social services and the fulfilment of longstanding promises on such items as child benefit and comprehensive education.

He concludes:

Considering how fierce and far-reaching was the world slump which hit us in 1974, considering how slender or non-existent our majority, taking the economic record of the Wilson-Callaghan cabinets from 1974–79 altogether, here was a situation which democratic Socialists could honourably defend.[45]

The assessment which the majority of party and trade-union activists made was quite different. They argued that the 1974–79 Labour government drifted, or allowed itself to be pushed, into monetarism, making it very much easier for Thatcher to claim that 'there is no alternative'. They further pointed to Manifesto commitments on industrial and economic policy which had been intended to develop that 'alternative' but which had been abandoned in the face of pressure from the City and big business. Foot concluded that the government did the best it could, *given* all the pressures and constraints that it was under. The majority of party members and significant sections of the trade unions saw such a view as giving up altogether.

A blunted sword

The crucial point of conflict with Michael Foot and the new left was that they had come to believe that Parliament on its own, and in one nation, was not a strong enough democratic power to exert control over the increasingly powerful, increasingly international, centres of unaccountable financial and industrial power that shape the British economy's future. The experience of Labour governments had shown that Parliament was not 'the sword at the heart of private property' which Michael Foot, following Nye Bevan, had believed it to be. Not only did the sword need sharpening, but those that wielded it needed reinforcements with more powerful weapons. Bevan himself did glimpse the bluntness of Parliament when, in the late forties, he warned how easily the nationalised industries could become subservient to the needs of private industry: 'When the state moves to take over private industry,' he said, summing up his point, 'private industry moves to take over the state.' But he did not suggest a solution. Thirty years and four Labour governments later, the problem was far more acute: the leading private corporations were much stronger, Labour's use of the state had become far more compromised – so much so that large numbers of working-class people no longer supported further nationalisation.

The whole strategy associated with Bevan, Foot and the old *Tribune*, of a Labour government plus nationalisation as an answer to the crises of the capitalist economy, was itself in crisis. This could not be blamed simply on the world slump and Labour's small majority; there was something more fundamentally wrong with the strategy itself. The steady collapse, from Harold Wilson's first government onwards, of this essentially parliamentary strategy of the old left underlay the new divisions in the party. It is no wonder that the tribune of this strategy, suddenly finding himself party Leader at the very moment when its collapse was recognised, should end up defending the structure, unable to comprehend the stirrings of the new soul.

3 Local experiences

The idea of making the powerful accountable is infectious. Once party members had shown it could be done, whether to a Cabinet minister or to a mafia of local councillors, party activists elsewhere applied it to their own circumstances. In many areas this meant, and still means, local government. The explosion of party and popular democracy in local government in the late 1970s and throughout the eighties is like one of those unpredictable fireworks that starts with exotic bursts and then seems to smoulder as if at an end, only to let off a new series of firecrackers and leap back into life.

The fuses were lit by the new-style GLC and Sheffield Council. Sparks spread to London borough councils and further afield to district councils in Scotland, Stirling and Edinburgh in particular. At the same time, opposition to the old regime was smouldering in Manchester, to flare up in new directions in 1984. In Liverpool, explosions went off in rather divergent directions, at first soaring higher than any other but then doing a zig-zag backwards into the ground. Then, while many tended to assume that the new radicalism of local government had had its day, small firecrackers began to go off in centres of moderation: in Birmingham for instance, in Tyneside, and in more recent centres of Labour control in the south-east.[1]

These developments were taking place at a time when local government – its finances, it democracy, its services and its employment – were under threat from central government.[2] Experiments in democracy do not always flourish best under pressure. A political leadership under attack from the government, but in a position of local managerial power, is not necessarily in the best position to lead a movement for democracy. There is always a temptation to go for the short cuts and to use the source of power most easily at hand – usually the least democratic. On the other hand, adverse conditions often provide the drive to find new sources of support and power. Which of these directions a local left leadership takes seems to depend on the popular base with which the left comes into office, and its relationship to that base; for instance, whether it was part of a campaigning opposition to a long-established Labour group; whether there are strong Labour parties or independent movements exerting pressure on the council. So we need to know the different histories of the left in each town and the character of the local political economy and labour movement to understand the ways they have used their control of the council.

Each experience is the product of a combination of local traditions and nationally influential ideas. And although my purpose is to generalise, details of local circumstances are important in order to discipline the generalisations. So I will first briefly sketch the distinctive features of three councils dominated by the left that were associated with the wider reform movement in the party: the GLC, Sheffield and Manchester. I will then draw the contrasts and the similarities to Liverpool, and finally describe the problems faced by the left in a town like Newcastle, with its competent, cautious and coolly authoritarian leadership, and make references to recent developments in a rather similar authority: Birmingham. I will also separately discuss Scotland, where the national question is overriding. Already, a central question there is how far the experience of the left local authorities is providing an alternative model to that of Westminster for the Regional Assembly proposed by the Labour Party.

First, then, let us consider the GLC, Sheffield and Manchester.

In Manchester and the GLC, the new left leaders came from experiences of opposition: opposition to previous Labour regimes and to policies of the 1974–79 Labour government. They were already part of wider community and trade-union campaigns before they achieved any power within the council. Such involvement was a more shared experience for the present leadership of Manchester than for the leadership of the GLC, whose political involvements were more scattered. From the start, the leadership in both cities were committed, and expected, to share power with these social and trade-union movements. Moreover, the majority of these councillors came from the new tradition of socialism formed in reaction to the old parliamentary left with all its optimism about the existing state, and the pragmatic right with all its complacency about the market. What was new about them was that they approached power not from the point of view of the party machine, but, initially at the very least, from the point of view of the campaigns and movements let down by that machine.

The left leadership in Sheffield too was strongly influenced by this tradition. But to a greater extent than in Manchester and London it straddled the old and the new. Labourism had been at its most transformative in Sheffield – its local history is interwoven with Communist and syndicalist traditions – and its local vitality continued well beyond its national decay. The left developed from it, rather than, as in other towns, against it. This is reflected in the way that the Sheffield left arrived in positions of leadership in a more gradual way, through a more internal route. They had not had to build new alliances or wage a prolonged struggle against the cuts of an old regime to the same extent. They relied on the strength of the left in the unions and frequently already had a position of some power in earlier administrations. This continuity in leadership has meant a rather more centralised regime, at least until very recently. Democratic initiatives in Sheffield have come even more from the top than in Manchester and London, though it is an unavoidable feature of all three.

The main theme which I bore in mind for this book, as I worked with or talked to people involved in these three councils, was their contribution to the ideas and practicality of a socialism based on popular democracy. This means many aspects of their work will be omitted or referred to in a summary manner. (This is not a potted history of the municipal socialism of the 1980s![3]) There are at least three questions implied by this theme. First, developing one of the themes of the reform movement discussed in Chapter 1, is the legitimacy and importance for socialism of sources of political democracy outside Parliament or councils. Has the new municipal socialism helped in practice to widen the scope of democracy? Has it strengthened extra-parliamentary sources of accountability in the public sector, in the community and in private industry?

Secondly, have the attempts both to make councillors more accountable to the party and in some instances to share power with community, trade-union and voluntary groups, produced any models or lessons – negative and positive – for the goal of a democratic socialist state?

And thirdly, by what political mechanisms can the achievements and lessons of these developments be defended, deepened and generalised? In other words: what has been the role of the Labour Party, and in what ways has its internal political life and democracy, its electoral position and its relationships to the trade unions and other non-parliamentary organisations been affected by the local experiences?

The GLC

Looking back, the Labour Party Manifesto for the 1981–85 GLC was nothing like as radical as the policies for which it later became known. 'There was nothing,' claims Ken Livingstone, 'that a good social democrat couldn't do on a warm day.' Born out of a struggle against the cuts carried out by previous Labour and Conservative administrations, it was an explicitly redistributive manifesto. It sought to maintain a tradition started by Herbert Morrison in the 1930s, of using the rates gathered from the wealthy London suburbs and the City to subsidise policies that would most benefit working-class people. Morrison applied this principle to housing. The Livingstone GLC tried to apply it to transport. The clearest single redistributive commitment in the manifesto was to 'Fares Fair', a dramatic reduction in fares on the underground and on the buses.

The Manifesto also included some bold and, for British local government, new ideas: interventionist industrial and employment policies, the creation of an Ethnic Minorities Unit, and a high priority for equal opportunities within the council's own staffing policies. But it was essentially a programme of modernisation and Fabian-style intervention. It was to be carried out largely by existing GLC officers plus a very small number of specially recruited, politically sympathetic experts. 'It was nothing particularly revolutionary,' concludes Livingstone.

What turned out to be revolutionary, at least in spirit, was the way that the GLC opened its buildings, its funds, its research and – very much more selectively – its decision-making process to some of the most radical and most needy sections of the public. Especially provocative was the way in which it provided what became in effect a national political platform for many otherwise disenfranchised groups. This was the content of the 'modern socialism' that Norman Tebbit frankly admitted the abolition of the GLC was intended to kill. 'We learnt,' says Livingstone in retrospect, 'that once you initiate that style of opening up, so that ideas can come in from outside, you accelerate and take off, in an increasing process of change.'

Political traditions

It is unusual for anything very radical to come from an electoral success. It is especially unusual when the electoral victory is slim (Labour's initial majority was only five, and was reduced further when two Labour councillors joined the SDP) and when the left's success is the result more of a factional coup than a firm base (Livingstone wheeled, dealed and charmed his way into the leadership rather than winning it because of a clear left majority). In effect, the left leadership at the GLC turned themselves, only half intending it, into a magnet for popular pressure. What happened was that a minority of high-profile councillors, Valerie Wise, Paul Boateng and Mike Ward as well as Livingstone, acted and talked in a way which raised expectations and gave a focus for movements which then pushed the politicians far further than any of them could have imagined they would possibly go. The process certainly took their notions of democracy much further than the original ideas of internal party democracy which in the late seventies had dominated Labour Party politics locally in London, as well as nationally.

The absence, among the leadership of the GLC, of the paranoia with which Labour local councillors almost everywhere usually regard 'outside' organisations and movements – including parts of the trade-union movement beyond a clique of full-time officials – was important in enabling this process to flow. The roots of this belief and trust in a political life outside County Hall lie in these councillors' experience, between 1973 and 1977, of being an opposition group during the previous GLC Labour administration.[4] During this time and in the following period of a Conservative administration their base was not in County Hall or exclusively within the Labour Party. Councillors like George Nicholson, Mike Ward and Livingstone himself worked closely with community and campaigning groups *against* the central and local state, including at times the 1977 GLC Labour leadership. This experience of a conscious political exile – an experience shared in a more dramatic way by the left in Manchester – influenced their view of the power and resources of local government and how they could be made use of. Frequently, they felt closer to and more allied to socialists and feminists outside the Labour Party than functionaries within it. They saw the potential of these resources from a stance outside the stifling and neutralising world of local government. Yet they had had sufficient experience of watching that world at work to know how to turn it upside down and to have the confidence, on occasions, so to do.

There is always a risk when writing after the events of making something very messy seem more coherent than it was and in the process losing some of the truth. There was much about the GLC's work which for insiders and outsiders *was* very messy and frustrating, as well as exciting and hopeful.

Both sides of this contradictory experience came partly from people having a taste of power (and only a taste compared to what needed to be done) for the first time in their lives. They also came from being part of a process that really was pushing one set, however marginal, of the secretive, elitist political institutions of the British state, a lot further than they have recently been pushed. It is important now to give some retrospective coherence to this process so that it can be taken further. I will focus attention on the political features of the new GLC, and, in particular, its approach to democracy. From this point of view several distinctive developments stand out.

Beyond representative democracy?
The first is the way in which several committees – notably the Women's Committee, the Planning Committee, the Police Committee, the Ethnic Minorities Committee and the Industry and Employment Committee – decided that policy development and implementation could not be carried out by themselves and council officers alone. For them, the normal model of representative democracy – that is, councillors elected on the basis of a manifesto which in theory is then carried out by civil servants accountable to councillors – was not enough even to implement the manifesto, let alone develop it. A further popular

input into decision-making was needed, particularly from people directly affected by the committee's policy.

The need to extend democracy in this way was felt most strongly by the women involved in creating the Women's Committee – the first of its kind in British local government – and particularly by its chair, Valerie Wise.

The Women's Committee

The crucial influence on Valerie Wise was not the campaign for democracy in the party, though she was part of this; nor was it the women's movement: she had been influenced in a general way by feminism, but had never been a member of a women's group. The decisive influence came from a trade-union organisation: the Lucas Aerospace Shop Stewards, and one of their leading spokesmen, Mike Cooley. Before becoming a GLC councillor, Valerie had been a secretary at the Centre for Alternative Technological and Administrative Systems created by the Lucas Aerospace Shop Stewards, and, she explained,

Mike always insisted that 'the workers are the experts'. I translated that to the idea of women being the real experts as far as the work of our Committee was concerned.

Being a woman myself did not mean that I had all the answers (I've learnt that a lot more since having Alan [her child]. Whilst I campaigned in support of child care and children, I do feel slightly different now I've got one of my own and I'm more aware of the problems). Nor was it enough to have sympathetic, feminist women working for us. They can never make up for the women with real-life experiences. It's best to go out and talk to women out there about their views.

'Go out and talk to the women out there' is exactly what Valerie and the Women's Committee did, within ten days of its formation. They convened a public meeting to ask women for their views about what should be the committee's policies. They also asked the meeting how they wished to elect women co-optees from outside the council onto the committee. Over a hundred women turned up. At this first meeting, the women were mainly from feminist groups and campaigns. From then on, quarterly meetings were advertised through all the women's press in London. The numbers grew to between 300 and 500. They included both representatives of groups and individuals; as Val says, 'Large numbers of women are unorganised, so the normal delegate meetings you have in the labour movement would not be appropriate.' She adds, 'I don't think we got it right, but we made a start that others can build.'

One very important way in which the Women's Committee was a start of something new was through its election of a significant group of women with full decision-making powers onto what became a major council committee. 'You can have as many public meetings as you like, but unless the women are in on the decision-making process then they are not really sharing power,' observed Valerie Wise. So eight co-opted women were to go onto the Council Committee of three Tories, one SDP and seven Labour. Six of these were elected annually from the open meetings. Councillors had no say whatsoever in these elections. They were elected under different categories: black, lesbian and disabled. Another two places were uncategorised and were also to be elected from the floor of the meeting, but, much to the initial resentment of the open meeting, the Labour Group insisted that they be allocated to two trade-union women. They were chosen by the Women's Rights Committee of the south-east Regional TUC. This use of the Labour Group's power was rare; in fact there was no other occasion where it was used against the wishes of the general meeting. But it does indicate the way in which these new developments were an extension, rather than a replacement, of the council's representative democracy. In other words, the councillors had final power.

The Women's Committee shared its power in this way to an extent that no other GLC committee even tried. For some time now many Labour authorities have co-opted tenants and community representatives, usually only in ones and twos, onto Housing and Social Service committees. But this, on the whole, has been a frustrating experience for the co-optees and has had little impact on the committees' policies. The community representatives tended to be in a secondary position within a structure unresponsive to their needs. There was little pressure on the committees to be directly accountable to a community power base, in the way that there was on the GLC's Women's Committee.

One reason why the Women's Committee found it easier to open itself to direct representation in a more radical way than other committees was that there was a more clearly self-identified constituency for such a process. Another factor was simply that Valerie Wise was more willing to buck conventions than most of the councillors:

I think I had a great advantage going onto the council very young (she was 24) without having got used to how one does things. It meant I didn't go in with set ideas. I didn't know how you were supposed to do things. I wasn't inhibited.

She had the support of the Leader and a core of committee chairs who were trying to achieve a similar sharing of power in their own areas.

Planning

One such area was planning. The chair of this committee was George Nicholson. A major part of the new planning policy was for the GLC to buy vacant land which provided prime sites for office development but on which the local community wanted housing and community facilities. Local community groups and campaigns, in some of which – Coin Street, Waterloo and Bermondsey – George Nicholson had played an active part, were given considerable decision-making power. This included power both in the development of the 'Community Areas Policy' and in the actual management of the sites.

Industry and employment

Another kind of power-sharing, more experimental and perhaps more difficult, was tried by the Industry and Employment Committee, chaired by Mike Ward. Here, the committee's approach was to provide financial support and develop a close working relationship with specific community and trade-union groups on, for example, campaigns for locally determined plans, resistance to redundancies, developing a strategy for a London-based industry and building an international shop stewards' committee. Here, too, new forms of democracy were tested, which gave a direct political voice and focus to popularly-based organisations. These tentative new forms were different from those of the Women's Committee.

The Industry and Employment Committee did not open itself directly to representation from any wider constituency. There was a manifesto commitment to co-opt London MPs and representatives of the south-east TUC. As the work developed this latter proposal bore little practical relation to the organisations on the ground with whom the committee was working, so it was never carried out. On the other hand, attempts to establish a forum – rather optimistically titled the 'Popular Planning Assembly' – for these exceedingly diverse organisations never gathered momentum. It seemed somehow artificial; perhaps the popular constituency and base for local economic policy will only cohere when there are the political conditions for both economic planning and constitutional devolution. At any rate, as far as the GLC's industrial policy was concerned, the making of an overall strategy was the work of councillors and council officers. Popular organisations shared power, to varying degrees, in elaborating and carrying out the details for particular industries, workplaces and communities.[5]

Several other committees had their own particular way of combining some form of direct democracy with the representational democracy of the council. For instance, other committees brought community representatives onto the panels which allocated grants. This was the case with the Arts and Recreation Committee; the presence of a majority of community and specialist representatives was part of a radical shift in the criteria and priorities of arts funding and they helped to shape the committee's whole strategy.[6]

The experience of the Industry and Employment Committee illustrates a second distinctive feature of the extension of democracy on which the GLC found itself embarking, often in response to the demands made on it. Many of the initiatives taken under the authority of this committee were on issues over which the GLC had little or no direct power. This meant that the new GLC put considerable emphasis on what the GLC lawyers would label 'the function of advocacy' (every item of GLC spending had to come under some legally defined function of local government, however innovative the interpretation might have to be). This meant support for organisations campaigning, or in some way struggling, for their needs and rights against another institution such as a transnational corporation, the government-established Docklands Development Corporation, or the defence industry.

The GLC saw its job as not simply a manager of strategic services and regulations, but as a political voice for the majority of the people of London against whoever was perpetrating an injustice.

Without a party card

The GLC's political voice was very much more than a Labour Party voice, in several senses. First, a party card was not a condition for working in a politically sensitive or high-profile job at the new GLC, nor for being involved in its decision-making from the outside. Many members of the Labour Group were unhappy about this. It was a principle that had to be fought for, especially where the 'outsiders' were to be co-opted onto committees. Several members of the Labour Group argued with Val Wise, for instance, that the women elected to the Women's Committee by the open meeting should be in the Labour Party. Val rejected this and was supported by Livingstone and others. The executive of the London Labour Party, however, and Ted Knight in particular, wanted further explanation. Val went to the executive to explain. 'It was not a left – right issue,' she recalls; 'people were worried about keeping control of the committee. They were worried there might be a takeover of the co-opted places. But let's face it, if a decision had been taken at the committee that the Labour Group fundamentally disagreed with, they could always have voted against it at full council.'

As it happened, a particular faction did at one point take over the Women's Committee's public meetings and managed in 1984 to win two of the co-opted places. But other women on the committee and at the public meetings, from a variety of standpoints and backgrounds, became increasingly aware of what they described as the 'bullying' tactics of the group. These women got organised and defeated the factional group at the next year's elections. And they did not need the intervention of the London Labour Party to protect them.[7]

The mistrust on the part of members of the London Labour Party Executive is not unusual. As I will describe in relation to the attitudes of some constituency parties to non-party women's groups or black organisations, a trusting relationship with people outside the party, however close their goals, is quite outside the Labourist tradition. The only non-party people who have historically been graced with such trust in the past seem to have been senior civil servants!

Ken Livingstone sums up the orthodox approach:

The concept of actually deferring to some group outside the mainstream movement about what you should do is totally alien to the leaders of the labour movement. I mean everybody expects you to produce a party card, whether they're a right-wing councillor in Tower Hamlets or a Militant in Liverpool.

There's a broad assumption that we only talk to party members, we only deal with trade-union leaders. We don't deal with people who haven't been organised out there. We take the sort of attitude: 'You want to change housing policy? Join the Labour Party, comrade.'

Well, you just can't work like that. We haven't got the God-given right to demand that people accept that we are somehow a good thing. We've got to prove it. We've got to prove our goodwill and integrity to the groups that have looked at us in the past and decided we didn't have any.

In London, perhaps more than anywhere else, such proof was near enough a condition for the GLC's success. The party's traditional, organised working-class base had collapsed more rapidly than virtually anywhere else in the country. The old shells are still there: the number of places on the executive for dockers and printers reflect their old strengths. But they no longer represent a mass force. There are now more municipal home helps than dockers in London, more hairdressers than employed printers. Instinctively the GLC leadership knew they had to reach out and appeal to a popular base beyond that of the Labour Party. And in so doing they demonstrated, in an unfinished form, the potential of extending the campaign for democracy beyond the party to the state – or rather a small part of it – itself. The problem in London since the abolition of the GLC has been the absence of a party able to build on the new political base which the GLC began to create.

Sheffield

In Sheffield the Labour Party was more secure, owing to its particularly strong links with the main unions and the fact that it is overwhelmingly a working-class city. Though, by the mid-1970s, industrial decline was beginning to shake the confidence of the more farsighted amongst party leaders. A group of them, mainly from the Brightside Constituency, including

David Blunkett, at the time of writing Leader of the Council, and Roger Barton, now Secretary of the District Labour Party and the Trades Council Labour Group, had the ability to read the political writing on the collapsing industrial wall and take action. Their base was in the party, *and*, through the Sheffield Trades Council, in the unions. Historically, the leadership of these two has been inseparable. In many ways it still is, but the trade-union composition of this alliance has changed dramatically in the last five years as a result of the decimation of Sheffield's engineering and steel industries.

It is important to understand the historical roots of these close-knit centres of power: Sheffield District Labour Party, Labour Group and also the Trades Council, and how, recently, they have changed. This background helps to explain the priorities of the District Party and the Labour Group: their strong emphasis on economic and employment policy; their comparatively low emphasis on policies concerned with the specific interests of women and black people, compared with London, where industrial decline and, with it, the decline of organised labour set in much earlier. It also helps to explain the character of the Labour leadership: its relative centralisation – compared to, say, Manchester and, in a slightly different way, the GLC.

Political and trade-union traditions

The most significant historical feature about the Sheffield Labour Party is its intimate relations with the trade unions, especially the engineering unions. This intimacy was maintained through generations (often quite literally different generations of the same families, like the Caborns, Flannerys and Bartons) by the unity of the Trades and Labour Council until 1974. Behind this unity lay the intense feeling, in the words of Lord Mayor Bill Owen, previously President of the Trades and Labour Council, that 'the trades unions had built up the Labour Party; it was *our* party. We never had much of a middle class like they did in Leeds, where the Jewish community and others contributed a lot to the Labour Party.'

In many towns, such as Leeds and Manchester, the Labour Party separated from the Trades Council in response to restrictions imposed on joint organisation by the 1927 Trades Dispute

Act. In Sheffield and Liverpool the mutual determination to remain united was strong enough for them to find a way round these restrictions and establish industrial and political wings of the one organisation. The two wings would meet together, but decisions concerning the industrial wing could only be taken by industrial delegates and those concerning the political wing by the party delegates. In fact the majority of delegates tended to be their branch delegates to both.

In 1974 the TUC and the Labour Party decided to insist on the separation of the sections into a trades council and a district Labour party. The move came particularly from the TUC, some of whose affiliates were not able to play a full role in the Trades and Labour Council because they were not affiliated to the Labour Party. The Trades and Labour Councils objected, but in the end they had to accept the decision. They have found ways of maintaining the close connection, institutional as well as informal. The main institutional mechanism is the office of joint secretary to the two organisations. At present Roger Barton works full-time as both secretary to the Trades Council and Secretary to the District Labour Party. These strong trade-union links, especially with a trade-union movement with a highly political culture (kept alive until recently primarily by the Communist Party rather than the Labour Party), made for a certain stability of membership even through the sixties, when parties elsewhere in the country fell into decline through disillusion and disappointment.[8]

Until the late 1970s the union–party relationships were dominated by the engineering and steel unions. The District Committee of the Confederation of Shipbuilding and Engineering Unions, which brought together all the engineering unions, was a major power in the city. A sign of this was that they would be consulted automatically by the Labour Group leadership on every major council decision. Fran Holmwood, who came to work with David Blunkett in 1980, remembers how, when she first came, 'big issues like the setting up of the Employment Department or the council's financial crisis would always be discussed with the Confed. In the last four or five years, though,' she says, 'this has all changed. The Group still talks to the Confed, but not regularly. They just don't have the same weight. It's the District Party that really matters.'

Another result of the decline of Sheffield's traditional industries is the change in the composition of the District Labour Party and the Trades Council. They are now both dominated by members of public-sector unions. It is now NALGO, not the AEU, which has the largest number of delegates to the Trades Council.

But this is jumping ahead, for when the present Group leadership came into office in 1980, they did so through a District Party and Trades Council dominated by the AUEW. It is to the story of their rise to office that I will now turn.

The continuity of the left

In Sheffield, there was no lost generation of the sixties and seventies, repelled by the Labour Party of Harold Wilson. The party's close political relationship with the unions meant that whereas in most other towns the party was bypassed by militant trade-union committees, in Sheffield it was drawn directly into the campaigns against the government's wage restraint and 'In Place of Strife'. Naturally the left stayed with and even joined the party as the base from which to fight. As a result there was not the kind of struggle, partly between generations, that happened in Manchester. Instead, the younger generation was assimilated relatively peacefully into the leadership with a leg up from the left minority in the generation before. 'It was a much more gradual shift towards democracy,' says David Blunkett.

Another result of this continuity was that the issues of party democracy came to the fore earlier in Sheffield than elsewhere. It was in Sheffield Brightside in 1974 that one of the first 'deselections' took place. This long, painful experience of deselection, like that of Newham, was an important stimulus to the national campaign for mandatory reselection. The Brightside deselection was an indication of the changes taking place in those few working-class constituency parties which were drawn into the industrial and community militancy of the late sixties, rather than bypassed by it.

It was a case of a clash between youngish, mainly working-class activists radicalised through their union, the AUEW, or through the impact of a local tenants' campaign and rent strike and an ineffectual, conservative MP. In earlier days such an MP would have got away with it, through a combination of applied charm and his committee's deference. Brightside was a closed and cliqueish constituency, the sort that would tell you that it was 'full up' if you wanted to join. The new activists and others in the party were trying to open things up, partly in order to survive in the new rebellious atmosphere that lingered on in Sheffield since a city-wide rent strike and Tory victory in the council elections in 1968. This election had marked the only gap in Labour's fifty-year rule. As one of them put it: 'The party realised more closely that it needed to fight for local working-class support, that it could not expect the local labour movement to go on supporting it just because it was the Labour Party.'[9]

The MP, Eddie Griffiths, was resisting this process of change. Eventually he was replaced by Joan Maynard. At the same time a similar desire for change was being expressed in the District Labour Party and the Labour Group, shaken by their brief period out of office and the militancy of 'their' tenants. Many, including the new leadership of the Brightside constituency, David Blunkett, Roger Barton and another leading councillor, Clive Betts, believed that the rent strike – in response to a rent rise – was a result of the Labour Group moving away from the District Party and taking decisions independently. Blunkett describes their view:

We were saying that the party and the group should be much more one and the same thing: the group shouldn't believe it could take decisions independently of the party; and if that were the case the party also carried a responsibility. It was not going to pass impossible resolutions. It actually had to play a part in how its resolutions could be implemented.

By 1980 the group and the party had established this close relationship under the leadership of many of those who had led the deselection process in Sheffield Brightside. An earlier leader, George Wilson, resigned, and Blunkett was elected to office. In this way people, mainly men but including strong, independent women such as Joan Barton and later Helen Jackson, of the same generation and broadly similar politics to those leading the GLC and, as we shall see, Manchester Council, gained control. But they did so without the long period of exile and campaigning against the council which the left went through in Manchester, and, to a lesser extent, in the GLC. And unlike the left on the GLC, they did so with the close involvement of a strong and active city party. These differences of history and in the character of the working class in Sheffield led to important differences in the kind of democracy that it pioneered.

Reform from the top

The first phase of the left's period in control was a process of reform from the top. It was, as with the GLC, a matter of the Labour Group deciding as a matter of political philosophy to 'open up' decision-making. The professed aim was 'socialism from below', but the process in Sheffield did not have quite the degree of independence and unpredictability that it had in London. 'Opening up' primarily meant consulting and campaigning, not sharing power in the same way as the GLC Women's Committee did, or Manchester's Neighbourhood Forums are trying to do. There are pockets of power-sharing, however. These are usually the result of radically minded officers being attracted to Sheffield by its image and its rhetoric, and on arrival taking the initiative to put the rhetoric into practice. One such pocket is the city's library service, where Pat Coleman, the recently appointed City Librarian, has introduced a unique degree of worker and user democracy. Another is in the Recreation Department, where Services to Community Action and Tenants (SCAT) have been employed to organise workplace and community discussion on improving services and working conditions. A recent one is in the Employment Department, where Keith Hayman, a community organiser from Coventry, has been providing funds and other kinds of support for organisations of the unemployed. The councillors have enabled these initiatives to go ahead, but have tended not to give the kind of high-profile political lead that was often given at the GLC.

There is a cautious, controlling strand in Sheffield's Labour Group; a wariness about raising expectations, which appears the opposite of the GLC's 'open up, accelerate and take off' approach. David Blunkett illustrates this when he says:

We've been in danger both with the community and the workforce of increasing expectations beyond the ability to rapidly carry them through. People are impatient and they get disillusioned very quickly – it is an indication of lack of political education in this country that people don't take a longer view.

No doubt this cautiousness stems partly from Sheffield's responsibility for running vast, increasingly tightly budgeted service departments such as Housing and Social Services. The GLC, as a 'strategic authority', had little responsibility for the delivery and maintenance of daily services, except for the Fire Brigade and, indirectly, London Transport. Moreover, until the tightening of the noose of abolition, the GLC's budget gave it far greater scope for innovation. But there is also an important difference in how democracy is understood.

In Sheffield, the democratisation that has gone on is at first hidden from a GLC-trained eye, especially one that looks in from outside the party, as mine does. For besides the pockets of activity described above, the trade-union and community participation that has taken place has done so through the party. It is party democracy rather than popular democracy. For instance, the running of the Employment Department has involved a regular meeting with the District Party's Employment Manifesto Committee, in which trade-union and party representatives monitor and contribute to the work of the department. In the past the strength and popular base of the party has been such that party democracy and popular democracy seemed one and the same thing. Compared with both London and, in a different way, Newcastle, there has been until recently sufficient real life in the Sheffield Labour Party to make such an assumption credible.

But, as we have already implied, the economic and social base of this life is crumbling. Councillors and party activists have seen this and, as a result, are adopting an increasingly outward-looking approach. The council and party campaigns in defence of public transport, against rate-capping and in support of the miners' strike show a party trying to reconstruct its base within a changing working class.

There is another political difference between Sheffield on the one hand and the GLC and Manchester on the other. It arises partly from the kind of working class that the Sheffield Labour Group assumes it represents, and the priorities that implies. This becomes clear from a description of Sheffield Council's initial approach to the needs and demands of women.

Feminism from underneath

The view of the Sheffield Labour Group – the majority – towards women had been that women would benefit from the council's general policies as tenants, mothers, council workers and citizens, as part, in other words, of Sheffield's working class. The assumption was that while the trade unions looked after the wage-packet and employment, the council cared for the home and the community. It was therefore automatic that council policies concerned women. The priority must be the council's general services; this was the way in which women's needs would be best met. The idea of women having distinct political demands and organisation was strange. Of feminism they were sceptical, to say the least: 'another trendy idea imported from the south' was the general response.

It was only in 1986 – five years after the left gained control – that a Women's Unit was set up.[10] Even then it was subordinate to the Director of Personnel and had only a staff of four and a budget of just £23,000 a year. But meanwhile pressure had been building up 'from below', down among the women – not from raised expectations, but from anger and frustration. It took several forms: on employment – one of the council's highest political priorities – women officers, trade unionists and Labour Party women organised to influence the direction of policy. As far as training, new technology and council staffing policies went, they have already caused material changes extending opportunities for women, but they have had less impact on the department's direct intervention in the private sector. On other issues, women have used the District Party's Manifesto Working Groups. The party's public commitment to democracy from below makes them and the Labour Group ultimately open to influence, even if it has been a struggle. Ann Howard is a long-standing socialist feminist who joined the Labour Party just three years ago. She is on the Health Care Working Group:

We've had to push hard for women's needs to be looked at in detail. But I've found all the work really satisfying. It's the first time I've had any power to really get things done. You discuss an idea, agree it, get it written into the party's commitments and then through also being on the council's Health Care Strategy Group you can keep a watch on its implementation.

In the end then, the women themselves, using evey available lever, are making gains potentially as radical as the GLC Women's Committee in terms of power and influence. One of their most important levers has been the party, through which they have increasingly questioned and then monitored the priorities of the Group leadership. At the GLC, the party was on the sidelines. In the absence of the party, women's influence was through a direct relationship with the councillors. This was possible because the GLC Group leadership, responding to a strong force within its own popular base, espoused a political vision influenced by feminism. In Sheffield the dominant view of socialism was on the whole anti-feminist. But the strength of the regime in Sheffield is that through the party they have created enduring democratic processes whereby these different views can be debated. Blunkett may be the Leader, but unlike the old-style Labour boss, his is less and less the final word. In a sense it is a measure of the left's original achievement that now a new wave of party activists, including a significant force of women, are re-asserting the independence and critical role of the District Party.

The independence of the party

Within the DLP, delegates are straining at the reins which have kept them tied to the day-by-day activities of the Labour Group. Several factors have contributed to the tension: most important has been the experience of the campaign against rate-capping and a sense that the DLP was too close to the Labour Group either to exert sufficient pressure or add much to the council's campaign.

Mike Elliott became Chair of the DLP after the 1985–86 rate-capping campaign. He explains his view of how the party should develop:

We must bring ourselves one step back from where we've been in the last two years. There was really no difference between a district party executive and a Labour group executive in terms of the issues we were dealing with.

We got to ridiculous extents on budget spending. Hours and hours we spent dealing with piddling sums of money in a way where we missed the politics of what we are about. We must not confuse detail with strength.

When Mike Elliott took over the chair he made a statement explaining the priority he gave to building up the party's distinct identity on matters of policy direction and on campaigning. His view of the campaigning role of the DLP draws on his experience as Treasurer of CND. It is a mark of how the party has changed since the days of the 'full' Brightside wards that he should stress the need to campaign together with other organisations, to get away from what he sees as paranoia about 'who are enemies and who are friends':

I'd have some form of campaign forum in which tenants' associations, community groups, women's groups, the unemployed as well as political parties, participated. We do that in CND. We're still stuck in this thing that everything in Sheffield emanates from the Labour Party. That's a mental bridge that we've got to cross.

In his view left-wing Liberals should come to such a forum where there is agreement.

Mike Elliott's view of where the local Labour Party should go takes the rhetoric of councillor accountability literally. He wants the District Party to be 'a counter-pressure on the Labour Group in the sense of making sure we are in control of the things that matter: timetables, political direction.' David Blunkett was probably making a similar point in 1978, but at least in 1987 the party and the group are agreed, in theory, that the party has the right to have such control. Elliott (who since I talked to him has moved to Bradford) believes that for this to be genuine the party needs to be strengthened. It will be an important test of party democracy and of how far a group committed to the left means what it says.

Manchester

The economic history and the history of the labour movement in Manchester have produced very different traditions to those in Sheffield. The comparison would make a fascinating and useful political study. I have merely scratched the surface because it seemed to me clear that the differences in historical tradition are vital in explaining the differing characters of the two left administrations and understanding their limitations. The most fundamental difference in the two histories revolves around the relations between the Labour Party and the trade unions.

Party and trade-union traditions

In Sheffield, as we have just seen, the relationship between the party and the unions at a city level has been extremely close. In Manchester, by contrast, the dominant unions, especially the engineering unions, have concentrated their energies, until recently, on building and preserving their industrial strength. In postwar years, they have not as a body treated 'the political wing' or at least the municipal wing as their priority – they have exerted influence over the choice of MPs in the Manchester area. The relative separation of the unions from the local Labour parties has its roots in the response of the Manchester and Salford Labour and Trades Council to the 1927 Trades Disputes Act. Like the vast majority of trades councils, Manchester and Salford decided to conform to the restrictions imposed by the Act on the political activity of trade unions. The Labour Party and the Trades Councils went their separate ways.

A further factor contributing to this separation was the growth in individual party membership among people who would be unlikely to attend the Trades and Labour Council, but who were part of the life of a commercial city like Manchester: the middle-class groups which Bill Owen describes as missing in Sheffield, the large number of clerical workers, and the Jewish community, at first unintegrated into the trade unions.

A heterogeneous party

This separation laid the basis for an increasingly syndicalist kind of trade unionism in engineering in Manchester, dominated by the Communist Party. In its own terms it was very successful, especially postwar. 'A feeling grew up,' remembers Eddie Frow, the historian of the Manchester labour movement, 'that the AUEW could run their own show; they were a power in their own right and they didn't need to look wider.' There were always a number of AUEW activists who did look elsewhere, to become councillors for instance, but they tended to be the more right-wing or those who lost out in the union's power struggles. (I came across the same kind of trade-union snobbery towards the job of a councillor when talking to NUM officials in Barnsley.) Eddie Frow again: 'Councillors were seen by union standards as a far lesser breed. Without being disparaging, they'd make good branch officers in the AUEW but rarely had the qualities to reach the District Committee.' (There speaks an ex-AUEW district officer!) Others in the party and union corroborate his general judgement.

The consequences were apparent in the mid- and late 1970s: the Labour Group was a mix of engineering workers and retired engineering workers, shopkeepers, printworkers and a small number of professional people who tended to dominate the leadership. The majority were over 45 years old. The party had suffered a massive decline of membership in the sixties and early seventies – the rotten harvest of the Wilson years, which affected so many areas. In a sense a whole generation was missing; those of the older generation lacked much will to fight, and were under no pressure to do so.

One aspect of this weakness was the lack of the strong and active trade-union connections which provided the Sheffield party with a continual source of renewal and stability – though, as we have seen, it was a renewal of a particular kind. Manchester Labour parties were more heterogeneous and, equally important, more tolerant of heterogeneity. This was due not simply to the absence of a strong bond with a particular section of the working class; there were positive traditions as well, for instance, a tradition of women's trade unionism, whose origins lie in women's experiences in the textile industry but which has permeated the whole tradition of the labour movement in Manchester. A friend of mine remembers watching the demonstrations against the Tories' Industrial Relations Act in 1973. 'We'd watch each region go past and it was men, men, men, men until suddenly came Lancashire and there were these mad women, gangs of them.'

The missing generation

When people from the missing generation of the seventies, the generation that had put their energies into community, feminist and trade-union politics rather than the Labour Party, finally decided to join, they joined a party in decline and lacking any strong political force. They had an immediate impact on its political character, becoming the leadership of the District in 1979 and leadership of the Labour Group five years later. I say 'they' because although the individuals concerned came from a variety of backgrounds and joined for slightly different reasons, they do, in terms of age and political experience, fall clearly into one 'generation'. For instance, in 1978 four out of the five of the new radical left councillors were between 25 and 35 years old. And in 1983, 20 out of 22 of the left were aged between 30 and 45. By contrast, 43 out of the 47 who supported the leadership in 1978 were over 40. And by 1984, 20 of the 33 who supported the right were between the ages of 50 and 70.[11]

These new recruits had similar reasons for joining, both pushing them and pulling them. Pushing them was a sense that the non-parliamentary movements or projects in which they were involved did not have, and, on their own, could not have, the political power that was necessary for radical change. Cath Fry, Chair of the District Labour Party in 1985–86, joined in 1974:

I went to a women's group at college – Bolton Tech – and I'd been to the odd meetings of IMG and the IS, as it was then. And I went along with all their ideals. But it seemed to me that theirs was not the way forward. That if we're going to achieve a real socialist state it had to be through the formal party structure, the political structure.

Another factor pushing this age group towards the Labour Party is described by John Shiers, who joined in 1976 and was Chair of the District Labour Party in 1984–85. At the time he joined he was involved in housing campaigns and other campaigns over community facilities and in the gay liberation movement:

So many of the problems people faced: housing, transport, education, facilities for youth, leisure . . . had to do with the local state. And I'd seen in Islington how urban aid (distributed through the local council) could be put to use to meet people's needs.

For example, Islington had used it to fund the gay movement to set up London Friend, for counselling gays and lesbians. I could see how the same thing could be done in Manchester. So to take our local campaigns any further it seemed natural to join the Labour Party and push them on the inside as well as the outside.

The factors pulling them towards the party were the signs of change in the party nationally. Graham Stringer, now leader of the Labour Group, feels that the national campaign for accountability was very important indeed. Others were influenced by their experiences of community politics in Manchester. They decided to join the Labour Party because the council was always the first obstacle that community campaigns came up against. With the national campaign for constitutional reforms, Stringer and his colleagues felt that this could be changed from the inside as well as the outside: 'The national developments gave us confidence. We weren't alone. We knew that if we got organised we could get something done.'

As well as becoming councillors and winning the leadership of the District Labour Party the other thing they 'got done' was the *de facto* deselection of Harold Lever. Officially Lever retired to the Lords, but this was only after the constituency executive had made it clear that they would no longer support him. They even suggested he accept a peerage; according to Stringer, who put this to him at a private meeting between Lever and constituency officers in his Whitehall office, he was 'visibly relieved at the suggestion'.

This was merely oiling the wheels of accountability compared with the eight-year-long struggle to make the Labour Group accountable. For the leadership of the Labour Group in 1976 accountability was a three-year formality – selection, reselection, reselection and reselection until retirement and beyond. The job of the District Party in this was to arrange and oversee the selection and reselection process and to organise the election campaign. The new DLP leadership had a different view. They saw accountability as an active working relationship with the Labour Group to carry out a policy drawn up by the District Party. The first stage of achieving this was to turn the DLP into a source of policy: the DLP set up working groups of experts within the party, who drafted detailed proposals on different aspects of the council's work; these drafts were then discussed and amended by constituency parties and trade-union branches. The amended drafts were then returned to the DLP and became, after further discussions and votes, the party's programme and therefore, in theory, the basis for the manifesto and the policy of the Labour Group. But many in the Group were suspicious of the new style and ideas being introduced into the DLP.

The old regime
It was not that the members of old regime were reactionary. They built up Manchester's services and housing stock throughout the sixties and early seventies. But their view of democracy – group

democracy, party democracy and popular democracy – was very narrow. The Group's meetings, rather like the Parliamentary Labour Party, had no written agenda or minutes; chairmen of committees were appointed by the leader. Discipline was rigid, views different to those of the leadership were not tolerated. For Councillor Val Dunn, even singing at a Christmas social – in the presence of a visiting dignitary – incurred the wrath of the leader, Bill Egerton, and led to a reprimand!

The District Party was treated as a formality. Its main task was to administer the party's work for council elections. As for any wider notion of democracy, it never went beyond the vote. The town hall was forbidding, an elaborate protection for councillors and officers: visitors by appointment only. The impressive Victorian halls were used only for municipal ceremonies and functions. Information was hard to come by. The council had no notion of consulting local people beyond the formality of notices on planning permission pinned up on obscure, dusty noticeboards.

None of this was in any way unusual in Labour groups throughout the last twenty-five years. There are still a large number who have remained like this. Take a random example from near London: Thurrock. An outstanding feature of the Labour Group on Thurrock Council is that they spend most of their recreation budget on looking after two specially made chandeliers in a vast civic hall, the inside of which is rarely seen, let alone used, by the people of Thurrock. Not much sign of popular democracy there!

The fundamental flaw in the old regime's approach, the source of its eventual downfall – in some ways similar to the GLC and Sheffield – was the growing gap between promises and delivery. As government cuts pressed down on local councils, many councils stopped even promising, but Manchester had built up a progressive image that it thought it could maintain by its ability to negotiate with Whitehall. Its response to a government which refused to negotiate was to make concessions in the hope of being allowed back to the negotiating table, and on the assumption that the swing of the electoral pendulum would restore Labour to power and enable them to get their spending programmes back on track. The option of resisting the government could not even be discussed. It was unthinkable.

A simmering conflict finally broke in 1980 when the Group leadership announced a budget involving cuts of £13 million. DLP policy was against cuts. Thirteen councillors decided to abide by DLP policy. The Group expelled them. For four years these councillors were in exile, together with the reinforcements who soon joined them through deselections and the winning of marginal seats from the Tories, and, in effect, the DLP itself. It turned out to be a very productive exile which laid the foundations for the Group leadership's present strengths.

The left in exile

Exile meant that the left councillors and the District Labour Party had a strong incentive to look outside the council chamber for support and direction. By the time the first cuts were announced a strong Anti-Cuts Campaign was already under way. The DLP and several Labour Party branches were involved with it but its support came more especially from housing campaigns, public-sector unions, advice and community centres, women's liberation and gay groups, and it was co-ordinated through the Manchester Community Resource Centre. It publicised and organised support for the case against the cuts through leaflets and meetings throughout Manchester, demonstrations, street theatre and adept use of the local radio. In a sense this alliance became what the engineering trade unions had long been to the left of the Labour Party in Sheffield: a non-parliamentary base of support and pressure. This base had an effect on the politics of the Labour Group, on its priorities and its methods. Graham Stringer points out its importance to himself and the rest of the present Group leadership:

During our three or four years in opposition we made alliances at all sorts of levels with all sorts of people who put feminist politics and the politics of the gay movement onto the agenda in Manchester. If we had not been fighting the cuts with them, they would have dropped off most agendas. Those sort of developments meant that our politics became more radical. I know my politics changed in that period. They were influenced by feminism and anti-racism which might not have been the case if we'd been in power in those years.

Traditions have their effect

The influence of the respective bases of the Labour Groups in Sheffield and Manchester shows in their priorities – and as the base has changed, so have the priorities. As we have seen, the traditional trade-union roots of the Sheffield Labour Party – and the threats to its survival – led the leadership of the group to put a high priority on industry and employment policy. Equal opportunities were well down the list, in practice. In Manchester, by contrast, employment policy (beyond the council's own role as an employer) was not given any significant new thought until 1986. The DLP's proposals on economic policy in 1983 were little different to the approach of the old Labour Group – grants to business, industrial estates, planning initiatives – except that all support for private businesses would be conditional on their compliance with certain council provisions on working conditions and trade-union organisation, and there was an explicit commitment to support for trade unionists resisting redundancies. The proposals on 'equal opportunities', on the other hand, were thought through in extensive detail and were radical in their implications for the main service departments, especially social services, education, and housing.

Equal opportunities can change lives
'Equal opportunities' is a grey term with bureaucratic overtones. but the measures pushed and co-ordinated through the Council's Equal Opportunities Committee and its Anti-Racism Committee illustrate the material changes that a carefully prepared equal opportunities programme could bring about in the lives of many people. The two committees were set up in 1984. Politicians had to intervene persistently to overcome resistance from departmental heads before they made real progress.

The first result was an agreement with the Education and Social Services Committee to build thirteen child-care centres providing care after school and during the holidays for the under-fives. Each centre is being planned to meet the needs of particular neighbourhoods. The hours and the uses of the centres are flexible too, to meet local needs. They might be used for washing and drying clothes, supplying clothes and second-hand furniture at small charges, self-help groups and so on. Four centres are already open.

Another area where major changes are taking place is in access to council buildings for the disabled. Builders have already started with the Town Hall, an inaccessible building for the majority of people, constructing ramps, fitting lifts, putting up notices in Braille and getting rid of other barriers to access. Then there are small, less costly improvements to day-to-day services: a library for Manchester's Chinese community, well stocked with books in Chinese and run by Chinese librarians; book lists in libraries including a category locating fiction and non-fiction likely to be of special interest to lesbians and gay men; a decision that all new or reconstructed roads will have a dropped kerb to make mobility easier for the disabled. These then are some of the changes that take place when 'The Hard Left Hijacks Manchester.'[12]

The alliances that the left made 'in exile' also influenced the methods of the Group, their internal democracy and the way they saw the relation between the council and the people of Manchester. To consider their internal democracy: most Labour Groups behave like mini-PLPs – some better organised, some worse. The experience of the left within the Manchester Group of unofficial opposition has given it a rare cohesion and informal as well as formal democracy. Its discussions are remarkably free of factionalism, or so I'm told by several participants. As with few other Labour – or Conservative or Alliance – groups, power is not concentrated in the hands of the leader. The most powerful group is the weekly meeting of group officers including the leader. These are the crucial strategic discussions to prepare for group meetings and through them the leadership of the Group is shared. Also, as with the GLC and Sheffield, the leader does not chair the group meetings. I would guess, though this is not something that I have asked about directly, that Graham Stringer's lack of personal ambition for a national political career has contributed to the greater cohesion of the left within the Manchester Group and District Party.

Councillors, bureaucrats and party members

The main problem now in the relationship between the Group and the party is not so much making councillors accountable but ensuring the party's independence and ability to monitor and, when necessary, put pressure on the council.

One problem is simply that as people become active in the party they get what was described as 'sucked' into the council.

It is a powerful process which seems to happen inevitably unless there is some strong pressure sucking in the opposite direction, towards the party. Val Dunn and her party branch fell victim to this process: she is a brilliant organiser, who led the bakers' strike in Manchester in 1977 and was applying her skills to recruiting for the party and building up her branch. But Hulme Ward wanted her to stand for the council: 'I felt it was an honour to be asked by Hulme, their problems are some of the worst in the city. But I was building things up in the party and was reluctant to go into the council. I know how easy it is to get swamped.'

For Cath Fry, the present Chair of the District Labour Party, it is the need to prevent councillors getting swamped and becoming 'bureaucrats' as much as the need to monitor policies which makes the party's independent strength so important. She made a conscious decision not to go on the council panel:

I've thought more and more about how important it is that there are active people in the party who are not councillors. If you're a councillor it can be very difficult to keep a political perspective. That's where the party is crucial. And it cannot play that role if it is just an appendage to the council.

Another conscious effort to break the umbilical cord between party and group is cutting the number of councillors on the party executive. At present twelve out of a 35-person party executive are councillors. The aim is to reduce this. In the last two years there has been an understanding that councillors cannot be officers of the party. The other strategy for building up the independence of the party is through extending its activity, especially around policy, education and campaigning. In the first three months of 1987, the District Party organised day conferences on race and socialist policies for education and organised an inquiry into the Stalker affair and the role of the police authority (since the abolition of the Metropolitan Councils this has been an ineffectual Joint Board). Again this stress on the party's campaigning and policy-making role is a conscious attempt to reverse the kind of trend familiar in the GLC, Sheffield and other left councils, whereby the left runs the council and the party sits back, a dangerous trend as councils come under increased government attack. Cath Fry again:

We tended to think once we were in power, that's it. A lot of us are recognising now that we – the party – have got a lot weaker. We've neglected the working of the constituencies and the wards.

Popular administration and control

The final, and fundamental, aspect of the new Labour Group's view of democracy is its relationship to the people of Manchester. Campaigning is one aspect, especially when there are threats from central government. But council campaigning tends to be a one-way communication: a flood of glossily produced leaflets. However in Manchester, alongside the campaigning, there is a real attempt to share power at a neighbourhood level. The Manchester Labour Party is aiming for more than administrative and physical decentralisation – something which many councils have attempted recently, especially with their housing and social service departments. The Manchester Group is aiming for political decentralisation. It is worth putting this in their own words, the words of the 1986 Manifesto:

The setting up of Neighbourhood Committees where local residents, non-statutory organisations, council workers, councillors and council trade unions can discuss together the needs of the area, the organisation of its services and develop local campaigning activities when necessary is an essential element of neighbourhood services.

Our aim is to devolve considerable decision-making powers to them. As quickly as possible we shall enable neighbourhood organisations to control the revenue budget for the area and play an effective part in capital spending allocations and overall policies set centrally by the council.

At present, this strategy is in its pilot stages. Five neighbourhood offices are being opened in 1987, and the political status of the neighbourhood committees is now being debated. There is nothing very new, or necessarily very useful, for local people about consultative neighbourhood committees. It just means more meetings. But the goal of neighbourhood committees with real political power over the council decisions which directly affect the neighbourhood is an ambitious one with far-reaching political consequences. It is, as an internal Manchester Labour Party leaflet puts it, taking seriously the second part of Clause Four – the Labour Party's commitment to social ownership – which is also a commitment to 'the best obtainable system

of popular administration and control over each industry and
service'.

'Popular control' implies more than workers' control; it implies
the power of all those people affected by the way the service is
administered. But for those at the receiving end of a service
rather than its provision, what can be the means of popular
control? The Manchester Group is proposing the neighbourhood
as the unit of 'municipal organisation', as the workplace is the
unit of union organisation.[13]

Of course there are important differences. In the first place, a
neighbourhood does not have the clear boundaries of a workplace, nor necessarily the clear focus provided by an employer/
worker relationship. So before the pilot schemes were decided
upon, the Neighbourhood Services Unit talked to large numbers
of people in different areas to discover what people identified as
their 'neighbourhood'. Another difference is that a neighbourhood committee, unlike most unions – unless they are in a co-op
and certain kinds of publicly owned enterprises – would be
wearing two hats. On the one hand they would be taking managerial decisions about how to carry out council policies and at
the same time they would be a focus for pressure, campaigning
and negotiation both in relation to the council and, in alliance
with others, in relation to national government. Furthermore,
like the Women's Committee at the GLC, they do not have any
precedent or models in British politics. And as with any new
move, numerous problems arise, especially concerning their
implications for traditional political institutions, including the
Labour Party.

In addition the Neighbourhood Forum proposals will involve
an administrative and political revolution in the way that departments work. It requires them to break down departmental
boundaries – often the boundaries of powerful empires – and
provide an integrated service. And at a local level it will require
council staff to work for community representatives on the
ground, rather than for councillors several steps removed.
Whether or not the political will can be sustained to see the
scheme through depends in part on what battles have to be
fought elsewhere, especially on the fronts of government and
national finance. But if the pilot schemes lead to neighbourhood
forums with resources and local power, they could by example

take the democratisation of local government an important step forward. This in turn, as with all the extensions of democracy described in this section, will then pose new problems for the party's ability to follow up the expectations that might result.

Liverpool

The GLC, Sheffield and Manchester have all been a thorn in the side of Thatcher's government: a constant reminder that she is not entirely in charge. The GLC, grinning provocatively across the Thames, behaved at times as if it was a government in exile, certainly an opposition in exile. There was a period when visiting foreign dignitaries would call on the government, the Queen and the GLC. Its self-confidence gave it the ability to make government and media smears bounce off, and to emerge more popular than ever. But popularity was not a sufficient protection against a government too ruthless to be deterred from its long-term aims by a local loss of popularity.

Confrontation

The council which came into most direct confrontation with the government's determination to limit the autonomy of local government was Liverpool. Liverpool has not figured in my description of cities where the left attempted to democratise the party and the council. It needs separate attention because two distinct issues are at stake: first, the courageous and popular resistance to central government and secondly, the abuse of power by a political group which put the aggrandisement of its own organisation before the needs of this resistance. These need disentangling because Militant's abuse of its power has been used to discredit the council's initial stand, by those – Conservative and Labour leaders alike – who were anyway against this stand.

Labour came into office in Liverpool in 1983 with 46 per cent of the vote, the highest share in its history, much to the amazement of London-based commentators and politicians (in fact, the whole story of Liverpool is punctuated with remarks of amazement from politicians and commentators, 'not realising quite how bad the housing problem was' – Patrick Jenkin, Conservative Minister for the Environment, or finding that the 'inheritance left by the previous Liberal–Tory administration was worse than I expected' – Jack Straw, one of Labour's front-bench Environment spokesmen).

The message of the Liverpool Labour Party's Manifesto was clear: no cuts, no job loss. Moreover it argued that this should not be paid for out of rent or rate rises; the government had already 'stolen' £270 million – in terms of grants withheld – from the city; people needed recompense. The Manifesto also included ambitious plans for house-building and refurbishment. The Liberals had allowed the municipal house-building programme to run down, so that from 1979 to 1983 no new council houses were started and a huge backlog of repairs was mounting up. The Liberals had a renewal strategy for private-sector housing but this provided no solution to the tenants awaiting rehousing from dilapidated tenements and high-rise blocks, or to the thousands on the housing waiting list unable to afford to buy a house or enter a housing co-operative.

The incoming Labour Group could do nothing, build no homes, create no jobs, improve no services, give no grants without either a massive rate rise (170 per cent to meet the Manifesto commitments; at least 60 per cent simply to preserve existing services) or a deficit budget and therefore, inevitably, a confrontation with the government. Unlike Sheffield, the GLC and Manchester, Liverpool had no reserves to finance even the maintenance of existing services, let alone the expansion that was desperately needed. The Liberals had used up what reserves existed in the late seventies and early eighties to subsidise a low rate. The pressure on the reserves had been made worse by the government's grant system. This had meant a reduction by over 20 per cent (£270 million) between 1979–80 and 1983–84 in the government contribution to the city's income. In the year 1979–80 the government contributed 62 per cent of this income. In 1983–84 it contributed only 44 per cent. The low level of government grant was also due in part to the Liberal inheritance. Their expenditure had been very low compared to that of other major city councils and it was this which was the basis of the government's grant allocation.

On the other hand Liverpool was a city in great need; not a special case but an extreme one. Unemployment in 1983, at 24 per cent, was nearly double the national average. Rents were the highest in the country and the housing waiting list was one of the longest.[14]

A popular stand

The intransigence of the District Labour Party's politics reflected people's desperate desire for something to be done. As David Sheppard, the Anglican Bishop of Liverpool, put it, they represented 'a cry of pain'. Their stand was shared by a wide range of councillors and Labour Party activists who had no sympathy for Militant: 'You've got to understand we were not all Militant, or Militant fellow-travellers,' says Tony Jennings, a member of the Liverpool District Labour Party from 1980, a councillor on Merseyside County Council until it was abolished in 1985, and now a councillor in Liverpool. They were shared by people like Tony Byrne, who cared about one thing and one thing only: to have the money to build the houses that he believed the working class of Liverpool deserved.

This was the background for the decision of the District Labour Party and the Labour Group in 1983 to draw up a budget according to the city's needs and their manifesto commitment to no rate or rent rises: that is, a budget with a £30 million deficit which they believed should be found by the government.

In March 1984 this budget was put to the vote. Liberals, Conservatives and six Labour rebels voted it down, but without being able to agree on an alternative. The government was playing for time, waiting for the rebellion to collapse. The risks of precipitate, high-profile action, such as putting in commissioners, were too high since the council workforce strongly backed the council – demonstrations in support of the council's stand brought 30–40,000 onto the streets. The government assumed that the electorate would be scared off by the 'extremism' of the council.

In fact, in May 1984, the electorate came out in force to protest at the intransigence of the government. Turnout in the May elections was 51 per cent which is high for a local government election. It was 20 per cent up on 1983. And, as in 1983, Labour got 46 per cent of the vote. It increased its precarious majority by seven seats, so that even if the six rebel councillors voted against them, they could get their proposals through council. Behind the vote was a popular readiness to take action. Support for the specific actions of the Labour Group was not overwhelming – 46 per cent of Labour voters supported the tactic of a deficit budget – but support for a strong stand against the government was. An NOP opinion poll taken during the week after the election showed 70 per cent of Labour voters in favour of the occupation of council offices if council workers were made redundant, and 55 per cent in favour of a general strike. Even 30 per cent of Liberal voters favoured an occupation and 14 per cent a general strike.[15]

This evidence, from the ballot box and from action in the streets, of popular support forced a change in the government's position. Its hopes that the electorate would be frightened off by Labour's stand had been dashed. Realising that for the time being it had lost the argument, it agreed to negotiate. It would not alter its targets, penalty system or grant allocation. These had all been fixed and approved by Parliament. But it did admit to some 'marginal flexibility' in the special urban programme. It allowed up to £3.1 million of the city's urban programme money to be used to continue support for projects which Liverpool would have to support on the rates, and made other concessions which were worth £17 million to Liverpool Council. Not an overwhelming victory – the council had demanded concessions worth £30 million – but a forced climb-down by the government, and an achievement for a determined leadership with popular support. It provided the basis for some creative accounting to allow a lower rate rise, and no cuts or redundancies consistent with manifesto commitments. Definitely something on which to build.

The seeds of defeat

However, fourteen months later, in September 1985, after the councillors had again persisted with a deficit budget and the city was facing bankruptcy, the council workers who had been committed to action in 1984 voted against a strike against the government. The decline in support showed itself again six months later, in March 1986, when only a bedraggled 400 turned out to protest against the court's ruling to surcharge and disqualify the forty-eight councillors. And the May elections too reflected the lower morale: turnout was down to 40 per cent;

Labour's share of the vote was down to 39 per cent. What had happened? Why had the council's support declined?

When the popular support for a stand against the government had been so clearly there, the answer has to focus on the kind of leadership it was given. First, how did the leadership of Liverpool Council interpret the support? Derek Hatton, the deputy leader of the council, claimed it as an expression of support for the Liverpool Labour Party. 'The people have spoken very loudly and clearly in favour of the policies of the Liverpool Labour Party.' The emphasis of council supporters outside the inner circles of the Labour Party was different: ' "It's our city that's under attack," that's how most people I talked to saw it', observed John Bohanna, a senior shop steward at Fords. 'Every Scouser loves Scouseland, they regard it as *their* city. That's what was at stake: our city, not the Labour Party, not Militant.'

The results of the NOP opinion poll back up this view. A vast majority simply believed that the government was not giving Liverpool a fair deal, and supported action to get a fair deal. The gap between the basis of popular support and the narrower way in which the local Labour leadership, in particular the supporters of Militant, interpreted it is important for two reasons.

Mobilisation without participation
First, it blinded Labour Party members to the need to consolidate alliances with groups of people who voted Labour and supported the council's stand but were not part of the Labour Party, even though they might have been trade unionists. The support for the council was not a solid mass lined up behind the Labour Party's banner. It was made up of all sorts of groups, whose support was trusting but also conditional: they were supporting the council because they thought it would support them. They had their own distinct interests: manual workers' unions, white-collar unions, tenants' groups, women's groups, black organisations, a range of voluntary and community associations, all with their own ideas of how they could work to save the city.

In different ways most of them expected to be involved, to be informed, to share in the building of a city-wide stand and to benefit from its achievements. The unions in the council, all of them, expected to be trusted and consulted as the Labour Group prepared its plans, plans that directly affected council workers. Black organisations hoped that the Labour council would take the needs of the 40,000-strong long-established black community more seriously and would give greater power and status to their organisations; tenants' groups pleased with the commitments on housing expected to be consulted, and the voluntary sector, especially the radical end of it, hoped for material support and felt themselves to be a vital part of the campaign. In other words, their support was associated with at least some expectation of involvement.

The council leadership's notion of support, however – though this was by no means always true in all the Labour Party wards – was mobilisation without participation. 'All policies are decided and supported by the Labour Party, not outside organisations,' declared Tony Byrne, the man responsible for the Labour Group's financial strategy and its housing programme. 'The best way to contribute to policy in the Labour Party is to be in it. In fact I wouldn't think there is much hope of influencing policy if you are not in it.'

This might have worked in conditions where the Labour Group had the resources they needed to run the city in accordance with their election commitments. But in conditions where they had to fight the government for these resources, the old politics of 'leave it to us, we know best' were no longer appropriate. People were being asked to take action and to make sacrifices; they assumed they would be involved at least in the decisions that directly affected them. 'We at least expected to be told the truth,' says Peter Cresswell, the NALGO secretary of the Joint Shop Stewards' Committee representing all council workers, which had worked closely with the Labour Group until late 1984, when first the white-collar unions and later, in 1985, the manual unions began to feel they could no longer trust the group leadership.

The first time Cresswell and his trade-union colleagues felt they were not getting the truth was after the government's climb-down. After the meeting with Jenkin, Hatton and others reported to the District Labour Party a 'massive victory'. 'There's no way', he claimed, 'that even Thatcher can take on the might of the working class of this city. And this is just the start . . .' Understandable jubilation perhaps, immediately after gaining something, however small, from the Thatcher government. The trouble was that this interpretation became the basis on which vital strategic decisions were made. The decisions consequently *assumed* the 'might of the working class' when a lot still had to be done to build it. For they had not won the £30 million they needed; they had won only just over half of that. The balanced low-rate budget they finally made depended on 'creative accounting' by Tony Byrne which assumed funds would be forthcoming from somewhere in the following year.

The budget was a compromise, and inevitably so. Short of a revolutionary or quasi-revolutionary situation, a local authority up against Thatcher's government, even the accident-prone Patrick Jenkin, would not get anything else. Perhaps Militant thought they were near to a revolutionary situation; certainly it benefited their organisation to create the impression that they were leading a revolutionary struggle. In fact, to admit a compromise would be damaging: how could they live up to their revolutionary pretensions when they were making – unavoidable – compromises with a Conservative minister?

Faction first

It is only looking back that trade-union and party activists feel that Militant were exaggerating the Jenkin concessions for their own factional purpose – to be seen as leading a successful struggle against Thatcher. It was the 'Sam Bond affair' later in 1984 which first alerted them to the fact that Militant was using their power for factional ends. Sam Bond is a black 26-year-old ex-building surveyor, Militant supporter, from London, with little experience of black organisations and anti-racist campaigning, who was appointed by the Labour Group to head a Race Equality Unit of seven people. His appointment was opposed by representatives of the black community who were formally on the appointments panel as part of the council's Equal Opportunities Committee. The trade-union observer on the appointments panel condemned the procedure as 'blatant political discrimination', believing it to have been 'fixed' in advance. The Liverpool Trades Council and many other trade-union, black and Labour Party organisations joined in an attempt to change the decision. They failed. But it was this experience that led many who believed strongly in the rightness of the council's stand to suspect that the

Militant leadership was allowing factional interests to determine their decisions.[16]

The final *débâcle*, in September 1985, was the half-hearted strike followed by the redundancy notices distributed by taxi. By then workers had become confused and demoralised by conflicting information, including rumours that the deficit budget on which the council was holding out could in fact be balanced with a loan arranged by Tony Byrne with a Swiss bank. Where would the strike lead? Was it really necessary? The questions were never answered. The strike petered out, the Labour leadership knowing the budget could be balanced in the end. In August Tony Byrne was working with the stockbrokers Phillips and Drew to arrange the loan. They knew it could be arranged. Their main concern was to stay in power and at the same time appear to maintain their political stand, hoping perhaps that they could once again negotiate concessions from the government. Making the workforce temporarily redundant was thought up like another accounting trick; the trouble was, it was no longer numbers that they were manipulating.

Leadership

It is a depressing story which makes it tempting to find scapegoats. Militant is the easiest, but other factors made their behaviour possible. It was a situation that required a kind of leadership that is very rare: trusting in the people who are the lifeblood of the resistance, but being able realistically and honestly to assess the strengths and weaknesses of their situation. 'Tell no lies; claim no easy victories,' said someone who in very different circumstances provided just such leadership: Amilcar Cabral, the leader of a guerrilla movement fighting Portuguese colonialism in Guinea Bisseau.[17] The one thing that makes his maxim relevant is that, like that of the Liverpool Council, the guerrilla movement in Guinea depended entirely on popular support for its success. Few of the leading actors on the Liverpool scene were equipped for such a struggle, or even thought in such terms. It was not just the factionalism of Militant.

Tony Byrne for instance, a powerful figure with a politics distinct from Militant, was always looking for *alternatives* to popular struggle, for accounting wheezes, for loans from anywhere. His motives were of the highest: he wanted to deliver the housing programme he had promised, and as long as he got the money he did not really mind how the deals were presented. And indeed one of the more cheering aspects of this story, as anyone who goes round the city will testify, is that over 5,000 families who would otherwise be homeless or stuck in high-rise blocks have and will have homes with gardens. Another 3,000 have had their homes refurbished. No other local authority has managed such a housing record under Thatcher.

However, not only did Byrne's concentration on delivery of his programme make him culpable in misleading the council's supporters, it also alienated support he might otherwise have won without jeopardising the housing programme, in particular from housing associations and community associations. Tony Jennings, at the time of writing 'caretaker' Deputy Leader of the Liverpool Labour Group, makes the point: 'It was wrong to generalise about housing associations. Some can be racist and bigoted but others have very good schemes. We should have supported those that met council criteria. The same with the voluntary sector.' The number of people in housing associations or connected with the voluntary sector is not vast but they have an influence, and publicity about the council's dogmatism towards these groups contributed to a drifting away of supoort.

The trade unions too were not all equipped for involving their members in sustained resistance. Take the GMB branch 80, of council workers. Its branch meetings were few and irregular, and the full membership was seldom informed that they were taking place. Its shop stewards were normally appointed by the existing stewards, in particular the convenor, rather than by election. And this was not the branch dominated by Militant. A member of the GMB describes how they all went to a meeting in the football stadium in mid-1984 – there had not been any branch meetings to discuss the issues: 'The G & M convenor addressed us very much in terms of "Look here, this is what you've got to do, I'm telling you" sort of thing.' That official, Peter Lennard, no member of Militant and now a leading critic, was one of those who went round in the taxi giving out the redundancy notices. The trade-union leadership was pleased with Neil Kinnock's attack at the 1985 Bournemouth Conference, on Militant's activities in Liverpool. But some of them would have reacted differently if he had given the conference the full story.

An emotional and political bind

The full story still needs to be analysed and lessons learnt – something that can only be adequately done in Liverpool. But one question which is raised by my summary of some of the issues is why doubts about Militant's tactics were not expressed more strongly and openly by the council's supporters in Liverpool. Part of the answer goes back to the basis of popular support: identity with Liverpool and its future. Militant, and Hatton in particular, had made themselves inseparable from this popular identity with the city and its struggle against the government. Derek Hatton's cocky personality came to personify the beleaguered but fighting city. To attack him or the council leadership was to attack Liverpool, to aid Thatcher; to criticise their policy was to be disloyal to Liverpool. It is this which explains for instance why the leader, John Hamilton, found himself an unwilling but powerless instrument of Militant. When Eric Heffer walked off the platform when Kinnock attacked Militant's tactics, it was not Militant he was defending, it was Liverpool. Even Militant's friends found it impossible to reduce the power and public image of Hatton once the symbolic identity had been achieved.

These emotions of local identity were powerful forces for a political faction to have on its side; more powerful than all the manipulations and intimidation – though as the identity began to slip, it was these that bolstered Militant's power. It was this which made it so difficult for any positive alternative voices within the Labour Group and District Labour Party to make themselves heard. In the end the voices came from outside, from the black organisations, some of which had a popular base of their own, an identity and loyalty to Liverpool of their own, which Militant's leadership denied and sought, unsuccessfully, to suppress.

Such independent voices should be able to speak within a socialist party, which is what the Liverpool District Labour Party claimed to be. How to create the conditions for this seems to me the issue, rather than expelling those who manipulate an inadequate structure. Expulsions, suspension and disbandment might do short-term wonders for the image of the present Leader, but I doubt if it does much to strengthen the political culture and popular base of the party, the weakness of which was, after all, the cause of Militant's strength. That would require, amongst other changes, the creation of greater opportunities for political education, freedom to form open factions, and the extension of affiliations to community and campaign groups as well as trade unions.

Newcastle

In the GLC, Sheffield and Manchester, extending democracy and defending services went together. In all three cases the Labour leaderships during the seventies were cutting services or raising rents *and* ruling the group and the party with a heavy hand. In all three cases the same councillors and party activists who were insisting on the democracy and accountability of Labour groups were also voting and campaigning against cuts and rent rises introduced by the incumbent Labour Group. Party democracy in local government, as in national government, became a matter of urgent action for large numbers of Labour members and trade-union branches, because Labour's representatives acted against Labour's constituency.

Modern paternalism

In Newcastle upon Tyne, things were and to a lesser extent still are different. Jeremy Beecham, the Labour leader since 1976 – two years after the imprisonment of T. Dan Smith – has been running as high-spending a council as Sheffield or Manchester with all the autocracy of an old-time city boss. At 43 he is of the same generation as Livingstone, Stringer and Blunkett, but he went down an entirely different political track. After Oxford he returned to Newcastle, his home town, became a wealthy solicitor and immersed himself in municipal politics. He has the pragmatism, political shrewdness and aura of smooth competence of a Wilson man without the technological hype. The politician he now most admires and gets on with is Roy Hattersley. He slipped easily into the political institutions – the political machine – which he inherited virtually intact from the T. Dan Smith era. And like Smith he uses that machine to further a distinct vision of Newcastle, a vision with which – after a few failed attempts at becoming a parliamentary candidate – he identifies his own future. Beecham's vision is of Newcastle as a capital city: capital of the northern region and the seat of regional government. People say that his ambition (which he denies) is to be Labour's kingpin on the Northern Regional Council, if it is ever brought into being; and Beecham will do his best to make sure that it is.

Throughout the late seventies and early eighties Newcastle Council was one of the country's highest-spending authorities on social services, housing and education. But with unemployment in that period never below 10 per cent, rising to around 30 per cent in the area by the river Tyne, and with an inheritance of poor-quality housing, its spending needs were among the highest too. Beecham was responsible for a very popular programme of house modernisation in working-class areas, as well as for building up the social services and the education system. He did carry out cuts but not of the sudden, massive kind which caused confrontation in Manchester. It was rather that, as the eighties wore on, 'everything became threadbare', as Councillor Nigel Todd, one of Beecham's main critics, put it.

Beecham has also been adept at diffusing opposition. For example, budgets were announced as containing massive cuts, these were translated in practice into cuts which, by comparison, seemed reasonable. The opposition was in any case weak for several reasons. First, within the group itself Beecham undermines protest, making the more able critics or potential critics chairs or vice-chairs of committees. The use of patronage is described in a book written by David Green, an academic who served as a Newcastle councillor between 1976 and 1978. He contrasts Beecham with Tom Collins, the previous leader:

The new leader's powers of patronage are used in a different way . . . Offices are distributed in the tacit expectation of support in future elections for group leader, but also with a view to getting particular jobs carried out effectively.[18]

The book goes on to quote one subcommittee chairman who was also a member of the group executive and the Policy and Resources Committee on how this patronage affected him:

I admit to a certain amount of being bought off by being made chairman of [a named] subcommittee. In return you are probably less critical of the person dispensing the patronage. It's not just that though. You need to specialise in order to get things done. Previously I was critical about many aspects of policy. Now I tend not to be critical of anything. It's the only way it can be done though.

Geographical factions

Another factor which secured Beecham's position in the early days was geographical, though this is now a source of revolt and factional struggle. His own ward is in West Newcastle, which is one of the areas most devastated by industrial closures and economic decline. In the late seventies he created several 'priority areas' for which special council subcommittees were formed with small budgets to meet local needs not covered by the main budgets.

For the first four years of the project, three out of five of these priority areas were in the west. Consequently, twelve of Beecham's neighbouring councillors owed Beecham the privilege of handing out crumbs of comfort to their constituents. But as other parts of the city have been similarly devastated by closures and collapse the 'priority areas' have taken on a life of their own. There are now fourteen of them, and where they are clustered together they have become the basis of geographical factions within the Labour Group. (The 'east-end mafia' is the most notorious, and the most hostile to Beecham. The word is out that a northern group is emerging. Will the west end fight back? Rumours abound. None of them are ideological or political in terms that would make sense beyond Newcastle.)

In fact, the absence of any explicit political tradition is another reason why the ground is stony for the left. A powerful combination of inertia and union machine politics has kept the whole party in Newcastle at a very low political temperature; sometimes so cold that it has been mistaken for dead. Take the Newcastle District Party for instance: during 1980 and 1981, a time when in Manchester and Sheffield over one hundred delegates were attending meetings, drawing up manifestos, organising campaigns, in Newcastle meeting after meeting was inquorate. Finally the quorum was lowered from forty to twenty. But district Labour parties only reflect the political life of the constituencies who send delegates to them.

Moribund parties

The Tynebridge constituency is one of them. Membership, 230; average attendance at GMCs between twenty and thirty – unless it's a selection meeting. The majority of ward meetings average between three and seven, though two, Elswick and Scotswood, are more active; their average is nearer fifteen. In November 1985 it had a by-election. This was soon after Neil Kinnock's Bournemouth speeches attacking Militant and Arthur Scargill, generally heralded as a triumph by the media and Labour's election tacticians. The next tactic was to treat the Tynebridge by-election as a popular endorsement. The party's new public relations machine was getting into top gear and was hoping to make the most of a by-election in a Labour heartland. Kinnock's campaign manager, Robin Cook, toured the constituency and realised the heartbeat was embarrassingly weak. The machine turned round and decided to wait for a more promising start. The turnout (38.1 per cent) at the by-election was the lowest in a parliamentary by-election for many years. Labour's vote was down by 40 per cent.

The membership figures for Newcastle East reveal a similar situation, though with slight variation. In five branches out of seven, three-quarters of the members are retired. The other two largest branches are significantly bigger, more representative of the economically active population. They are also dominated by the left. These figures contradict the interpretation that some commentators hostile to the left have made of the high proportion of 'unwaged' in Labour's membership figures. Ferdinand Mount, for instance, commenting in the *Sunday Telegraph* in June 1986 on the fact that 140,906 out of the 313,000 party members in 1985–86 were unwaged says this is 'the most startling illustration' of the way that

the decay of so many urban Labour parties and their easy capture by the bedsitter left has disastrously narrowed Labour's social circle . . . the Labour Party's membership must now be stupendously untypical of the nation as a whole, further estranged than ever not only from the professional and business classes but also from the skilled and supervisory workers.[19]

The figures from Newcastle East, not typical of the party as a whole but certainly typical of many older urban constituencies, indicate that, as in the case of Newham, it is only where the left does take over that the party becomes more representative of the social composition of the city. Moreover, the branches dominated by the entrenched 'unwaged', as they are in Newcastle East, are no easy prey for takeover. Would-be new members are told that the branch is 'full up'. You would need more than a bedsitter to live in to wait for these branches to 'open'.

A union built to rule

One reason why these branches feel they need not recruit is the strength of union affiliation, especially that of the General, Municipal and Boilermakers' Union, the largest union in the area. Their delegates and members dominate the Newcastle East constituency, much of which is, or rather was, a dormitory for the shipyards and the heavy engineering company, NEI - Parsons. Their MP, Nick Brown, is GMB-sponsored, as are several other Tyneside MPs. He used to work for the GMB's northern region, as political officer. The G&M has changed since the days of Andy Cunningham – the G&M boss who provided trade-union clout for the T. Dan Smith–John Poulson operation – but the machine is still there. In fact, it has been rebuilt on more efficient lines. Tom Burlinson, the energetic secretary of the northern region, is proud of the fact. He explained the background to me:

After the Cunningham affair, the union lost heart in many ways. Representation in the party dropped significantly. The Cunningham episode demoralised people. They felt inhibited. I needed to pull the machine together.

He went on to say:

I'd say we have more influence than Andy Cunningham, and it's more sustained.

The influence is used for different purposes. Mainly, it is an influence for party stability. In Gateshead, for instance: when it came to selection of the candidate for what was a safe seat there was someone on the short list who supported Militant, and they had a good chance of winning. In the end Joyce Quinn, a 'moderate' MEP, won the nomination. Burlinson comments:

We used our representation. I wouldn't say we didn't control. The system is there to be used.

He still talks with the swagger of a union born to rule, especially on Labour Party matters: 'Dave Clelland for Tynebridge,' said Tom Burlinson in answer to a question about their role in the selection of parliamentary candidates, 'when Harry Cowans died, we put him there. Joyce Quinn was another one . . .'

But their political position is not much more secure than their industrial one. Their main rival is NUPE, which in the north-east has come up from behind. Its northern region bears all the signs of a union which has had to struggle for its position. It is one of NUPE's most radical campaigning divisions. And one of the reasons for this is that it had to organise the unorganised and the difficult-to-organise, while the GMB had long ago sown up the main municipal workforces. Their political influence will soon be felt in Newcastle's Labour parties. (It has already been felt in North Tyneside, where NUPE delegates and officials played a vital role in supporting the left against a traditional leadership who in the end resigned and stood, disastrously, as independent candidates against the new radical left regime.)

Prospects for the left

Without such union support and thereby a shake-up of some of the constituencies, the left in Newcastle's Labour Group and District Labour Party does not stand much of a chance. The left within the party and with a toehold in the Labour Group came together through a Newcastle branch of the Labour Left Co-ordinating Committee, in the wake of the national constitutional reforms. The Secretary of the local LCC comments on the significance in Newcastle of these national developments:

They were very important for us. They provided significant 'bench-marks' for us in the north-east, and a feeling that we were not alone. Tony Benn's campaign was important too. Many of us did feel that there was the chance of real transformation within the party, even though we knew that we were quite marginal within the Labour Party in this part of the country. Benn's rally in Newcastle and his appearance on a regional TV programme gave us a real boost!

Their monthly newsletter tells mainly of their attempts to rebuild the District Labour Party. There are reports of the attempt to take the writing of the manifesto away from the Group Leader and party secretary and put it in the hands of an elected working group, who would prepare drafts for discussion at

party and trade-union branches and for agreement at a day-long
conference. There are plans for meetings with trade unions,
tenants' groups and other interest groups to build a campaign
against the cuts. There are proposals for a women's committee
and an ethnic minority committee which would have its own
budget and staff and representatives from women's groups. In
other words there are signs of most of the ideas of party democracy, of working with outside movements, of paying specific
attention to the needs of women and black people that have
begun to change local government in London, Manchester and
Sheffield. There is one announcement, however, which reminds
one of the difficulties such ideas face in Newcastle:

The LCC will also give active support [i.e. leg work] to those of its
supporters and members who seek to recruit members to the Labour
Party in order to revive moribund ward branches, women's sections
and so on.

The left has gained support for many of its proposals in the
District Labour Party. But this has counted for little. The group
leadership ignores the DLP when it wants to, or adapts its
proposals in ways that change little. Take the proposal for a full
women's committee: Beecham says, 'I set up the Women's
Committee and the Ethnic Minority Committee and I'm very
proud of that. I faced resistance from the more traditional
members.' There is a significant block of 'traditional members'
– historically they have been part of Beecham's power base.
But according to women on the DLP, there was not much in
Beecham's Women's Committee to resist. His proposal was a
'working group or subcommittee' without any special powers,
authority or even budget. There has been little that the two or
three left councillors could do. And until recently, the left have
not been able to do what they did in other cities, that is, gradually
replace the majority of existing councillors with representatives
prepared to be accountable to the party. The left has absolutely
no influence over the majority of 'moribund ward branches'. It
will take some major social movement to open these up.

In the meantime the left, broadly defined, has improved its
position by winning seats it does not normally win. Beecham's
position has shifted somewhat. His recommendations for council
committee chairs are more frequently challenged. He is under

some pressure from the local mafias as well as from the left. His administration is also under pressure from community groups outside the Labour Party, in particular the Newcastle Tenants' Federation, who have won several victories by drawing up their own proposals and then forcing housing officers to negotiate over development plans (though growing unemployment and poverty is eroding the confidence and unity of what used to be a strong and lively movement). While the left is hemmed in within the party, restricted to a limited base within the ward parties, it seems that these community pressures beyond the party, along with those from NUPE, will be vital to achieving a democratic revolution in Newcastle.

The challenge of democracy

Newcastle is in many ways more typical of Labour local government across the country than Manchester, Sheffield or the GLC, though as in Newcastle, the methods and ideas of the more radical councils are spreading in a variety of forms. The modern baronialism of the kind that rules in Newcastle is resistant to challenge. And where it has been competent it has a base. In local authorities with this kind of regime the challenge of the left is primarily in its demand for democracy.

The reaction to democracy

An indication of how radical a demand this is in local government, as in a different way in national government, is the response with which it is greeted by both the council establishment and the press – fed by supporters of the former. An episode in Birmingham illustrates this well. Birmingham's Labour Group, like Newcastle's, remains in a semi-baronial era. A reliable indicator of this is usually the amount of horror with which the slightest threat of democracy is greeted. Birmingham rated high on the horror scale. On November 19 the *Birmingham Post*'s main headline was 'LEFT GEARS UP FOR POWER QUEST', followed by 'MODERATES IN THE FIRING LINE AS LABOUR EXTREMISTS PLOT BIRMINGHAM TAKEOVER'. These were headlines for a report on a group of socialist councillors, most of them women and black people known as the Summerfield Group after the name of the Community Centre in which they met. They had come together to try to democratise the Labour Group. Their targets for the next twelve months included:

– Labour Group standing orders to be made available to Labour Group members and to delegates from District Party.

– Labour Group minutes and Group Officers' minutes to be made accessible to Labour Group members and delegates from District Party.

– To implement in May 1987 the party policy that the election of the Leader, Deputy Leader, Chairs of Committees and Group Officers take place at a joint meeting of party and group. (At present the Leader, Dick Knowles, appoints the chairs of committees.)

– To open up the Council House to party organisations and the wider labour movement.

Here again then, at local level as well as nationally, it is the democratic pressures of the left which are feared and portrayed as extreme, rather than policies which are distinctively socialist. But for this left, whether Tony Benn at the Department of Industry or the Summerfield Group or the Manchester Cuts Campaign in the council chamber, the threat is precisely that its socialism is contained within its democracy. Their demands for democracy include trying to establish accountability within the parliamentary structures, that is, within the Labour Group or the PLP, but these are part of an attempt to widen the idea and reality of accountability and democratic power, so that working-class people have the kind of access to public resources which have previously been the monopoly of well-connected businessmen and the elite of the professions. Thus they do stand for fundamental change. The press is not wrong to signal this, even though they grossly distort its character.

Scotland

The radical democratic challenge, which in England focused on change within the party, produced in Scotland, in 1975, a breakaway from Labour. The strength of feeling for Scottish independence and the possibilities of democratic and socialist advance free of Westminster dominated all other political issues during the seventies. This is again the case now, in the mid-eighties, though in a different form.

Breakaway

The 1975 breakaway was called the Scottish Labour Party. It was led and, ultimately to its detriment, dominated by Jim Sillars, one of the boldest and most charismatic Labour MPs to have emerged from the Labour Party in Scotland since Jimmy Maxton, the leader of the Independent Labour Party – itself in the end a British breakaway. The SLP was short-lived; it collapsed in factional chaos and bitterness in 1976. Its membership was 900 at the time, probably larger than the then active membership of the Labour Party. They came from the Labour Party, the left of the SNP, CND, independent Marxist and republican writers and journalists and Trotskyist groups, in particular the International Marxist Group. It was never tested at the national polls, though it did not do well in local elections. But it so quickly became divided that there was never a real test of the potential political base for such a project.[20]

Electoral shifts in Scotland over the late sixties and mid-seventies had been dramatic. In 1966 Labour won 55 per cent of the vote; the Tories 31 per cent and the SNP 13 per cent. By contrast, in 1974 the Tories were third with 24 per cent and the SNP came second with 30 per cent, not far behind Labour.

Although a lot of past Tory voters had clearly switched their allegiance to the SNP, the SNP was more than a band of Tartan Tories. It had a considerable left, including many of the student generation of the late sixties who had joined the SNP in revulsion from Wilson. The nationalist coalition could not last for long once the debate began in earnest about what a Scottish Assembly should actually *do*: how it would govern, with what policies. Here was one source of potential support for a socialist and nationalist party.

A further source lay in the combination of the moribund state of the Labour Party and the increasingly strong nationalist influence on militant trade unionism following the UCS work-in. In Scotland, due in particular to the strength of the Communist Party, it was in many areas the trades councils rather than the Labour Party which had historically been the focus for political campaigning. Moreover, few Scottish trades councils have had the kind of close links with the Labour Party which the Sheffield Trades Council had with the Sheffield Labour Party. Consequently, rather than influencing the party as a whole, which the

Trades Council did in Sheffield, they tended to attract away from the party the energies of some of the most active members of the Labour left. In periods of heightened political awareness such as the late sixties and early seventies there was therefore a constituency of socialists who would not join the Communist Party but were frustrated by Labour's almost obsessive orientation to Westminster. Potentially this too was the base of the SLP.

Whether the SLP could have succeeded, given the timing of its formation and the fact that the Labour Party moved fairly rapidly to support devolution – soon after the SLP was formed – is open to speculation. What is certain is that its collapse seriously weakened the nerve of those on the left who had anything to do with it, many of whom were the generational and political equivalent of the left which led the challenge to municipal Labourism in many English cities.

The Labour left

Since 1976 the left in the Labour Party, including some of those who came back from the SLP, have regrouped under the banner of the Scottish Labour Left Co-ordinating Committee. This is associated with the National LCC but has a high degree of autonomy, and has been significantly more active and campaigning. The immediate stimulus for the left to form their own organisation within the Labour Party was the need in 1978 to plan a left strategy towards the Scottish Assembly, which then seemed likely to be in existence by 1979. Mark Lazarowicz, leader of Edinburgh Council since March 1985:

People on the left came together at the time of the Assembly campaign. Many of us saw it as an opportunity for radical policies, rather on the lines of those since carried out in some local authorities – Stirling, Edinburgh – following the example of the GLC. I mean at that stage the party had – still has – a very strong right wing and we didn't want the Assembly to be a traditionalist kind of authority writ large.

Another stimulus was the advance of the SNP and the evidence that Labour would crumble unless the party was rebuilt. On both issues, the Assembly and rebuilding the party, the left had to overcome this 'very strong right wing'. Throughout the seventies the Scottish Labour Party conference, more often than not following the lead of the Scottish TUC, was passing radical resolutions on economic policy – for campaigns against unemployment and cuts – and on devolution, with which the majority on the Scottish Party Executive was completely out of sympathy. A political time-lag existed between the increasingly political character of many of the unions and the influx of a new generation of left party activists on the one hand, and on the other an executive surviving from the sixties because little effort had been put into getting them out.

It was not until a Scottish Assembly became a real possibility that the Scottish Executive was seen as a significant centre of power or potential power in the Scottish labour movement. It was little different from a regional executive in England. Its staff were, and still are, appointed in London. Its budget is decided in London. So a corollary of the left's view of the Assembly as an opportunity for radical policies was to organise for the executive to reflect the view of conference and lay the basis for a more independent party, though this latter objective is likely to become a major issue only when the Assembly is finally a reality.

Scottish region of the Labour Party

The LCC won a majority on the executive in 1984. Soon after this change in the political control of the executive, the party did something previously unheard of: it drew up a specifically Scottish manifesto. (There has always been a document referred to as a 'Scottish Manifesto', but normally it was written in London; according to Bill Spiers, recently elected Chairman of the Scottish Party: 'What would happen was that after the general manifesto had been agreed the spokesman on Scotland would get together with a researcher to "Scottishise" it, over a pot of tea or more likely a bottle of whisky.') To many people's surprise, Neil Kinnock has publicly committed himself to establishing a Scottish Assembly with devolved powers if Labour is elected. The electoral reasons for so doing are overwhelming, although in the past Kinnock has opposed devolution.

The left's success in taking control of the executive and winning control over several local authorities was as much a result of the electoral defeat by the SNP of the traditional, pro-UK right-wing councillors, as of their own initatives. The electorate gave the Labour Party a much-needed spring-clean. Throughout the seventies the SNP was winning safe Labour seats at by-elections, taking control from Labour in several new town councils and several traditional centres, helping to defeat long-established Labour councillors in Glasgow, Strathclyde, Edinburgh and Stirling, and maintaining opinion poll results of between 20 per cent and 35 per cent. One of the political spin-offs of this intense electoral competition within the working-class electorate – a competition for which the Labour Party was totally unprepared – was the clearing of the left's road to power within the Scottish party. It served the same function as a mass deselection, and more generally it weakened the authority and credibility of the leadership, both in Keir Hardie House and in Westminster.

The LCC's control over the executive did turn the party outwards. The party creaked into becoming a campaigning party. Local government was a particular focus because the government first tried out its rate-capping policy on Scotland. Plant closures were another focus, with the party executive leading strong support campaigns with workers at Lee Jeans, Plessey, British Leyland and Kinneil Colliery.

Some constituencies took to the party's change of direction more readily than others. The West Lothian party took it on wholeheartedly. So successfully did it turn itself into a campaigning party that its activities and those of local trade unions now sustain a thriving political print and graphics company. The membership of the party grew from around 200 in 1977 to 800 in 1983. 'In the old days,' says Bill Gilby, who used to be Secretary of the West Lothian constituency, 'when there was a strike or a closure, the party might invite a speaker and pass a resolution of support and maybe arrange for the stewards to meet the Secretary of State. That was all the trade unions had come to expect. But we established a campaigning approach. We printed collection sheets and went round with the stewards to get local support. We produced badges, leaflets, everything. The habit has stuck.'

Other constituencies, for example in Glasgow, were more conservative. Also, the extent to which the campaigning momentum has continued has been very uneven. Centrally, since the miners' strike and also the collapse of the campaign against rate-capping, the Scottish LCC appears to have been marking time. This is partly, no doubt, due to the uncertainty of the 1986 –87 pre-election period. It is also due to the difficulties of having

Scottish regional officers who are nationally appointed and are out of sympathy with the politics of the elected leadership.

It also comes up against the problem I mentioned earlier, that in most parts of Scotland the Labour Party has little campaigning, activist tradition. In the past, socialists would join the Communist Party for that. The kind of people who joined the SLP would have tried to establish such a tradition as they have tried in England. The LCC have tried to do just this, but with little on which to build. Moreover, since the collapse of the SLP there has been an atmosphere of caution reinforcing the pre-existing conservatism within the party. As a consequence, although the LCC achieved some major breakthroughs for the devolutionist left within the party – the majority of its founding members are either in leading positions on the party executive or on local councils, or they are prospective parliamentary candidates (Mark Lazarowicz is Leader of Edinburgh Council; Mike Connerty, Leader of Stirling; Jack McConnell, Secretary of Stirling Labour Group; George Galloway, MP for Hillhead; Maria Fyfe for Maryhill) – it has not always had the momentum as an organisation to follow up these positions.

The Scottish TUC

Insofar as any part of the labour movement is giving a lead on the national question, as distinct from reflecting the prevailing sentiment, it tends to come from the Scottish TUC, with their new General Secretary, Campbell Christie, and from several trades councils and individual unions. The LCC has also been an influence in the STUC. There is in many ways a stronger socialist republican tradition in sections of the trade unions, particularly the trades councils, than in the Labour Party itself. This is partly the historic impact of the Communist Party, but it is deeper than that and has been sustained in several periods by the independent and proudly political character of the STUC. The STUC is no mere Scottish wing of the TUC. Its origins and contemporary character are entirely different. In general its policies and its action have been far to the left of the TUC, except for the period between the 1950s and 1960s when the ice of the Cold War had a grip on the whole of the British trade-union movement, or at least its leadership.

Political trade unionism

The distinctive lifeblood of the STUC flows from its origins as a federation of trades councils and small Scottish-based unions, brought together at the turn of the century by socialists in the ILP, the SDF and other political groups.[21] It is the outcome of relations between trade unionism and political activists quite opposite to those at the core of the Labour Party. Whereas in England the TUC created a political party as far as possible in its own image, in Scotland it was the other way round: politics – the politics of radical socialists – led trade unionists to form a united national (Scottish) organisation based on local trade-union organisations, especially trades councils.

One result of this is that, on the whole, the STUC has a less corporatist, more campaigning character than the TUC. For a period, until 1920, governments refused to talk to it. It now has an involvement with most Scottish institutions including the Scottish Office, the Scottish Development Agency and so on. But as Campbell Christie, the present General Secretary, puts it:

We've never seen that as an alternative to organised militant trade unionism. It has been seen as just a vehicle for expressing a trade-union point of view and we should maintain that, but it's no substitute for organisation and campaigning.

As a national official for the SCPS, Christie saw the TUC's approach at first hand. He makes the contrast:

For the TUC, campaigning feels uncomfortable; they don't want to give leadership. Whereas campaigning groups positively look to us for a lead. The TUC would spurn that.

The Scottish trade-union movement therefore has not been through the humiliating and debilitating experience of the 'new realism': the humble petition of the TUC to be allowed back into the corridors of status. 'We just accepted,' said Campbell Christie, 'that of course we wouldn't expect to have the same relationship with Conservative ministers. We would have to turn to organisation and campaigning as a way forward.'

This the STUC did: organising one-day strikes against the public-sector cuts, conventions against unemployment, support for the health workers in their successful attempts to hold back privatisation, support for the teachers in their successful strike over pay and conditions. General surveys, usually by London-based journals and newspapers, make generalisations about the state of the trade-union movement without taking into account the specifics of Scotland – or any other particular region, for that matter.

In Scotland, unlike many other parts of Britain, unemployment and industrial decline has not been followed by a shift to the right in trade-union politics. In the AUEW, for instance, the shift in the eighties has been to the left. And surveying the Scottish trade unions as a whole, though there has been an obvious decline in the industrial membership, the public-sector unions have maintained the political tradition that was dominant in the industrial unions. As an aside: one way in which these traditions are carried on is through the large number of redundant shop stewards and convenors in engineering who have become organisers and full-time officials in public-sector unions such as NUPE. In other words, Campbell Christie and his General Council have an organised and potentially active base for their political initiatives, especially on devolution.

However, socially it is on a very different basis. It includes a growing proportion of women. This could have more political consequences than seems at first obvious. Campbell Christie's thinking is one indication:

I think the debate that women have forced onto the trade unions is having a politicising effect. It takes you beyond traditional trade-union concepts and makes you think about the structure of society. It raises issues of public services, support for families, of questioning existing differentials. It takes you down paths that trade unionism has not travelled.

He's not typical, by any means, but he indicates a thought process which is working away in what is still a very male-dominated trade-union movement.

Issues raised by women have also been a stimulus to advancing the debate on the question of the political character of the Scottish Parliament. 'We want to get away from the Westminster model,' says Jack McConnell, Secretary of the Labour Group on Stirling Council, 'and it has been issues raised by women's sections that have produced some practical ideas for new democratic structures and methods of operation. Designing these new methods must start now; otherwise we'll get an Assembly that is more like Strathclyde Council than the GLC.'

The failure of the People's Party to win sufficient support amongst the people of England means that for the time being Scotland will not get any assemby at all. Work on the left has moved from institution-building in the air to struggles growing on the ground: against the poll tax, to save Ravenscraig steel works and with it much of Scotland's traditional industrial base. For it is the strength of resistance over these issues which will determine the possibility of forcing a constitutional crisis, for instance by non-co-operation and creating a *de facto* assembly. There is no doubt that the conditions for a constitutional crisis are there: a ruling adminstration that has lost the confidence and the ability to rule and a population that no longer wants it to rule. The question is whether the leadership of Scottish labour is sufficiently different from the English to challenge the power of Westminster when the opportunity arises. Certainly the pressures will be on them to do so.[22]

Conclusions

What do these local and regional experiences reveal to us about the new soul emerging out of the collapse of Labourism? First, that its emergence is not a clean break. On many issues it involves an alternative to Labourism in its rhetoric, but only occasionally does it provide one in practice. Moreover, these innovations have usually been *ad hoc*, the initiative of individuals, the result of outside pressures rather than the result of a concerted strategy on the part of a reformed local Labour Party. For instance, the political innovations of the GLC were dependent on a minority of like-minded radical councillors with politically sympathetic staff, responding to and stimulating popular pressure. The majority of the GLC Labour Group were straight out of the Labourist mould: 'unreconstructed characters from 1946,' said Reg Race, a frequent observer to Labour Group meetings. 'The first time I attended the Group,' he says, 'I was truly appalled; they were as reactionary as any Labour Group.'

The left's successful leadership, and in some cases conversion, of this centre-right majority illustrates a feature common to the demise of Labourism: the absence on the centre-right of any confident idea of what they want to *do* with power. In many cases they desperately want to hold on to it, but at the GLC they lacked the unity even to achieve this. The left, on the other hand, had a positive vision and a determined leader. For a period this swept much before it. But the left's minority, or precarious majority, placed limits on what it could achieve. Meanwhile the appearance of strength given by its position of leadership created complacent illusions through the London labour movement of a powerful left dominating a strong party, when in fact the party and left within it were in a fragile position.[23] In Manchester the transformation of the party and the group was more thorough-going. In Sheffield it has been more gradual; its Labourism had been strengthened by other socialist traditions. In Liverpool the party's transformation was led by a political group that championed many of the values of Labourism in an extreme and dogmatic form: its faith in extending the existing state, its assumption of a homogeneous working class, its deep party chauvinism and mistrust of movements independent of the party. Militant combined these values with a strangely static kind of Marxism – Marxism pickled in Labourism. Its sectarianism meant it was incapable of uniting the diverse popular energies of Liverpool.

Bearing in mind this uneven strength and coherence of the new transformative tradition, its local experience illustrates three distinctive features. First, on the issue of the state about which Labourism, left and right, is so resolutely conservative, the new left has been confidently radical. Its challenge to the state institutions of local government comes from two directions which have influenced the character of the challenge. On the one hand, it has come from those – mainly councillors – whose recent political experience has been predominantly within the Labour Party. They focused their attention on the power of senior local-government officials. Their priority was to turn formal political power into real political control.

At the same time these left councillors believed their power base lay outside the council and consequently put much emphasis on mobilising this base in the face of external threats – mainly from the government. They at least illustrated, even if they did not always stick by, the idea that external constraints need not be the occasions for compromise, as they have repeatedly been for Labourism. They showed how so-called 'constraints' can be faced, through the creation of wider, popular sources of power. In this they were influenced by Tony Benn's experiences at the Department of Industry. Mike Ward, a leading GLC councillor, observed that:

The things Tony Benn said about the exercise of power, about the state, the Civil Service, about the need to be open about the difficulties you face, were very important to the ideas and the practice of the GLC. We couldn't have begun the process of writing and carrying out the manifesto without that body of ideas.

The second strand in the new left's challenge to the state came from those based more in community, feminist and trade-union organisations than in the Labour Party. They focused their challenge on local government's relations with working-class people. Their experience had been of campaigns against cuts, closures and privatisation in the late seventies in which they found, and shared, ambiguous feelings about these and other public services. This experience was summed up in an influential book called *In and Against the State*.[24] At one point, its authors say:

The cuts and the fight-back against them have raised questions . . . Perhaps it never was *our* welfare state? We are still certain that it is right to fight against the sale of council houses . . . to fight against turning medicine over to private practice . . . But perhaps we should not be looking to defend the state, even the 'welfare' state, as it is, but fighting for something better?

After discussions with people involved in 1978, 1979 and 1980 in trade-union and community attempts to defend different parts of the welfare state and local government, they conclude:

In each of these situations we have made positive gains not by 'winning power' in any formal sense but by taking a degree of control, counterposing our forms of organisation to theirs. From practical experiences in struggle, not just from utopian dreaming, we have concluded that we must forge our own forms of organisation.

Where real changes have come about in the institutions of local government towards stronger control by councillors and a greater sharing of resources with working people, it has been a result of these two strands of new left politics in combination. This is what occurred in many parts of the GLC, Sheffield, Manchester, Stirling and Edinburgh councils.

In general those Labour groups with the commitment to transform local government have succeeded more in their external relations with the public than in their internal relations with their senior officers and major departments. GLC leaders say they did not achieve full political control over all the council's corporate management until 1985, four years after their election. Most of their achievements were in new areas where departments were freshly created.

One reason for this difference between the external and the internal relations of the local state is that externally there were already popular energies pressing for change, making the most of every opportunity and demanding more, whereas internally the pressure was predominantly in the other direction, in defence of the *status quo*. Senior local-government officers, like civil servants, are unaccustomed to radical shifts in policy with changes in political control. Neither are they used to councillors who follow through the detail and wish to know the options and research behind officers' recommendations.

Local-government unions have tended, from a different point of view, to reinforce this conservatism. Unless the Labour leadership has somehow established a strong political bond, as they had in Manchester with the manual unions, in the course of campaigning together against the previous regime, the unions see no reason to treat the new administration any differently from previous political managements, especially when local government is under financial pressure from national government. They are understandably wary of losing their independence and with it their negotiating power.[25]

A third explanation is simply the left's relative inexperience in *managing* anything beyond small-scale projects, as distinct from *organising* campaigns and movements of opposition.[26] Its organisational experience and skills are considerable, but these are most immediately applicable to the outward-going side of local government. There are no ready-made models for running large departments in a democratic and creative way. In the past the Labour Party's representatives have left it to the 'experts', that is, to the senior officers themselves. Labourism, left and right, has treated management as politically neutral. The new left believes that there are political choices to be made in the internal management of local government, in the relations of officers with councillors and between departments, in how the delivery of services and other achievements are measured, in what information is given to whom, and in the division of labour, pay and status. They have learnt how to make these choices through trial and error.

The second issue around which some local parties are breaking from Labourism is in the left councils' idea of whom they represent. In both Manchester and London, for instance, the left have developed an acute sense of how the working class has changed and of how it is differentiated, especially by race and gender. The first expression of this recognition came in the adoption of policies to consciously achieve equal opportunities for women, black people and the disabled in the councils' employment. But movements and organisations among these groups had for years been developing and campaigning around changes far deeper than equal opportunities. On the whole, these wider collective needs had no political expression. The Labour Party had always subsumed these groups into the 'working class' in the way that we saw in Sheffield. The commitment by the GLC, Manchester and others to the needs and, most important, the self-organisation of women, ethnic minorities and the disabled opened up a flood of unrepresented demands.

Neither the council administrations nor local Labour parties coped easily. The first change they had to make was to their structures of representation. The creation of women's equal opportunity, race equality or ethnic minority committees reflected the new left's recognition that the old institutions of municipal socialism could no longer respond to the population they now represented. Many quickly found new structures did not solve the problem; rather they opened up areas of politics entirely new to the mainstream of the labour movement. Again they are learning through trial and error.

However, the Labour Party, even where it is dominated by the left, has not always proved a good forum for learning positively from mistakes. It is on this third issue of the party that the break from Labourism is least apparent. As Crossman implied in his description of 'the party militants' doing the organising work without power, for Labourism the local party meant the troops – the rank and file – for rounding up the voters. It also meant a pool of recruitment to the officer class, the councillors, and finally it meant a seal of democratic approval for policies drawn up by these officers, or at least their leadership. Within Labourism, left and right fought each other for control over this machine.

The new left, intuitively, had a different kind of party in mind. Inspired by experiences throughout the seventies of political movements outside the party, they had tried in various ways to stretch out of the factional caucuses towards a party with a socialist culture with a participatory membership, campaigning outside the electoral timetable and reaching people on the problems of their daily life. However, creating or participating in the elements of such a party through women's groups, trades councils, cuts campaigns, anti-racist movements of a broad embrace like the Anti-Nazi League was one thing.[27] And around specific issues, the new left, from inside and outside the Labour Party, has created a richer socialist politics. Turning the Labour Party in such a direction has been an entirely different matter.

In London, the left organised the caucuses and took over the machine, beating Labourism within its own rules and winning the GLC. They then, without perhaps intending it, created some of the elements of a new kind of party through the GLC *itself*. The London Labour Party, though formally under the control of the left, remained its old unreconstructed Labourist self, demanding to see the party card of those co-opted onto GLC committees, but not so much as blinking an eyelid or moving an amendment when the Labour Group made what turned out to be the disastrous mistake of employing a high-flying 'neutral' professional manager from the private sector to run London Transport.[28] The gap between a left simply winning control over a machine and the left attempting to create another kind of political agency yawned widest when the GLC was under threat. The party proved almost incapable of campaigning to defend GLC policies and ultimately the GLC itself. It was the party – but not the Labour Party – employed in County Hall which reached out to encourage and support the action of community, black, feminist and trade-union organisations throughout the city.

This created a lasting political culture, but of a diffuse character, rather than focused through the Labour Party. This has put those London Borough Labour groups who share the GLC's approach in a vulnerable position. They do not have the resources and the public platform that were available to GLC councillors. Consequently the weakness of the party leaves them suspended in mid-air, making radical gestures but without a party able to provide either an independent critical intelligence or a means of popular persuasion.

In the absence of such a party the borough councils can easily become misunderstood, isolated from their constituents, especially at a time when government cuts make it impossible for them to significantly improve their services. Or they become dictatorial and puffed up, behaving as if the weak and rootless party over which they preside is a mass movement at their command.[29]

The importance of a strong and critical party with a political life to some degree independent of the council is illustrated positively in Manchester, where there has been a conscious attempt to establish such a party. Leading activists such as Cath Fry and John Shiers, the present and past chairpeople of the party, decided not to stand as councillors specifically in order to work for this aim. One of the most vital by-products of this collective effort has been the existence in Manchester of a group of experienced people not directly subject to the day-to-day pressures of the council, but fully informed about its work and problems, and able to think ahead, to anticipate difficulties, to help formulate group and party strategy.

With the GLC this was the one party function for which no number of advertising campaigns and politically sympathetic staff could substitute. This strategic political intelligence is perhaps more than anything else an essentially party matter, depending on relations of trust and common political purpose. And it requires an input independent of the immediate political rivalries of the council chamber. The absence of this strategic intelligence had its impact with the rate-capping campaign and the *débâcle* of the GLC's role in it. The main points in the story of the rates campaign illustrates its importance.

The rate-capping campaign was a national response to the Conservative government's Rates Act in 1984. This Act set a legal limit on the rate which specified 'overspending' local authorities could raise. The Act was a powerful enabling act; it gave the government the flexibility to pick and choose according to the political and financial circumstances of different councils. If it had been implemented as rigorously as many believed it would be, the cuts in services and loss of jobs would have been devastating, especially in the district councils and London boroughs, that is the lower-tier local authorities, but also for the metropolitan councils. Throughout 1984, at the same time as the miners' strike, a strong campaign got under way involving all the rate-capped authorities, metropolitan councils such as the GLC and the lower-tier authorities.

In the boroughs and the district councils such as Sheffield, local campaigns built up a very powerful popular momentum. In these areas local government and its provision became the centre of political attention. The national unity of the campaign, however, was a condition for its success. This unity was built on the assumption that all authorities faced fundamentally similar problems. In fact, the metropolitan authorities were in a different legal situation. Their 'rate' is in fact a precept which is collected from the public through the rate-collecting authorities, i.e. district and borough councils. The precepting authorities were legally bound to set their precept by April 1. The lower-tier authorities on the other hand faced a legal constraint which was less precise and predictable. Their legal constraint was determined by the judges rather than by statute. It depended on the point at which the judges considered that the council was being 'unreasonable' in not setting a rate and therefore forgoing income and getting into debt. Their constraint was a financial one (though retrospectively the government and the courts have made it a legal one too). The GLC and other metropolitan councils would therefore be in effect in the front line. Yet the left in these authorities were, numerically, among the weakest. At the time, the momentum of the campaign, the background of the miners' strike and the assumption, based on the success of Liverpool's 1984 negotiations with Jenkin, that the government would concede, this difference did not seem to matter.

Early in 1985 the government further deepened the difference. It increased its assessment of the necessary expenditure of some of the rate-capped authorities and raised the Grant Related Expenditure Assessment (GREA) rate support grant. The effect of this on the GLC was to wipe out much of its alleged overspending and enable it to gain some rate support grant. The result was that the GLC Labour Group could then make a growth rather than a cuts budget – £30 million of growth to begin with, and building up to £240 million. Many lower-tier authorities, however, still faced the prospect of serious cuts if they did not resist rate-capping. In the interests of unity, so went the argument, the GLC would continue to campaign as if they would similarly suffer. The GLC leadership, including Ken Livingstone and John McDonnell – who took opposite sides in the final decision to set a legal precept – continued to put out publicity claiming that rate-capping would mean cuts and job losses at the GLC.

They also, for the same reasons – the unity of the national campaign – gave the Labour Group only a partial picture. Consequently the Labour Group, though they did discuss the GLC's strategy, did so without full details of the council's legal and financial position. The London Labour Party contained many leading borough councillors whose council services genuinely did depend on the success of the national campaign. The national campaign had been built on the identical action of all authorities. Consequently, discussion at the London Labour Party of any distinct approach by the GLC was taboo. In London Labour Party circles it would have been judged to be a betrayal of the national campaign to raise the possibility of the GLC using its favourable position to help the boroughs (which in the end it did, but in an acrimonious, divisive atmosphere) and to concentrate its campaign on abolition (the GLC's rate-capping campaign never really got under way; it was as if people sensed its unreality). In the end one faction in the GLC, led by John McDonnell, stuck by the national campaign and voted against setting a precept. The other faction, led by Ken Livingstone, proposed the growth budget which they had known they could propose for two months. The left throughout London then took sides. The split was given a misconstrued national significance: 'Livingstone has realigned [towards Kinnock]', said the ever-hopeful pundits. Individuals were painted as heroes (non-macho ones, of course) and villains, as in some medieval drama.

These interpretations were based narrowly on the positions leading councillors took 'on the night', that is the night when the Labour Group decided to set a legal precept. A full understanding needs to extend its focus to the rate-capping campaign as a whole and the GLC's position within it. It needs to ask how it was that a group of councillors which led or at least symbolised the creative, open socialist politics which were evident at the GLC should get themselves – both sides – into such a corner. An important part of the explanation lies in the absence of a party which not only shared the political outlook of the new left in the Labour Group, but had an independent base which provided a counterbalance to the short-term and sometimes over-personalised interests which can swamp even the most left-wing town and county halls.

To sum up: the emergence of a new transformative tradition therefore is uneven, not only geographically but even within one political authority. It has achieved breakthroughs but has not always transformed the local party through which such break-throughs can be sustained and followed up.

This applies not only to the strategic thinking needed for such follow-up, but also to the popular support which the new left can clearly gain. The examples in this chapter show that popular support *can* be won for radical policies which represent both an extension of democracy and the spread of socialist values. They provide practical illustrations of the sociological and psepholog-ical studies of Heath, Jowell *et al*, by showing that Labour can be electorally successful by winning support on the left, by conviction, rather than competing for the centre. The problem is that parties accustomed simply to the routine of identifying the Labour vote and bringing it in on election day just do not have the reflexes to articulate an active desire for change. And mere *takeover* by the left without a *transformation* cannot create them.

4 Women and Blacks: What is all the Fuss About?

A central assumption of Labourism is that the Labour Party speaks for the whole of the working class. It is an assumption shared by parliamentary and trade-union leaders on the right and Militant on the left. It has fundamental implications for the internal political culture of the party and for its relationship to popular movements and organisations.

First, historically it has established an attitude, deeply rooted in all the party's institutions, which takes working-class support for granted, built into the party's history and structure. This too is an assumption which until recently has been shared by the left and the right. The right takes for granted the loyalty of working-class people to the party leadership: 'If I go to working people in a particular ward where we have problems and say, "We need your vote to get out the loonies", they'll come,' says John Golding. 'I can go to a trade-union official and say, "We need so many delegates", and I'll get them.' With this goes a contempt for political argument and debate. 'Debate?' scoffed Golding, when I asked him whether the pressure to get more delegates might not rebound on him and provoke debate in trade-union branches about how these delegates should represent the branch, 'you must be joking.'

In Liverpool, we saw a similar assumption of loyalty, though from an opposite standpoint: an assumption that once in control of the party's structures, 'the might of the working class' was behind you. Militant represents an extreme version of a view that used to hold considerable sway on the Labour left: that winning control of the Labour Party would of itself mean gaining the leadership of the working class. This tempting but debilitating illusion springs easily, if mechanistically, from the trade-union–party link to the idea that the party is the class, or as near as makes no difference. This was the attraction of the early Labour Representation Committee for small socialist parties at the beginning of the century. This has always, unconsciously perhaps, been the attraction of the party for middle-class social-ists. There is little of the uphill work of convincing people to join and build a party. It is a matter of joining a party with a ready-made appearance of solidity sustained by the trade unions, and then, one way or another, getting to lead it.

One consequence of this is the weakness and sometimes total absence of any of the activities associated with political per-suasion: political education, political organising in everyday insti-tutions – the workplace, community associations, youth clubs and so on – sustained campaigns and a political culture reaching beyond the party faithful.[1]

Many individuals from the new left, the left that both initiated and were attracted to the party by the reform movement in the late seventies, began to change this. They got their constituencies to appoint active political education officers; they started to hold regular public meetings, to organise stalls and campaigns. They began to go canvassing in between elections in order to win members and discuss the party's activities. They learnt from the tactics of mass movements like CND, the women's movement and black community politics. This persuasive, outward-going kind of politics is particularly clear in the behaviour of the new breed of MP and parliamentary candidate: Jeremy Corbyn in Islington, Bob Clay in Sunderland, Peter Hain in Putney, Kate Hoey in Dulwich, Jean McCrindle in High Peak, Dawn Prima-rolo in Bristol and Bernie Grant in Haringey, to mention a few. They all see their role as persuading and reaching people alienated from the Labour Party and politics generally, and giving support to local campaigns rather than just expecting support for the party and themselves.

The two groups in the party who most fundamentally challenge Labourism's complacent conservatism and the institutions which go with it are women's sections and black sections (though they too can produce arrogant and presumptuous leaders). With only 34 per cent of working women, and with a negligible number of black trade-union officers in spite of a high rate of black membership, the assumption that the labour movement repre-sents the working class has none of the natural quality it has to many of the party's white male stalwarts. Women do make up around 40 per cent of the membership of constituency parties, but until recently women officers of the party were exceptions.

In the seventies and early eighties many socialist women and black people joined the party because they thought it was changing. Sarah Perrigo, a socialist feminist active in the Labour Party women's section, writing in *Feminist Review* in 1986, summed up the shifts in the party which led probably the majority of women who had made up the 'socialist–feminist current' in the women's liberation movement of the late sixties and early seventies to join:

The campaign for Labour Party democracy was pressing for changes in the constitution . . . Heavy electoral defeats at the same time were leading to a renewed debate around the need to question some of the assumptions of existing statist and bureaucratic socialist models. Decentralisation and the extension of local government democracy were seen as ways of both resisting Thatcher and of building real community support for a socialist programme in the future.

All of this appeared to offer more favourable ground for socialist–feminism to develop than had been the case in the past.[2]

Younger women too, who had not been part of the original socialist–feminist movement, joined in the early eighties because the party seemed the kind of party through which they could do something. Ellen McLaughlan, now a member of the Maryhill Constituency women's section in Glasgow, joined in 1983 when she was 24 years old. Her parents are working class and, when they vote, they vote Labour, but she had not bothered to make any direct contact with the party until then:

My image of the Labour Party was that MPs and important people had all the power, so there was not much point in people like me getting involved. Then with all the changes and the campaign for democracy, I thought ordinary members would be able to influence the party and how policies were made.

Black people were also attracted in larger numbers than ever before by the changes in the party. Hassan Ahmed, now Chair of the black section in Nottingham, had been a trade-union leader in Pakistan and, like many black members of the Labour Party, had had considerable experience and a family tradition of labour movement activity. He joined in 1980 because, as he puts it, he was 'moved' by the campaigns to democratise the party: 'there seemed a chance to have an influence.'

These new recruits were not under the illusion that there was a structure simply to slot into, or to take over. In general they joined because they believed that the old structure was breaking up and that they could reshape it to fight for a kind of socialism which would mean liberation from the oppressions of race and gender as well as class.

In this chapter I intend to describe the efforts of women's sections and black sections to achieve this reshaping of the party, and to identify the difficulties which they encountered. I will start with the experiences of women and the politics they brought with them when they joined.

Women's sections: feminism and democracy

Socialist feminists of the old school, and many younger women influenced by feminism, brought a politics and an approach to organising which amounted in practice to a distinct view of democracy. Feminism encouraged a participatory democracy which at times fitted ill with some of the inflexible structures which had grown up around the representative democracy of the constituency parties. The way that feminists dismantle traditional forms of leadership and hierarchy also aroused the antagonism of some of the older women involved in women's sections. At the 1986 Women's Conference I spoke to some older working-class women from the Gateshead women's section who felt that 'their' conference – the annual National Women's Conference – had been taken over by 'outsiders', that is young educated feminists. The symbol of this 'takeover' was the decision to put an end to the tradition of a rally with the party Leader on the Saturday of the conference. 'That was the high point for me,' said one of the Gateshead women. Now, much to their dismay, the Leader is not even invited, and at the 1986 Conference, Larry Whitty, the General Secretary, was lucky to get five minutes.

The modern women's movement developed its democracy *ad hoc*, to suit its needs and to find a political voice. It drew on the ideas of other movements: the direct action of the black civil rights movement, the anti-authoritarianism of the student movement. But its forms of participatory democracy have not been theorised;[3] neither have there been sustained, documented debates about its strengths and weaknesses.[4]

As with many libertarian movements there has always been a tendency to start afresh in each new situation without a collective historical memory of what lessons had been learnt in the past. Consequently, feminists joining the Labour Party or women becoming feminists through their experiences in the party did not have a model they could point to and hold up, to contest the established procedures and to sustain their distinctive ways of organising. What they brought with them were various habitual practices and 'commonsense' (from their point of view) assumptions – assumptions and practices which came from exploring and testing out the kind of democracy that is necessary for women to have not just equal rights, but equal power. In the case of the Labour Party, equal power meant sharing in the leadership of the party, but without co-option; that is, on the basis of women's autonomous organisation.

When you look at the values and ideas of feminism's participatory democracy it is obvious that there will be tensions, to say the least, between the women's sections influenced by feminism and the more traditional forms of representative democracy in the Labour movement, especially its more rigid interpretations. First, the democracy of the women's movement places a high value on the social and economic organisations, formal and informal, created by women to press their needs directly without parliamentary or council mediation. This follows from the starting point of much modern feminism that the liberation of women is not a matter of political equality alone. Unless women also have economic independence, and control over their own bodies and sexuality, unless child care and other domestic work is reorganised, then women will still, whatever their formal rights, be subordinate. This approach frequently leads the new women's sections to work with groups of women involved in social, community and economic issues which the rest of the party, left and right, does not consider 'political'.[5]

Then there is strong scepticism towards Parliament. This comes from the experience of the last fifteen years, in which parliamentary leaders have promised much but delivered little (sometimes worse than little), and when they have delivered something they have failed to give it the power to make it work.

Denis Healey's cutbacks on child benefits in the seventies, and the ease with which employers evaded the equal pay and anti-discrimination legislation, all deepened women's doubts about leaving the needs of women to the Parliamentary Labour Party. From such disillusion came a stress on taking action yourself with others in a common predicament, not waiting or pleading for someone else to act on your behalf. Getting organised and confident, defining together your needs and demands and only then, from a position of strength and independence, making allies, calling on Parliament or the council; that was the women's movement's distinctive approach to politics.

The idea of combining self-organisation with a struggle for power within the established institutions of the Labour Party rolls easily off my pen, but from all that feminists in the party say, it is a fraught process. They feel torn between the visible impact and sense of collective strength that comes from direct action – joining a demonstration at Greenham Common, protesting to keep open a local school – and the often humiliating, long-drawn-out process of lobbying for support for resolutions, constitutional reforms and positions of power in the party.

They also are wary of the way in which arguments in the Labour Party quickly polarise, and political ideas which need exploration freeze into rigid positions. The unavoidable pressure of the constant battle between left and right means that to be tentative is seen as playing into the hands of the enemy. 'It's very difficult in the Labour Party to say, "I don't know",' sighed Sarah Perrigo. It is not that these women wish to abstain from political conflict: it was recognition of the need to engage in it that led them to join the party in the first place. But they do not want the internal conflict to dominate and determine political thought and action. Women's sections often provide some relief from this pressure, and some opportunity to explore problems rather than take positions. As I have remarked in earlier chapters, the left generally has not established the independence for this, to its cost.

Some women have taken to these internal struggles. Melissa Benn describes its attraction and points to a danger:

There is nothing more exciting than learning the rules of a previously

mystifying game and then to play it better than the people who taught
you how. But in playing that game – in getting 'your' person elected
Chair of the GMC – it is easy to forget what feminists are doing in the
party in the first place.[6]

Other women remain uneasy, and as a result find their proposals
defeated. Sarah Perrigo describes how, in Leeds,

many of us felt distinctly uneasy at engaging in the sort of 'politicking'
that appears necessary if we are to be successful in Labour Party politics.
We tend to resist organising 'behind the scenes' or indulging in 'fixing'
things in the bar.
  At the same time we are constantly surprised when we are outman-
oeuvred by others who are clearly prepared to be utterly ruthless in
pursuit of their aims.[7]

The tension remains unresolved. But a new kind of 'politicking' is growing up, based on spreading information rather
than holding on to it, and on making personal contact with the
members of a resistant union rather than trying to 'fix' things
with the leadership. 'It means a lot more consultation and involvement, it takes more time, but in the end it pays off because
we bring women with us, for instance trade-union women,'
observed Jill Page, a delegate from Leeds to the party's National
Labour Women Committee, adding that 'with the old-style fixing
we'd just get cut off by the "femocrats" who are always off to
London'.
  Many women joined the Labour Party in the early eighties in
reaction to Thatcher and the attacks from the right. They found
it easy to do so because they had gained sufficient confidence
through earlier independent women's liberation groups to feel
they could remain, somehow, a distinct political force. 'Many of
us had gained enormous experience and confidence through our
involvement in feminist politics,' said Sarah Perrigo, 'and felt
more able to enter (or in some cases re-enter) the more formal
arena of Labour Party politics and make our voices heard.' In
this way they joined the Labour Party with an already deeply
held political view: one which naturally led them to look outward
and to think, how best can the party support the initiatives
women are already taking? Their attitudes clash with the deferential representative process where matters pass upwards: CLP
resolutions, for instance, have in the past tended, almost exclus-

ively, to call on a higher authority to take action – if only to call on an even higher body. This has begun to change, but such resolutions are still the main subject-matter of the majority of constituency parties.

Outside the party, out of bounds

The emphasis of many women's sections brings them into conflict with that of the constituency party. Most women's sections see one of their purposes as being to work with women outside the party. An episode in the recent history of the Maryhill Women's Section and Constituency Party illustrates a contrast in approaches which is not exceptional.

Judith Parsons from Maryhill Constituency, Glasgow, described how their women's section

has a short business meeting and then an open discussion which women outside the party attend. We often invite outside speakers. And many of our members are involved in campaigns and movements that aren't run by the party, Anti-Apartheid, CND and so on.

On September 20, 1986, the evening's speakers came from the Maryhill Women and Girls' Action Group. This is a group of unemployed women based at the local Unemployed Centre. Ever since a highly successful 'Women's Week' in 1985, they have been running the centre for a day each week for women only. But they wanted more facilities and in particular they wanted a mobile crèche. Their idea was that crèche workers would take play equipment and set up a crèche on demand, at adult-education classes for instance, or health centres or community centres.

The Women's Action Group carried out a detailed survey to assess the local need and to work out how many crèche workers would be necessary. Then they calculated the costs with help from two local community workers.

The Action Group turned all this into a proposal to the regional council for a grant, but their local councillors did not seem to understand what was needed. 'Don't hassle us', was the impression they gave to the Women's Group. They allowed the proposal to go through with amendments which had not been discussed with the women: 'the changes completely undermined our chances of success,' commented Ann Ayre, a member of the Women's Action Group.

Labour Party women had got to know some of the Action Group through street collections and leafleting during the miners' strike. At the women's section meeting, representatives of the unemployed women explained the difficulties which the group faced at the regional council. After hearing these, the Labour women lobbied councillors and joined the Action Group on a demonstration outside the council chamber. Then they won support, on an uninterested nod, to invite members of the group to speak to a CLP meeting. This they did, on October 27, 1986. But the party did not give them the same welcome that the women's section gave. Ellen McLaughlan tells the story, with shame:

The party did not treat them nicely at all. The chairman was abusive. He didn't ask them to come to the platform, but made them speak from the back of the meeting. He didn't introduce them. He quibbled about how much time they should have. 'Well since you're here I suppose we must let you speak,' he said. In the end, we had to get up and welcome them. It was awful.

The two unemployed women who witnessed this had been on the point of joining the party; it had seemed the logical step to take when they realised that their group would soon get stuck without wider political support. They are not so sure now, though they keep in touch with the women's section. In fact, they organise joint socials and they hope to set up a women's centre together.

Ann Ayre describes the impact the experience had on her. There were several other women on whom it had a similar effect:

I come from a staunch Labour family and have always voted Labour. I've often thought of joining, and I'd still like to join the women's section. They really supported us and I always feel at ease at their meetings. But I couldn't join the party as a whole. I feel disillusioned about them. I would have thought they would have been keen to involve new people. But when I went to speak at their meeting they made me feel like an intruder. It was like a secret society.

It turned out that the local councillors had not represented the group's case to the committee accurately. In the end the committee chair had to apologise publicly to the women, and agree to their grant. The reaction to all this by the CLP was, according to Ellen,

that we should have done it all quietly. 'You are party members,' we were told, 'your first loyalty is to the party and you have brought it into disrepute.'

They were protecting the councillors, you know. They were more concerned with the image of their councillors than with helping people in the area.

And Maryhill is by no means a right-wing constituency. It passes left-wing resolutions. It has selected a woman for its prospective candidate (now its MP) and has always supported the proposals for the greater accountability of the MP. It is just that this concern for democracy tends to remain very much a party affair.

Women, local parties and the miners' strike

The response of women's sections and, by contrast, of some of their CLPs, to the 1984 miners' strike also illustrates the divergence of the two views of democracy. At Maryhill, soon after the strike began, the women's section made contact with miners' wives at Polkemmit pit. They then worked to establish a support group: 'All the women just devoted that year to organising support for the strike. We did a lot of campaigning on the streets which the party had not done before', observed Judith MacDonald.

The support group began as a Labour Party group but soon other people wanted to join it. The CLP were not too pleased. Even though the membership was 75 per cent Labour Party they argued with the women's section that 'it might get taken over by an outside group'. The strike was into its ninth month and the support group into its sixth before the CLP formally endorsed the idea of allowing other groups to participate.

In the Easington Constituency, County Durham, it was also women who took the initiative, dragging only one or two of the branches behind them. The details of the story are different – Easington is a mining town and the party is dominated by miners or retired miners – but it tells another version of the same tale: a party worried more about its rules than about the needs of the people it seeks to represent. Heather Woods, an active and well-known party member in the area, started to organise an

Easington support group, initially under the banner of SEAM – Save Easington Mines. It was natural for her to try to involve the local Labour Party branches:

I wrote to Horden branch, but they weren't interested. From my own branch I just got a lot of stick. I was so busy with the strike I didn't have time for branch meetings – they carried on having branch meetings going through the normal agenda as if the strike wasn't going on at all. I got into trouble.

Why was this, given that so many of them were miners?

What they were worried about was stepping on toes. They were worried of doing things the union would not approve of.

Heather understood the fear, but knew such procedural niceties were by then beside the point:

What they couldn't see was that all we should do is go to union and say 'Look, what we've got to offer is this. This is what we want to do; we want to carry on as long as is necessary. Do you want us to do it or don't you?'

The local NUM certainly wanted what the Easington support group had to offer: collections, food, soup kitchens, publicity. And a close relationship grew up between the women and the NUM:

All along the way we consulted the union. They consulted us. Nobody ruled anyone.

The Easington Village Labour Party has not been the same since. A group of women from the support group joined Heather in the party and by the end of the strike women had been elected to all the key posts in the branch (in other branches where there were no women like Heather providing a focus, the situation remained unchanged). There was one wider repercussion however, which sheds an interesting light on the potential of the changes where they occur. Soon after the strike Heather stood for the county council in a seat which on a very low turnout had fallen to Labour a few years before. She won, turning a Liberal majority of nineteen into a Labour majority of 2,000. The turnout was up by 15 per cent. 'For once people had seen Labour people in between elections,' said Joan Whitty, another member of the Easington support group and a recent recruit to the party:

We'd been round the houses collecting and distributing food. We'd organised Christmas parties for the kiddies. We'd given out leaflets and held meetings. People who'd abstained last time were determined to vote. And people had only voted Liberal last time because they'd got fed up with being taken for granted. The strike raised people's awareness and we went out there.

So participatory democracy can win elections too!

Socialist values in practice
Another aspect of the women's movement's participatory demo-cracy was an emphasis on creating democratic relationships, personal and political, here and now, in the organisations for which we were in some way responsible. This concern was partly a matter of necessity: the women's movement would never have gained the momentum it did, if in its own ways of organising it did not provide some immediate relief and support for women. The importance this is given comes also from women's experience in male-dominated movements – the student movements, the Labour movement, the early peace movement – whose professed aims are emancipation.

Modern feminism grew partly out of the confusing and frus-trating experience of perpetual contradiction in these movements between their aims and the way in which the men treated women, and indeed each other, in the daily life of these movements – certainly not in a way which gave one the feeling of being part of an emancipating process! The unselfconsciousness about what was going on in meetings; the way some people were silenced while others enjoyed noisy dominance, the way newcomers were left in loneliness while old hands indulged in the cosiness of a clique, was (and often still is) truly off-putting. As was the lack of awareness of the often involuntary absentees, the 'class-struggle widows' at home looking after the kids. Women joining the Labour Party in the late seventies and eighties had in many cases to face this all over again – having faced it in student organisations, in the trade unions, in their jobs. (It is an indi-cation of how severely isolated the Labour Party was from the radical politics of the sixties and seventies that an explicitly feminist organisation – the Women's Action Committee – was not formed until 1981.) And frequently they faced it from their very first encounter.

These were the comments of Sue Petney and Doreen Humber, miners' wives from Blidworth, near Nottingham, after their first Labour Party meeting: 'We were obviously a nuisance, to them. We felt it was geared against people. It was a little clique.'

The Blidworth branch is a very traditional, stable working-class branch, not used to new members. The Maryhill branch in Glasgow is made up mainly of professional people, many of whom have joined over the last ten years, but Ellen McLaughlan did not find it any more welcoming:

I must have been very naïve. I thought people would say 'great, you've joined, now what do you want to do?' That's what they did when I joined the SWP as a student. But no one talked to me. Nobody explained things. I couldn't see any way of getting involved in the party. It was like attending a monthly debate, just to observe. I couldn't see how to participate.

Consequently, Ellen helped to set up a women's section. Here the atmosphere is different:

We make sure new women are welcomed and encouraged. We explain the structures, the ECs, the DECs, the SECs, NECs . . . how you can get things before them, how you can get on to them. We get individual women to talk on what they know about. That way we all learn. I really *enjoy* women's sections. The other meetings are duty.

It is because of this kind of experience that many women now join the Labour Party through the women's sections who would not otherwise join the Labour Party.

Political culture
The new wave of women's sections sustains educational and cultural activity far more effectively than most CLPs or branches: reading groups, day events for local women, regular socials often with other organisations, regular open educational meetings are typical. Time and time again, in Coventry, Newcastle, Bradford, Bristol, Birmingham, Nottingham, women told me either when I interviewed them or participated in their meetings that the women's sections 'have the best political discussions in the party', as Val Manchee from Newcastle put it. 'Some men are getting jealous and want to come along,' she adds, 'they feel they are missing out on something.' It is no wonder that in some areas

there are many women who attend only meetings and activities organised by the women's section. There are constituencies, however, where feminist women are less enthusiastic about their women's sections. Women report, from experience, that some of the London ones are as bogged down in 'resolutionary' politics as some of the worst CLPs.

Women's sections are not a ghetto. From their independent base they have had an influence on many branches and constituencies. Child care is perhaps the most material achievement. In Val Manchee's branch, the Heaton branch of the Newcastle East Constituency, they have changed the time of meetings to suit parents and provide two hours' paid child care. The Maryhill Constituency now has a budget to pay for members' babysitting arrangements. They have also influenced the branch's attitudes to how they treat new members and how they treat each other. In one branch in Bradford, for instance, they have a social at the end of every other meeting specially for the new members to meet people.

Bradford, city-wide, is a good example of a Labour party wavering between the traditional and the feminist. The two traditions were in evidence at a pre-Christmas public meeting and social in 1986. The 160-strong audience was seated formally in rows facing a platform at least 15 feet high, in the Prince's Suite of the rather grand Alhambra Theatre. At least half of the audience were women. And at least half were under forty. Almost all of them white.

On the platform, towering over the audience, was a row of eight dark-suited men: the six local MPs and prospective candidates for the area plus the Asian chairman Mursha Singh and Tony Benn. Only Pat Wall and Tony Benn showed any self-consciousness at this situation, with Benn pointing to the eight of them and saying 'we must rebuild our movement so that women have a voice'. Several of the men would preface their speeches with remarks like 'this speech will reach the *Guinness Book of Records* for brevity', only to continue for another twenty minutes. The chairman kept mentioning the intention to end the speeches by 8.30 – ten minutes each.

At 9.30, the speeches over, the chair called for questions. A desultory few. Then the secretary of the party was given the microphone to present a huge bouquet to 'Edna May for all the work she has done to organise this meeting and the social which is to follow'. Edna May accepted the bouquet with embarrassed grace and encouraged everyone to tuck in. A good time was had by all.

But there were some mutterings at side tables by women like Sarah Hodgson, a woman who was part of the women's liberation movement in the seventies and would describe herself as a socialist feminist. She is now the women's officer for Bradford West Constituency.

It's a bit like I imagined political meetings in the fifties, isn't it? But having been round some of the wards at my insistence as women's officer, it does reflect the party on the ground.

I went to one which was all white middle-aged men plus a woman fund-raiser who was entirely silent. They seemed to have no idea about what women had done in the past in Bradford. It was women in the Independent Labour Party who had won school meals in Bradford schools, for instance. The women were politically very active in the party then, they were a real thorn in the council's flesh.

Democratising the style of meetings, welcoming new members, insisting on collective responsibility for child care, all seem rather mundane matters without tremendous political importance for a parliamentary party. But glimpses of alternatives in accord with the values that you are fighting for come partly out of these everyday concerns. And, potentially, these enrich the policies and vision for which the party is seeking popular support.

This emphasis on prefiguring in the movement the practices and relationships of a socialist society, 'starting as we mean to go on', as Raymond Williams puts it,[8] goes against the grain of a party that has sought to prove itself sufficiently respectable to be accepted into the club of the British elite. Somehow the contrast between those dark-suited MPs towering over their audience, and on the other hand Sarah Hodgson's stories of ILP women in Bradford in the thirties, symbolised what Labour's uncritical acceptance of that Westminster-style 'democracy' has done to the potential vitality of the labour movement, outside as well as inside the trade unions.

The upward-drawing process of parliamentary 'representation' has sucked dry so much of the activity and self-organisation of women and men at the base. Without implying a golden age, the evidence is there of an erosion of cultural and educational activity and social campaigning in favour of parliamentary acceptance.

Annie Davison, a Glasgow socialist, described the importance of socialist activity other than voting, for her generation, in the thirties:

There was also for many years a Socialist Music and Drama Festival in Glasgow, and many young people learned a lot about music and drama in those annual competitions. These children are now mostly the back-bone of our Scottish institutions, like in the trade unions, acting, orchestras, writing, poets, CND, Women's Lib, etc. It was very well organised in Glasgow and all of the socialists – the Labour voters as you call them nowadays – they were really early socialists who wanted a change of society and their children to learn that socialism was a way of life and what was good for one was good for all, and so this was the moral attitude they had . . . they didn't just want to vote Labour.[9]

The process by which, in the course of thirty-odd years, it became a matter of 'just voting Labour' – she was talking in 1967 – is complicated and obviously not only a process affecting women's activity. No one has explored such a process fully. It would require a rare historian to focus on both national political developments and the detail of political activity in the localities and then follow the relationship between the two. The fate of women's campaigning and political activities can illustrate them both. But two periods seem especially important. A brief descrip-tion of them will help us to understand the position of women in the party today.

Women and the party's power structure

The first period was in 1918, with the writing of the Labour Party's new constitution. The Women's Labour League, a separ-ate but affiliated organisation of Labour women, merged into the party and its groups became the early women's sections. The Labour League's paper *Labour Woman* was taken over by the party and, with the exception of the letters page, became very much a party paper, reflecting none of the debates and activities going on among women in the twenties and thirties. The women's sections had no formal power within the party's decision-making. For a time they were merely temporary expedients, in effect a sop for closing down the WLL (about which many delegates were extremely angry). Jill Liddington, in her book about Selina Cooper, a leading socialist suffragette in Nelson and Colne, describes how 'party officials remained terrified lest women in their sections acquired too much power and took off in a separate direction from the rest of the party.'[10]

Rather than 'take off in a separate direction', women pressed for more power within the party. Instead they received just further advisory bodies: an annual Women's Conference and the Women's Advisory Committee. They were also given a reserved seat on the NEC – later expanded to five – but this was to be elected by the conference as a whole, and therefore determined by the trade-union block vote rather than by the constituencies or the women's sections themselves. As Caroline Rowan, a historian of women in the early years of the Labour Party, points out, this had more to do with the leadership's concern to weaken the position of the left than with promoting the interests and organisation of women – an insight applicable to the present-day arguments about the position of the women's organisations in the party:

Henderson's intention [Arthur Henderson, leader of the party, with intervals, from 1906 to 1932] had been to weaken the left of the party, particularly the ILP, who had always supported women's rights, and to strengthen the unions by the introduction of the block vote at conference. The method of election of women to higher bodies was consistent with this trend, shifting the balance of power away from the constituencies and towards the unions at a time of high female unemployment and when women's position in the unions was weak.[11]

Then came the party leadership's long struggle for respectability.

One of the first of the women's section activities to fall foul of this was the campaign for public provision of birth-control advice. Many women's sections were actively involved in organising birth-control advice at municipal welfare centres. Women like Dora Russell, Selina Cooper and Stella Browne tried to make this national party policy. First they sought to put it to the Women's Conference. The attitude of the leadership is indicated by the attempt by the Labour Party women's organiser to get Dora Russell to withdraw the resolution. When she refused, the women's organiser, Marion Philips, told her: 'Sex should not be dragged into politics; you will split the party from top to bottom.' Nevertheless the motion was won by 1,000 votes to eight. But Marion Philips's view finally prevailed. For the party nationally believed that birth control was an electoral liability, and refused to back up the women's sections' support for the birth-control campaign and the clinics which were slowly being established in different parts of the country.

In the thirties, many women's sections became involved in support for the Spanish Civil War and the Popular Front against Fascism. They risked expulsion from the party through this work as it involved working with Communists. Some of them were expelled – like Selina Cooper, the 80-year-old founder of the Nelson and Colne Labour Party – others kept a low profile or drifted off into the broad-front activities of the Communist Party. The third phase in the erosion of the political life of the women's sections was in the fifties, at the height of the Cold War, and again was the result of distrust of any kind of independent activity, especially if it involved working with non-Labour Party organisations (and therefore suspected communists' organisations).[12]

Women's sections in political decline

Under the pressure of this mistrust and disapproval, women's sections became increasingly apolitical. Occasionally an energetic and stroppy woman would ginger up a local section; like Evelyn Gorham, a miner's daughter in Doncaster. She joined the party in 1970: 'My husband had died, so there was more time to get involved.' She joined the women's section: 'I thought women were getting a raw deal. Men got all the top jobs.' She found the women's section inactive. 'The older women [Evelyn was in her early fifties!] weren't very lively; they didn't push their case.' So she and a friend worked to build up the section and get women a voice in the party and on the council. But apart from rather individual exceptions like this, women's sections were either dead or simply the tea-makers and bazaar and jumble-sale organisers (no mean task!).

Women's sections in revival

It is not surprising, then, that when the feminists joining the party in the late seventies tried to set up political women's sections they were often met with ribald laughter, downright refusal, or subtle subterfuge. 'What do you want to do that for? To discuss Lenin's views on lingerie?' was the retort of the

Secretary of the Newcastle East Constituency, no doubt thinking he was being very witty. In Glasgow two women's sections wanted to create a women's council to co-ordinate the work of all the women's sections in the city. The Scottish Regional Women's Officer – a man in his 40s who doubles up as youth officer – said that they could not have the names of other women's section secretaries. They then asked him to announce in the regular regional mail-out to all Labour parties that there would be a meeting, on a specified date, of all Glasgow women's sections to explore the idea of a women's council (something which now exists in most major towns and cities). The details went out. But on the day before the meeting the Secretary of the District Party got a phone call from Gerald Petty, the Women's Officer, to cancel the meeting. 'It is unconstitutional,' he said. But the women could find no rule against women's councils, or meetings to discuss them.

Sarah Perrigo describes a more general aspect of the problem:

The Labour Party is extremely bureaucratic and its network of communication generally leaves a lot to be desired. In relation to women's affairs it is appalling. National decisions, drafts, and policy proposals and information on conferences fail to reach us or arrive too late to be of use. Recently Leeds Women's Council was asked to discuss and comment on the proposal for a Ministry of Women's Rights without receiving a single copy of the draft proposal.

There is a regional officer, one of whose responsibilities is servicing the women's section of the party, but either because of pressure of work or the low priority given to women's affairs relevant information is not circulated; conferences, day schools and so on are not advertised properly or the information is sent to constituency officers who fail to publicise it.[13]

In the face of these bureaucratic obstacles as well as a thinly disguised misogyny, Labour Party women decided they had to gain a stronger position in the power structure of the party. As Judy Sadler, Secretary of the Labour Women's Action Committee, put it:

We have learnt that many men will not willingly give up their power – no matter what the justice of the case for women's equality. We are now demanding a position of strength in the labour movement and will organise together to obtain that position.[14]

Judging by the overwhelming support for WAC proposals at the Annual Women's Conferences over the last four years, Judy Sadler was speaking for the majority of those Labour Party women who play a part in women's sections. There are many, especially older women, who are not involved in women's sections. It would be wrong to equate women's sections with women in the Labour Party. Some activists are against them, as second best: a NUPE shop steward in Newcastle who had applied to join the party told me very strongly, almost contemptuously, that she would not have anything to do with a women's section. Others do not join because the local section is run by feminists and they do not share a feminist view of the role of women's sections.

Since 1981, WAC has been the national focus of this struggle for power. Only a minority of women in women's sections identified with WAC organisationally, and there has been resentment at its London focus, but its demands and its original spirit expressed the views of women far beyond its rather London-dominated active membership. It has come to symbolise the recent struggles of women in the Labour Party but does not embrace the majority of women involved in these struggles. Its demands have been adopted by the National Women's Conference since 1986 and are now being pursued through the party's constitutional maze, under the leadership of the National Labour Women's Committee.

WAC came directly out of the Campaign for Labour Party Democracy. Its creation was a classic case of how women in avowedly radical organisations become angry and organised: a campaign led largely by men; a small minority of women playing an important backroom role (it is difficult to imagine Frances Morrell in a backroom for long!); the women applying the radical aims of the campaign to their own predicament. WAC took the theme phrase of CPLD about 'the fundamental shift in the balance of power and wealth in favour of working people' and rephrased it for their own objectives:

To campaign for action, including positive discrimination, to ensure that women are fully represented at every level of party life, and thereby to strengthen the fight for a fundamental shift in the balance of power and wealth in favour of women as well as working men.[15]

WAC's arguments are for power for women in the party as women and as representatives of Labour's women's organisations. Power at every level of the party, from the constituencies up to the NEC and the CLP.

Women's demands

They argue that the Annual Women's Conference should have formal recognised decision-making status within the party (until recently it did not even have its own minutes, so insignificant did the party consider its decisions); that five of its resolutions should automatically go before party conference, and, most significantly of all, that it should directly elect the five women's representatives on the NEC. In a sense WAC is taking the party's claim to be a federal party at its word and claiming that women's organisations should be a recognised part of that federation with all the autonomy and power which the idea of a federation implies for its constituent parts. In arguing its case it both draws on the arguments of feminism for the right to autonomy ('only women know enough about the condition of women to fight for major change on their behalf', asserts a WAC pamphlet) and appeals to some implicit criteria of representativeness to claim legitimacy as a part of Labour's federation. Later in the same WAC pamphlet the author criticises the Labour Party and the unions for not agreeing to 'power being conferred on a body which is far more representative of the women of our class, where trade-union women *are* represented – the Labour Women's Conference.'[16]

The implications of their claim are far-reaching. For the Labour Party is only a federal party for the trade unions, as we shall see when we recount the obstacles which the women faced in pressing their reforms.

The achievements of WAC and of the pressure of women's sections themselves have been impressive. The successes have been mainly at a local level – though the fact that these basic rights are called 'successes' indicates the problem. Since 1983 women can form women's sections as of right; they no longer have to ask for permission. And since 1984 every constituency has to have a women's officer, and that officer has a vote on the General Management Committee executive. The pressure for this came as a result of a CLP, Pudsey, which went ahead and elected a women's officer with a vote on the GMC executive. At first the NEC threatened to prevent Pudsey from carrying out the reselection of its parliamentary candidate. The 1984 conference rallied behind Pudsey's initiative and voted for women's officers for every CLP. At a regional level too there have been some successes. In some regions, notably the West Midlands, the regional women's conference directly elects the women's seats on the regional executive (before they were elected by the party's regional conferences, and therefore predominantly by the unions' block vote).

WAC and radical women on the National Labour Women's Committee, learning from the tactics of CPLD, have also provided the tactical nous and co-ordinating ability to get women's demands discussed with growing support at party conference. This shows partly in the rapid increase in the number of resolutions to conference on women's organisations, from a total of six between 1974 and 1981, when WAC had been set up, to a total of 74 between 1982 and 1985. It also led to a greater sense of solidarity between women. Mildred Gordon, a delegate to the 1982 conference and now MP for Poplar and Bow, remembers:

I think WAC did a very good job at conference, helping women delegates, organising composite motions so that we could get women's issues on the agenda – something we'd never succeeded in doing before. It was the first time the party had heard our whole case, so it was an important conference for us. And there was considerable feeling among us as women, feminists, together.[17]

Trade-union power

But there are major barriers between the party hearing the women's case and the most powerful section of the party, the trade unions, accepting it. For the demands for women's power nationally, especially on the NEC, directly challenge the balance of power tilted so carefully by Arthur Henderson in 1918 in favour of the unions and further consolidated in that direction in the 1930s.

Some of the WAC women had had considerable experience, through CPLD, of winning trade-union support for constitutional changes to which the trade-union leadership was initially hostile. This experience made them confident about WAC's long-run chances of success. Ann Pettifer was trade-union liaison officer for CPLD. She had had to wheel and deal, persuade and cajole in order to deliver sufficient block votes behind the favoured proposals for constitutional change:

Getting it through the union conferences isn't going to be the problem. The brick wall in some unions is getting the delegations to take any notice of conference resolutions. For that, you have to make it difficult for those guys to oppose. What we had to do [in CPLD] was threaten them so that they'd lose something if they did.

You see I fundamentally believe that trade unions can't ultimately be corrupted. In the end the trade-union leaders have to look over their shoulders. Look, Sid Weighell was sacked, literally sacked for ignoring his members' views. The Labour Party never sacks a General Secretary or NEC members for ignoring a mandate. But the NUR sacked Sid Weighell.

There is, however, an important difference between the CPLD's proposals and those of WAC. CPLD's proposals meant an extension of trade-union influence, nationally (through the electoral college for the leader) and locally (through the role of trade-union delegates in reselection), whereas WAC's proposals involve a challenge to the power of the trade-union leadership. The outward signs of this have been becoming more apparent in a simmering conflict between delegates from the majority of feminist women's sections and trade-union delegates at the Annual Women's Conference. This tension was not only about a threat to trade-union power. It also reflected a remarkable cultural and political gulf between the constituency and the trade-union women. I say remarkable because feminism *has* had an influence among trade-union women, for instance in NUPE, USDAW, the T&GWU and ASTMS. Ironically, there is something about conflicts within the Labour Party which has polarised trade-union women from constituency feminists in a way which bears little relation to the urgent economic and social problems that groups of women face.

There is no trade-union block vote at women's conferences. Trade-union delegations have as many votes as they have delegates. If, for instance, they had sent to the 1986 conference the total number of delegates that they are allowed – 520 – they would have had 45 per cent of the vote. They sent only 141 – a sign of the conferences' lack of power – 24 per cent of the vote. 286 women's organisations or CPLs sent 427 delegates out of a possible total of 572. They had 73 per cent of the vote (Socialist Societies had 3 per cent).

The reason for the weakness of the trade-union representation is of course that nothing was at stake at women's conferences. The conference has no power. Votes do not count for anything; as I have already mentioned, they are not even minuted. But, increasingly, the Women's Conference has been developing a *de facto* power by the growing attendance, the seriousness with which women's sections insist that they are treated by their CLPs, their propaganda impact within the party and the confidence they build up among Labour women for the battles to be waged in the preparations for the party conference.

'It all started at Malvern [the 1979 conference]', people say, with a sigh of regret or a proud, mischievous smile, depending on who you are talking to. In 1986 the women's conference went off to the Isle of Bute, off the coast of Scotland, just about the most difficult conference centre to reach in the whole of the British Isles – though for Scottish women, Bournemouth the year before must have been nearly as bad. Over 600 women turned up. 'Before Malvern' 200 was the normal attendance.

By 1986 the majority of women on the National Women's Committee supported WAC's demands. With its success, WAC had reached something of an impasse. They had full support in the constituencies plus support from a minority of left unions: the NUPE, NUM, ASLEF, ACTT. They felt they had to do something to force the pace. They decided to get the Women's National Committee to organise a shadow election for women's seats on the NEC and then campaign for the unions and CLPs to support the five Women's Conference candidates. Most of the union delegates boycotted this shadow election. The trade-union delegates were in a predicament: here was a conference grabbing power and yet they were being marginalised; without the block vote they were not equipped for a struggle over power.

In such circumstances, trade-union officials without the block vote are like generals without reinforcements: they get into a discreet flap. Certainly they become united against what they define as a common enemy. At the Conference Centre at the Isle of Bute unlikely knots of officials, the right-wing EETPU talking to the left-wing TASS and the T&GWU, could be seen gathering in the foyer with the substantial figure of Ken Cure, chair of the

NEC's organisation subcommittee hovering in the background. An almost common front developed of trade-union delegates against WAC supporters from the women's sections. Misinformation and caricature spread like wildfire. Several of the more right-wing officials whom I interviewed told me that the problem was 'feminists and Militants'; 'they are all the same,' as Eileen Gallagher, a tough full-time official from the EETPU put it.

On the other hand, WAC women accused the trade-union delegates pretty indiscriminately of being manipulated by their male officials: 'There are plenty of slaves who would kiss the feet of the slave-owners,' said Ann Pettifer at a fringe meeting. There was little opportunity to break down the divisions socially. As at party conference, the union delegations stayed very much to themselves. As Jo Richardson put it: 'They didn't socialise at all after the conference or inside, they stuck together.' But then the constituency women had not done any preparatory work identifying the allies in the union that they undoubtedly have.

The division had happened before at previous Women's Conferences, but never quite so starkly. There was a basis for common ground with some of the unions. It was contained in a resolution put by NUPE which essentially supported the WAC proposals, but recommended further consultation without specifying a timetable. It was seen by the majority of WAC as a compromise that would delay progress rather than promote it. It was defeated, as were most of the resolutions on the WAC slate for the NEC at the party conference later in 1986.

At the Isle of Bute it was stalemate. But the trauma caused an unusual degree of movement at Walworth Road. The pressure of the women could no longer be ignored. A temporary compromise has been agreed which involves the NEC and the National Labour Women's Committee preparing proposals which will give the trade unions some form of block vote at the Women's Conference; integrate the decisions of the Women's Conference into the party structure with a clear line of communication into the Annual Party Conference and the NEC; and 'review the system for electing the five reserved women's seats on the NEC'. The Women's Committee are very clear what they want: a 50/50 voting proportion at the conference, with trade-union votes being based on block votes of their *women* members and conference electing the reserved seats on the NEC.

The implications of this would be very threatening to many assumptions behind much of the Labour Party's structure. A Women's Conference with real powers and with a gender-based trade-union block vote would mean political recognition of distinct interests within the working class. It could also open the way to the affiliation of other women's groups from outside the party but in agreement with its aims. In effect, it would establish the precedent of a mass presence in the party of an autonomous force other than the unions.

An immediate political consequence would be that five seats on the NEC would no longer be part of the unions' pool of seats over which to bargain and exchange – a process which, as Arthur Henderson intended, has historically favoured the right-wing or at least loyalist (to the parliamentary leadership) trade-union leaderships. Block votes of women trade unionists would not be easy to control. In most unions it would now be very difficult for the unions to select the delegations other than by election.

Already, in the consultation period, some unions are lining up in favour of basing the block vote on *all* members. More significantly, a firm 'not on' is being given to the idea of the women electing the NEC seats. As Margaret Prosser, the T&GWU Women's Officer, puts it in a response to the Women's Committee's consultation document:

I believe it is unrealistic to expect that either our own union or many of the other unions affiliated to the party would give up the current system of election. This is not to say that I believe the current system to be without fault or that I believe it should continue indefinitely. However, I believe this to be the reality of the situation.

She is probably right. But her note of qualification is also significant. Unions like the T&GWU are not in a very strong position to sustain their opposition, when they are launching massive publicity exercises to appeal to and recruit women. The GMB is in a similar position: 'without more women members we don't have a future,' says John Edmonds, the GMB's General Secretary. The personal view of Tom Sawyer, the Deputy General Secretary of NUPE, the union with the largest number of women, is to support the direct election of the women's seats by the conference – a conference in which NUPE would be one of the most powerful single voices.

The unions that increasingly depend on women have established or are setting up structures and educational provisions which promote women in the unions. These rarely go far enough, but in most manual unskilled unions they have gone too far for the union to halt a momentum towards increased power for women.[18] As the issue of women in the Labour Party is debated, it will be very difficult for reluctant executives to protect their position within the party from the processes of change going on in their own unions.

Black Sections: a stronger voice

Black sections, like women's sections, are demanding a distinct voice in the party's power structure, where before they have had no voice at all. 'Black sections,' says Diane Abbott, one of their leading advocates, 'are about a new Labour Party with a place for all its constituent parts.'[19]

Black people, like women, were joining the Labour Party in the early eighties in larger numbers and with higher expectations than ever before, because change was in the air, or so it seemed. And many of them, again like many women at that time, came from movements outside the parliamentary, party-political, world. They had had enough of petitioning, lobbying, pressuring white politicians; they wanted direct representation of their own. Consequently, when they joined the Labour Party many of them were interested in power. This is one of the goals of the black section movement, as Narendra Makenji, Secretary of the Black Sections National Committee, explains:

We're not a social organisation, or a cultural organisation; we're not people who go to black sections because we can't go to adult education. We're about power. It's absolutely blunt: we want power and we will go wherever power is, whether it's branch meetings, whether it's community organisations, whether it's trade unions, councils or Parliament, we will get organised and take it.

He focuses on power in a provocatively single-minded way, as if to emphasise his sectional priorities. This theme recurs in the recent rhetoric of black-section spokespeople. Amongst others though, the emphasis was less on power and, as Ben Bousquet, one of the founders of black sections in 1984, put it, more on [getting] the party to open itself and to open the trade-union movement, which is the real arm of the Labour Party, so that black people feel that they are part of the labour movement and can get to all levels of strength.

In the last three years black sections, in spite of their unofficial status, have made significant advances both in terms of opening the party up to black people and achieving positions of power within the party. In order to understand these advances it is revealing to look at the history of the party's attitudes to race, through the experiences of black members themselves.

Narendra Makenji is a long-standing member of the Labour Party. He joined in 1974. But until recently he, like many black members, had been excluded not only from power but from any effective participation. He is now a councillor in Haringey, but ten years ago, when he was a member of the Labour Party in Coventry, he and the only other black member in Coventry were not even encouraged to canvass, never mind stand for the council:

You'd go in at election time and say 'I want to go out canvassing.' 'Oh, no, no, no. We've got better things for you to do,' they'd say. We'd spend the time indoors, out of sight, sitting stuffing envelopes. You mustn't underestimate the level of racism in the party.

It was under the shadow of the Wilson–Callaghan years that racism spread like a fungus throughout the party. It was their policy for immigration controls in particular which made racism seem somehow 'official'. Just two years before Wilson became leader, Hugh Gaitskell was leading a campaign against the Conservative government's introduction of immigration controls. Under Gaitskell's leadership the Labour Party's position was unequivocal and unconditional. In 1961 the Secretary of the Parliamentary Labour Party (under Gaitskell) answered a letter from Cyril Osborne, a leading Conservative campaigner for immigration control, in the following terms:

The Labour Party is opposed to the restriction of immigration as every Commonwealth citizen has the right as a British subject to enter this country at will. This has been the right of subjects of the Crown for many centuries and the Labour Party has always maintained it should be unconditional.[20]

The Labour Party's good name lived with the first generation of black voters in Britain on the credit of this opposition to immigration controls, as well as the role of some of the best-known leaders of the left – Fenner Brockway, Nye Bevan – in campaigns against colonialism. It is still seen as *'on paper* the party that stands up for black people', as Hassan Ahmed, Chair of the Nottingham black section, put it. But the second and third generations remember mainly Harold Wilson and Jim Callaghan.

During Wilson's premiership, Labour's policy on immigration became a matter of electoral expediency rather than political principle. This meant, in effect, outflanking the Conservatives in the expression and encouragement of racialist prejudice. In 1963 Wilson talked of 'loopholes' in the Conservative legislation. He called for stronger legal powers, tighter health checks and greater powers of deportation. Within the party, immigration became a taboo subject; to raise it was a sign of 'extremism'. During the 1964 election campaign, orders went out from Transport House that on no account was immigration policy to be raised on the platform of prospective candidates. When the 1965 Immigration White Paper turned Wilson's election propaganda into legislation, all thought of sticking to a principle was gone. Richard Crossman, all too aware of the principles that had been dropped, summed up the government's main considerations. It is worth quoting this passage from his diaries in full:

This afternoon we had the statement on immigration and the publication of the White Paper. This has been one of the most difficult and unpleasant jobs the government has had to do. We have become illiberal and lowered the quotas at a time when we have an acute shortage of labour. No wonder all the weekend liberal papers have been bitterly attacking us. Nevertheless, I am convinced that if we hadn't done all this we would have been faced with certain electoral defeat in the West Midlands and the south-east. Politically, fear of immigration is the most powerful undertow today. Moreover, we had already abandoned the Gaitskell position when we renewed the Immigration Act, and any attempt now to resist demands for reduced quotas would have been fatal. We felt we had to out-trump the Tories by doing what they would have done and so transforming their policy into a bipartisan policy. I fear we were right; and partly I think so because I am an old-fashioned Zionist who believes that anti-semitism and racialism are endemic, that one has to deal with them by controlling immigration when it gets beyond a certain level. On the other hand, I can't overestimate the shock to the party.[21]

Jim Callaghan took the 'out-trumping' of the Tories several

steps further with the 1968 Immigration Act, which put new limits on the entry of British passport-holders from the Commonwealth. This Act had racialism built into it because its provisions did not apply to those who could prove 'a substantial connexion' with the UK. As if in knowing guilt, the government rushed it through the House of Commons with thirty-five Labour, all twelve Liberals and fifteen Conservatives voting against.

This provoked even greater anger within the party than the 1965 White Paper. In his book on *The Politics of Harold Wilson*, Paul Foot describes the shock the Bill caused among the 'principled' right of the party: 'Resignations were reported all over the country from intellectuals and Fabians.'[22] But what was the response of black members, intellectual and activist? Sharon Atkin, at the time I talked to her the parliamentary candidate for Nottingham East, who comes from a Labour family, whose father had been a member of the People's National Party in Jamaica, and who joined the Labour Party in 1958, remembers:

There weren't many black people in the party then (in some areas they were kept out). Those of us who were in began by being vocal in our opposition to the immigration policies; then we retreated. We felt very alienated from the party, not only because of its immigration policies but also because of what it was doing internationally; talking about defending 'our white kith and kin' in Rhodesia and sending troops to 'put down black rebels' in Anguilla.

Certainly, most politically-minded members of the second generation of black families felt little motivation to join the party at that time. It was not until the early eighties, when it looked as if the old leadership was out of the way and things were beginning to change, that many of those responsible for setting up black sections joined.

Hassan Ahmed, for instance, a founder member of the black sections movement, joined in 1980. He joined the Nottingham East Constituency which, like many others throughout the country, still bore the mark of the Wilson years:

I was lucky with my ward where I knew several people, mainly on the left. It was they who got me to join. But on the GMC it was different. If you tried to raise issues beyond the normal agenda, especially international issues like the movement for democracy in Pakistan or even the issue of South Africa, they were ignorant and they did not want to

know. They looked at you as if you were an outsider for raising these
issues, as if you had no right to be there. You felt shunned.

At first when Ahmed came to Britain, he says, he did not think
of himself as black but as a trade unionist and socialist. 'My
black consciousness sharpened more and more as a result of my
and others' experiences in the Labour Party.' Talking to others
who had been in the party longer, he found a common complaint:

I heard many stories of how black people had tried to get nominated
for the council but they never got through. Or they'd try to become
officers and never get support. Yet when the Labour Party wanted their
support these black members went to their community to get the
support and they did get it. After that they were just forgotten. They
were just used. They were never looked at as political equals.

The statistics bear him out. In 1980 the figures for Nottingham
East show a ladder on which black representation declines with
every step towards power and status. Eighteen per cent of the
population of the constituency was black; 5 per cent of the party
membership was black; two out of 100 constituency delegates
were black. There were no black officers and no black councillors. London constituencies fared no better. The figures for the
Streatham Constituency, which includes a good part of Brixton,
are outstanding. Until 1980 there was one black member. On
further inquiry it turns out that in the memory of one long-
standing member – ten years – the constituency never discussed
race. Clearly Harold Wilson's taboo had held.

In other constituencies the racism was both patronising and
involving patronage – the 'Hatterjee' or 'Bidwell Singh' syn-
drome. As Asian people came to Britain in the fifties, initially to
work, then to settle, they naturally looked to their MP for
help. As the immigrant community became a more and more
significant part of the electorate, the MP in turn looked to them
for support. In certain constituencies a pyramid of reciprocal
understandings and relationships grew up. At the top was the
MP, with the power to get people through immigration, and to
put pressure on the local council for housing, employment, and
planning permission, and at the bottom were Asian families,
powerless and dependent. In the middle were Asian leaders who
had power partly through their access to the MP or the council,

and who maintained this access partly by their ability to 'deliver' significant sections of the Asian community as votes.

This kind of situation, especially in Sparkhill, Birmingham, and in Southall, was made the subject of a controversial Channel Four *Bandung File* programme[23] which explored the relationship between councillors, MPs and the black community. The programme provided evidence of this recruitment. Asians were filmed telling *Bandung* how they were asked to sign forms (for Labour Party membership) they had not filled in, containing subscription fees they had not paid. This reproduces a colonial mentality. 'The older generation of black people in this community were subservient to Bidwell [Sidney Bidwell, the MP for Southall] and still are,' says Mahdar Patil, an Asian councillor and chairman of the Southall black section. 'He does everything for them.'

In both Sparkbrook and Southall before the emergence of black sections there had long been a large black membership, but they have never had any power. Only recently have they become councillors or constituency officers. Those that have won office have normally done so by organising independently of the old patronage system, often with the support of the local black section. But another aspect of the colonial mentality has been the weakness of any independent politics. Najma Hafeez, who has recently become a councillor in Birmingham, talks about the kind of party she would like to see the Labour Party become, and the way the patronage form of recruitment makes such a goal so difficult to achieve:

We should be a mass party in the sense we ought to go out as the Labour Party used to do in the twenties, thirties and so on, where we recruited people and educated the people and told them what socialism was about, why it is most important to get involved in order to change society. Although we would like that, some of us are complaining that the sort of mass recruitment that's going on isn't a campaigning recruitment, it is simply for voting and for support for certain candidates . . . That is actually preventing those people who are serious about politics, serious about political involvement and serious about change, it's preventing them from getting involved. They see it as just, well, if you want to put it strongly, a corrupt game. And they don't want any part of it.

Black sections were formed therefore not simply to achieve power within the party as it is, but to transform the party, 'to rebuild the new Labour Party', as Elaine Foster put it during the 1984 debate at party conference; 'we're about renewal of the party,' emphasised another black speaker.

Rebuilding and renewal has certainly been the effect of black sections in several inner-city areas in London and in Nottingham, where branches were in a state of collapse. In Tottenham the black membership has gone up from around ten in 1983 (the year that the black-section movement came together) to over eighty in 1986. In Nottingham East the black section has recruited over 200 people in two years. This is not the passive, opportunistic recruitment that Najma was describing. It illustrates the campaigning kind of recruitment that she was advocating. On average, around seventy attend the monthly meeting of the black section. Public meetings on issues such as the movement for democracy in Pakistan, on South Africa and on Nicaragua have attracted between 300 and 400.

The section in Nottingham organises in two directions: within the party for representation and policies, and within the black community. Within the party they have made impressive headway. There are now twenty-seven black delegates to the GMC where before there were two. Four or five members of the black section are chairs of their ward parties and Hassan Ahmed is chair of the constituency. This year there are four black candidates in winnable council seats where before there were none. The prospective parliamentary candidate for Nottingham East, a marginal constituency, was, until removed by the NEC, a black woman.

But the Labour Party is not the be-all and end-all of the Nottingham black section's politics. The black section has taken a lead on several international issues: after the bombing of Tripoli they organised a demonstration of 600–700 people. They are heavily involved in community issues, especially immigration and the education of black children, on which they work in close co-operation with other organisations. Hassan describes their approach:

There are several black organisations who have been doing this work for several years and they are very radical. If we tried to monopolise the issue we would be undermining the other groups. So we try to work with them. The issue isn't how big a headline the black section can get, it's how we can have an impact on the problem.

Southall too has seen the rapid growth of a black section. But here the focus was initially on the party: the reselection of the MP and an attempt to replace Sid Bidwell, now in his seventies. The black section has recruited around 300 members in thirty-three years. In Streatham, progress has been slower, but without any base on which to build. In the Sparkbrook Constituency of Birmingham an active black section now exists, attracting thirty or so to its regular meetings, where before black membership consisted of several 'community leaders' and people who would turn up at their behest to vote.

So black sections vary. As with any new movement, a lot depends on the character of their local leadership. There is a considerable difference between sections whose leaderships have emerged out of frustration with the lack of black representation within the party – the impetus in Southall for instance – and those who have wanted a more political focus for the younger generation in the black community – the Nottingham experience. What they have in common is that in building themselves and seeking power within the party and influence in the black community, they have in several areas turned the party into something more like a representative force. In inner-city areas it is mainly due to black sections that the Labour Party still receives most of the black vote. In the council elections in Haringey, for example, where the black section has led a thorough registration campaign and a high-profile campaign in support of the council, the number of voters on the electoral register went up by 20,000, a majority of whom were black. This was reflected in an increase in both the turn-out of black voters and the size of the Labour vote.[24]

Parliamentary representation
The national black-section movement was founded with a three-pronged strategy – 'the three R's', Narendra Makenji called them: Registration, Recruitment and Representation. I have illustrated the first two prongs; what of the third? It means representation at all levels, but not surprisingly it is the black sections' pushiness in organising for black MPs which causes the most offence and controversy – as well as, among many black activists and the black community, the most elation.

Enoch Powell sees it as a source of crisis, or at least confirming what he sees as the crisis that is already upon us. He said in an article in the *Guardian* in March 1984 that the demands of the black sections were:

symptoms of approaching crisis; for where numbers are political power, as, supremely, in Parliament, the numbers game of ethnic monitoring and quotas becomes a matter of life-and-death that will disturb even the pacific complacency of the British public . . .

He goes on to say that black M Ps will not

know how to use that capability to attract power from the rest who are bidding and counter-bidding for their votes. Power exists to be used where it can be seized, and its practitioners are ready learners.

The builders of the Tower of Babel were destroyed by differences injected into them from outside. We on the contrary have prepared the downfall of our Tower of Babel by insisting on enforcing differences upon ourselves.[25]

For the unity and sanctity of the British state of which Enoch Powell is the ever-watchful custodian, the black sections and the growing assertiveness of the black community, of which they are just one expression, *are* a threat. For a start, the black sections' approach to Parliament is distinctly unBritish. It has neither the deference disguised by cosy familiarity to be found among many Labour M Ps and would-be M Ps, nor the dismissive syndicalism to be found on the trade-union side of the labour movement in Britain. Its approach so far has been confident and demanding. It sees Parliament as an instrument of power to be used, not deferred to. The majority of black M Ps, in their rhetoric at least, imply that they feel little allegiance to the Crown and the state it stands for. Their allegiance is most directly to their constituents, but particularly to their black constituents to whom they feel they owe a special effort to make their voices heard. They also see themselves as accountable to the constituency parties that have selected them, to the black section within it and to the struggles of black people throughout the country and internationally. Just how these different pressures will influence black M Ps, and whether they will in fact be any different from the orthodox Labour M Ps will not be clear until the commitments are tested. The black M Ps have already taken one step away from orthodoxy by deciding to form a black caucus with the Parliamentary Labour Party.

Once in Parliament they will come under the pressures of patronage and respectability to which the majority of Labour politicians succumb. But the black MPs who owe their position mainly to the black sections are not going to find it easy to forget their accountability to black people. The media of the black community are already putting the spotlight on black MPs and establishing a very public form of accountability. And local leaders of the black sections constantly remind their members of the sections' role in achieving so many black candidates.

The black sections' organisation was indeed decisive in the latest round of selections: they targeted constituencies with a high proportion of black voters and then worked with supporters in the relevant constituencies to get trade-union or party branches to nominate someone from their 'blacklist'. One of the main arguments used in such campaigns was the one for representing the black community – in some cases a majority of the population – more adequately than could a white MP, however committed. These prospective MPs see their accountability to their constituencies as involving a special relationship with the local black section, whose role is to express the needs and demands of the black community. 'It's important not to pretend we can be superwomen,' says Sharon Atkin, 'but we must keep close links with black struggle in this country and make sure their causes are raised and strengthened.'

In contrast to the majority of Labour MPs, members of black sections hope their MPs will give a high priority to international issues, and in particular on changing Britain's relation to the world. Hassan: 'We want to stop this country getting involved in exploiting other countries. Because we love this country we want it to play a democratic and equal role. That is what I would highlight if I was an MP.'

Among a minority of the black-section leadership, determination to use Parliament is combined, at least rhetorically, with a critical attitude to the notion of a parliamentary career. 'I think they should be there for ten years at the most. They wouldn't be much good after that. They should make way for someone more in touch. I'll get out and do something more based in the community.' Narendra Makenji argues that there ought to be a constitutional limit to how long someone can be an MP. 'I don't see why, if Ronald Reagan can only run for two presidential terms, then has to retire, we can't have a similar constitutional position for parliamentary candidates. They could come back in five years or stand for another constituency. But you'd get a significant turnover. You wouldn't have people growing cobwebs round their bodies. You would shake up the way that Parliament operates.'

Not everyone in the black-section movement would be sympathetic to this idea. But black sections are not a politically homogeneous organisation. They do not claim to be. Many of them resent a tendency among white supporters to give their support to the political positions of the black 'leaders' (as distinct from the right to organise support for black sections) as if there was no critical debate going on within black sections, and more fundamentally within the black community. Black sections are in many ways a microcosm of the Labour Party: they include activists with a wide range of views.

There is intense debate. Many socialist blacks, inside and outside the Labour Party, are critical of some of the leadership of black sections. They are critical not of their campaign for recognition in the Labour Party, but of what they see as a certain personal opportunism among some of them. This is why Ben Bousquet, a councillor in North Kensington and a member of Lambeth Council's Police Monitoring Unit, decided to leave the black-sections movement:

I found some of these people wanting. Some of the newer national leaders were interested only in themselves and were using us as a front to push their own political careers.

Ben Bousquet too has his political career; he is parliamentary candidate for North Kensington (where he had played a significant part in defeating the hold of the right-wing Social Democratic Alliance on the council in the late seventies). His criticisms are no doubt fired by defeats he and others – most of whom stayed – suffered within the black sections' national organisation. But the suspicion of opportunism, which he does not make indiscriminately, is shared by black community activists outside the Labour Party[26] and needs to be taken seriously. There is the same suspicion about women involved in WAC. (And it is almost taken for granted about most Labour Party men who aspire to power!) There is no doubt that some people use black and women's sections to further their political careers. But why not? In a party full of white and male careerists, black people and women surely have the right to organise amongst themselves to overcome the prejudice, material disadvantage and lack of confidence that have in the past excluded them from positions of power and influence.

This caution does not however weaken a firm unity on the issue of black representation. It is such an overriding commitment that membership of or even support for black sections is not a condition of being on the black sections' 'blacklist' of candidates to promote. 'The overwhelming view from within the community was that we wanted black representation. The assumption was that anybody who was black could be nowhere near as bad as anybody who was white. They could not run away from the problems of the black community,' says Narendra Makenji. The fact that some black people will use black sections opportunistically to get positions of power for their own interests does not deflect them from the priority of increasing black representation. They feel that they have sufficient momentum to influence, through the accountability that their strength will impose on the MPs, how that representation is used.

The black sections' case is not well understood in the white men's movement. The vote for their motion at conference to recognise black sections and give them full rights in constituency parties – including the right to participate in the selection of councillors and MPs – has remained in the last two years at around 1.6 million. Apparent political opposites symbolised by men like Derek Hatton and Roy Hattersley, and in a different way many million trade-union members, share a common blindness: a blindness to the idea that a group of working-class people, who face oppression and exclusion of a particular kind, might wish to come together independently of others who, whatever else they might have in common, do not share that oppression and at times even benefit from it. To Hatton and Hattersley, Militant and the parliamentary leadership, such a prospect threatens 'the unity of the movement'. The assumption is that 'the unity of the movement' can solve the problem of racism. During the 1985 Conference debate on black sections, Hattersley referred to a united party that is united against racism; which does not divide its members according to race . . .' Or as Ray Apps, a supporter of Militant, put it in the same debate: 'To sectionalise the labour movement . . . means dividing our movement on racial lines and threatens the unity of the working class and impedes the struggle against racism, which threatens us all.'

The problem of unity

Black members of the party have not found the unity of the movement quite so kind. Nottingham Labour Party was united, but it shunned the concerns of its few black members; Streatham Labour Party was united, but it ignored the problems of the black people in its midst; constituencies with large black populations throughout the country are united but they end up, without intending it, excluding black people from power or representation. The party nationally claims to be united but has few black members of staff. The self-organisation of black members, at first informally and now mainly (though not exclusively) through black sections, has begun to change this state of affairs. Their success in increasing the participation and power of black people *within* the party demonstrates the strength of their case.

On the basis of experience so far we can point to a clear relationship: the stronger the local black section, the greater the degree of active participation and power of black people within the party as a whole. Above all, they have shown that there is no single thing that can be called 'unity'. There is unity of different kinds, of different qualities, resting on different relations of power and different kinds of involvement. 'Unity' is no longer a password that can be accepted uncritically. Black party members have achieved in several constituency parties a new kind of unity: a unity in which black people are not just equal 'on paper' but in the power they share in running and representing the party. They have done this by organising independently, by developing among themselves and with others in the black community a common analysis of racism in the labour movement and a common set of aims for confronting it, and by presenting a force that could not be ignored.

The inability of both the Hatton and the Hattersley sections of the party to understand this has a further aspect to it: a deafness to what the black-section movement is actually demanding. Both wings of the opposition to black sections seem congenitally deaf to demands from rank and file members of the sort which say 'we found it necessary to do certain things – organise together for the recruitment, registration and representation of black people – and we wish the party now to support our right to do so and allow us the constitutional position to exercise that right.' They mentally receive this as a different demand, a demand that the *party* set up black sections. The black-section resolutions to conference are very clear. For instance, a resolution moved in 1984 by Bernie Grant says: 'Conference recommends the creation of black sections, where there is a demand for this . . .'

It goes on to propose an instruction to the NEC that it:

submit to the 1985 Conference amendments to the rules for constituency parties which allow black sections to be formed, *where black members so desire*, with the right to send delegates to general and executive committees in the same ways as women's sections and young socialists [my italics].

The party leader has on occasion talked about an 'enabling state'. What the black sections are demanding is an 'enabling party'. They got a little bit further with Neil Kinnock, but suddenly the door was slammed in an extremely disabling manner. It is worth telling the story in full because it reveals a surprising view of the party from the party leader. A view we shall be exploring in more detail later.

The enabling leader?
In 1985 Kinnock was speaking at an event to celebrate the work of Paul Robeson. At one point he said that Paul Robeson would have been against black sections. Paul Robeson Junior was present and said that, on the contrary, Paul Robeson would have been a great supporter and activist for black sections. When Robeson Junior asked Kinnock afterwards the reasons for his opposition Kinnock complained that they wouldn't talk to him. Whereupon Robeson arranged for Sharon Atkin to go and see him. Sharon Atkin, at that time a Lambeth councillor, takes up the story:

He obviously expected me to be a Ted Knight acolyte. He seemed very surprised by the way the conversation went. I mentioned people who he approves of who were against black sections and are now in favour.

By the end he was remarking on how well we'd got on. I had to leave to go to a council meeting and he said, 'Look, I'll drop my opposition to black sections if you can come back to me with a legal definition of "black".' He suggested the 'Poale Zion' option by which the Jewish Labour Party is affiliated and has rights of representation on GMCS and so on. But in order for them to enshrine something in the constitution they would need a legal definition, checked by lawyers.

Black sections have many members who are lawyers, so Sharon agreed to the idea of a further meeting the following week. Sharon discussed the idea with other black-section members who agreed she should go ahead with a further talk, armed with a legal definition. She would come back to the committee before anything was agreed. The meeting was put off for several weeks. Finally she got a date and prepared to go with Diane Abbott. However, on the morning of their meeting, in June, *The Times* carried a report of a fierce attack on black sections by Neil Kinnock. Sharon takes up the story again:

I told him what the response had been to the Poale Zion option. He turned on me . . . as if I'd never been there before, and said, 'The people who agree with that are spineless jellyfish, and I don't want anything to do with them.' . . . It was as if we'd never had the first meeting. He wasn't interested in the legal definition. He went on about Ted Knight and *Labour Herald*. In the end I just left and called a press conference.

To Kinnock and many other senior Shadow Cabinet members, black sections are just another base for what they call 'the hard left'.

Kinnock's apparently irrelevant remark about Ted Knight and *Labour Herald* and their support for black sections illustrates the point. It is a decisive point, given the importance in Kinnock's strategy of marginalising the independent left. Behind the hard-left accusation is a more general fear, the fear of any part of the party that has any autonomy of its own and to which the leadership have no easy bridges.

It is also an instinctive conservatism about Labour's bid for electoral popularity. A bid, as we saw in Chapter 2, that has British nationalism at its core. And British nationalism depicts the nation as homogeneous. It absorbs, or tries to absorb racial differences into a single British national identity: an identity inherited from Britain's imperial past. Kinnock presents Labour as the party best able to preserve this identity. The assertive organisation of black members disrupts this strategy. It presents a very different appeal: to identities of region and race. The construction of such an appeal is entirely outside the framework of Labourism.

The arguments put against black sections by the party establishment – including accusations of apartheid – are by now wearing thin with party members who support the leadership in other ways but are looking at the arguments for and against black sections on their merits. Adrian Ham, adviser to Denis Healey under the last Labour government, is such a member. Until 1985 he was strongly against black sections. But since observing the impact they have had on the recruitment and participation of black people he has changed his mind and thinks they should have formal rights within the party.

Arguments about the definition of 'black' illustrate the thinness of the leadership's case. In the case of Poale Zion, it has been a matter of self-definition: that is, for the purposes of the Labour Party you are a Jew if you join Poale Zion. Why cannot this be so for black sections? Anthony Bevins, now Political Editor of the *Independent*, discussed this with Neil Kinnock soon after Kinnock's second meeting with Sharon Atkin:

Kinnock: The definition offered for those who would be entitled to be part of black sections are people of Afro–Caribbean or Asian origin *or* those who consider themselves to be black. Now I think a certain bankruptcy is demonstrated when they've got to coin definitions of that kind.
Bevins: Don't you think that people who are black know they're black by the very prejudice they suffer?
Kinnock: My point exactly.
Bevins: But therefore they are best self-defined. That's not bankrupt surely?
Kinnock: No, wait a minute, that's not what they are talking about at all. In defence against the proposition that this would be a segregationalist constitutional change, people say this can't be segregationalist because anyone who considers themselves black can join. So I asked the question: All right, can I consider myself to be black? And they say patently not, because you are so obviously white. And if that subjective definition can't be accepted, how can anybody else's subjective definition be accepted?

Bevins: I hate to make the point, but when did you last come across colour prejudice in your own life?
Kinnock: Well, you define colour prejudice to me.
Bevins: They are the best people to define it, they have it every day of their lives.

Indeed, the Labour Party itself in another sphere where a challenge to the leadership is not involved, the monitoring of ethnic employment in the party, seems to accept self-definition as the basis for positive action.

Neil Kinnock ended his conversation with Anthony Bevins with a parting attack on the press: 'If you insist,' he said, 'on considering the actions of fifteen or twenty constituency parties and making it run then I suppose it will . . .' And run it has. But not without considerable encouragement from senior members of the Shadow Cabinet, one of whom told the *Sunday Times*:

I want these characters out and I don't even mind if we lose a few votes to the SDP in the process. It is an insidious disease that has been allowed to spread. It is political AIDS.[27]

The gap between the vitriol with which members of the parliamentary leadership respond to black sections and the reasonable nature of their case is remarkable. The fact that constitutional recognition of black sections has been rejected by party conference with a large majority is not sufficient to explain it. It would be quite consistent with conference policy for black members to organise informally (like other campaigns) and at the same time seek to win support within the unions and the party. Instead the leadership has chosen to make an issue of black sections, and to positively encourage press hostility. From every reasonable angle their case is strong: it is a case of 'freedom and fairness', the freedom to organise against injustice as those suffering the injustice see fit; the precedent is there in the Labour Party with young people, women, Jews; the benefits have been considerable in terms of recruitment and the political life of the party. If handled with confidence, it could be an electoral bonus in many areas. The only angle from which the black sections are a problem is the party's internal power structure; an angle about which it is difficult for a leader to be explicit. Black sections and women's sections upset an otherwise highly successful process of centralising the party under the leadership's control. These two are the most independent and sometimes the most radical sections of the party. That is what all the fuss is about.

5 The Unions: Business or Politics?

The Labour Party is first and foremost a trade-union party. In the words of Walter Citrine, TUC General Secretary in the 1930s, it was created by the trade-union movement, 'to do those things in Parliament which the trade-union movement found ineffectively performed by the two-party system'.[1] Since then Labour has consolidated its position as a party of government. In doing so, it has added other, sometimes contradictory, national ideologies to the essentially sectional themes of Labourism. But it has not lost the character of a trade-union party so firmly imprinted by Citrine and his predecessors. It is this which binds the left and the right together in a single party.

The left and right each need the bond with the trade unions, but for different reasons. These differences only become apparent during periods when the party is intensely polarised. In the late seventies such polarisation in the party was, in part, the political expression of an earlier militancy in the unions. Since then, new divisions in the unions have emerged, concerning the very purpose and character of trade unionism itself. In this chapter I will explore the reverberations of both these developments in the relationship between the left and the unions.

Although much of the groundwork for the creation of the Labour Party was done by socialists – mainly members of the Independent Labour Party – the decision to form a parliamentary party, and the power to decide what kind of party it was, lay with the TUC and therefore the leadership of the national unions.[2] This has meant that the organised working class is represented – indeed is in a dominant position – within the party, formally through their unions. They are 'not', as Ernest Bevin used to enjoy reminding the socialist constituency delegates, represented 'as conscious socialists'.[3] Thus the Labour Party has the unique character of being a workers' party based primarily on workers not as individuals joining the party out of socialist commitment, but as trade unionists formally, often unknow-ingly,[4] incorporated into the party by virtue of their trade-union membership. They are the 'dead souls' of Labourism.[5]

This relationship between the party and the unions has contra-dictory and unstable consequences. It makes the Labour Party potentially both very radical and deeply conservative. Which potential is realised depends on the consciousness of the trade unions, which in turn depends on the conditions of the economy and industry; and also on whether or not Labour is in govern-ment.

The limits of trade union–party loyalty

On the one hand, trade unionists expect the Labour Party in government to advance their interests. When such governments fail, trade-union interests eventually and, on the part of the leaderships, often reluctantly, come before loyalty to Labour. Trade unions consequently take action to defeat government policies, as they did over Wilson's 'In Place of Strife' and the Callaghan 5 per cent wages policy in 1978–79. As a result, Labour governments since 1964 have never fully succeeded in controlling the unions sufficiently to allow for a sustained restoration of profits[6] (though the 1974–79 government came near to it). Some sophisticated industrialists thought they might: this was one of the reasons why, in 1974, the president of the CBI, Campbell Adamson, even went so far as to publicly recommend voting Labour. But in the conflict between labour and capital, the Labour Party cannot for long desert labour and remain in office. For this reason, MPs of the right and centre of the party periodically get together to discuss whether or not the links with the unions might be broken or renegotiated to be less embarrassing. These discussions take place in the wake of electoral defeat. Normally, the idea gets dropped because very soon right-wing MPs find themselves relying on the loyalty of the union leaderships to stabilise the party against the left.

In 1981, however, the Gang of Four followed these specu-lations to their logical conclusions and created a new party. They had reason to believe that electorally they no longer needed to depend on an alliance with the unions. So long as they had been dependent on this alliance, and so long as the trade unions had not supported any serious challenge to the autonomy of the parliamentary party, the founders of the SDP had been quite happy with the block vote and the benefits it brought with it (for Shirley Williams a seat for 11 years on the women's section – elected by the trade unions – of the NEC).

The limits of bargaining

On the other hand, the rationale of trade unions is to bargain and compromise within the present economic system. They would survive and adapt to a socialist transformation but, as trade unions, they are unlikely to have the drive to bring it about. So the left too face a dilemma. They too have discussed breaking the party–union links, or at least radically changing their form.[7] They face the problem that while socialism cannot be achieved without the active participation of the majority of workers, these workers are attached to the party in ways which inhibit socialists from encouraging such participation. The assumption of the early socialists, and many socialists since, has been that they would be able to influence trade-union members through the party; that union affiliation meant a captive working-class audience. However, the relationship between the unions and the party has in general not been favourable to the process of political persuasion or indeed to any kind of political involvement by party members, as party members, in the unions. On the whole, it has been a one-way relationship: the unions intervening in the party, but not vice versa. Until recently, the Communist Party filled the vacuum and formed a politicised cadre of trade-union activists who worked closely with the Labour left.

Old taboos break down

From 1970 onwards, in the wake of the Wilson government's 'In Place of Strife' and in the face of industrial restructuring which required political as well as industrial action, these conventional inhibitions were broken. Trade-union activists established direct connections with the Labour left, often against the instructions of their leaderships. For instance, in 1975 the executive of the Confederation of Shipbuilding and Engineering Unions passed a resolution forbidding shop stewards from attending meetings with Tony Benn; similarly on a local level, trade-union officials tried – unsuccessfully – to discourage shop stewards from resisting factory closures, and from working with left MPs such as Eddie Lloyden in Liverpool and Audrey Wise in Coventry.[8] Trade-union activists in local branches started to take an interest in what their leaderships were doing with the union's block vote. Trade-union leaders were elected, for instance Jack Jones in 1968, who initially responded to this assertion of rank and file power.[9]

These changes simmered away beneath the surface until 1978 –79, the collapse of the Social Contract, the 'Winter of Discontent' and the defeat of the Callaghan government. Until that point many of the more militant trade-union activists and officials believed that they or their leadership could influence the parliamentary leadership through threats of action combined with backroom pressure. On the whole they believed they had power over a Labour government; Harold Wilson's eventual climbdown over 'In Place of Strife' helped to convince them of that.

The breakdown of the Social Contract was a devastating disappointment for its trade-union architects. Jack Jones blamed it on the way in which the Prime Minister and the Chancellor of the Exchequer became entirely dependent on the advice of their civil servants and stopped listening to the TUC.[10] Others believed that Jack Jones and the TUC were too loyal; they should have begun to exert their industrial bargaining power before it was too late.

With Tony Benn, they should have built on the high expectations and industrial strength on which the government had been elected, to exert a counter-power to the pressures from the City and business. The conclusion drawn overwhelmingly, whatever the disagreements about what Jones and Benn should or should not have done, was that the Leader and the Parliamentary Party had become too distant from the party. More policy resolutions were no solution. Constitutional changes must bind the PLP and the Leader to carrying out party policy. This view and the momentum behind it pushed several unions, whether the leadership liked it or not, into a more active political role.

In some unions, for example the National Union of Public Employees (NUPE), it was the leadership, reflecting the anger of their low-paid members, who decided to intervene in the party. They supported the constitutional reforms from an early stage and affiliated to CLPD immediately after the IMF cuts in 1976. In other unions, it was the active membership who took the initiative, rebelling against their leaderships' support for Callaghan. Changes in the General and Municipal and Boiler-makers' Trades Union (G&MBTU or GMB), normally the most loyal – and leadership-controlled – of unions, provide the most notable illustration. A subterranean disaffection exploded into public view with the defeat of Derek Gladwin, the powerful Southern Region Secretary, in the union's election for its Chair at the 1982 conference.

Gladwin had been Chair for the previous four years and also, as Chair of the powerful Conference Arrangements Committee for the Labour Party, was at the centre of union attempts to protect the Labour government from an increasingly rebellious party. He was heavily outvoted by Dick Pickering, a branch secretary who worked as a manual worker for Manchester Council and whose campaign was directed at the old union and party hierarchy. 'We were dissatisfied with the union's centralised involvement with the Labour Party and with the Labour government,' explained Pickering. 'We wanted the union's involvement to be open and democratic, and very much more of a constituency affair.'

Pickering traces the growing discontent back to 1976 and the IMF cuts. From then on the 'lay' membership of the GMB executive shifted gradually to the left. The elections for the Labour Party Deputy Leadership also indicated that the sands were shifting beneath the leadership's feet. David Basnett, the reassuring face of trade-union barony, was general secretary at the time of the Deputy Leadership campaign. John Edmonds, his successor from 1985, describes how Basnett's expectations were upset:

We had lots of consultative meetings throughout the country and there was a fairly clear message coming through of 'a plague on both your houses [Benn and Healey]'. This was a bit of a shock to us, actually. And especially to the then leadership, who were assuming that there would be a cast-iron, no-trouble support for Healey, which there was not.

In the end, Healey succeeded with the support of six of the ten regions. Benn won the support of three. For the GMB this was a sign that the views of membership could no longer be taken for granted; a good number of the 650,000 voters behind David Basnett's block votes had distinct views of their own. John Edmonds interpreted it as

an important signal to the leadership that their silent majority theory – you know, that the activists tend to be left, but really there's this majority down there who if they said anything would be supporting people like Healey – wasn't actually true.

Some trade-union leaders were unwilling even to put the theory to the test. When Tom Jackson, General Secretary of the Union of Communication Workers, heard that union members were planning a fringe meeting with Tony Benn at the union's annual conference at Eastbourne, he wrote a letter to Ron Hayward, the party's general secretary, asking him to prohibit Benn from speaking. Hayward replied that such a move was not within his powers. The meeting went ahead; 600 delegates attended. The UCW conference voted two to one in favour of Denis Healey.

A similar sequence of events took place at the ASTMS Conference, though this time with the decision going in favour of Benn. The executive recommended for Healey. Along with most trade-union leaders, Clive Jenkins, the general secretary, had been against the Deputy Leadership election in the first place, preferring Healey to be elected unopposed, and he had been among the trade-union leaders who had visited Michael Foot in December 1980, promising that they would ensure Healey's election. He conveyed this message to Benn himself with a specially made mug engraved with the words: 'Tony, Don't Do It. Elections Can Be A Poisoned Chalice' (Clive Jenkins has never stood for election for his position as general secretary).[11] He tried to prevent a fringe meeting for Benn. It went ahead and was attended by over half the delegates to the conference. The next day they voted, narrowly, in favour of Tony Benn against the executive's recommendation.

The Deputy Leadership did indeed prove to be a poisoned chalice: but more for Clive Jenkins than for Benn. The left in the ASTMS has grown, and so has the number of elections in the union. For instance, until 1979 all thirty of the ASTMS delegation to the Labour Party conference were executive members and other full-time officials. From 1980, sixteen out of the thirty were elected by the region.

In the end, Benn lost the campaign in the unions. He won 2,383,000 votes to Denis Healey's 3,969,000. The size of his vote is a measure, not so much of the number of 'conscious socialists' paying the political levy, but of an awakening among a minority of the union membership to the union's role in the party as a means of active political expression. The campaign itself had a lasting significance in two ways.

First, it began to shake up and put pressure on the old top-heavy procedures which governed the unions' relationship to the party. It led people to find out the part their union played in the party. It led them to demand information; for instance, it led to a resolution passed at the 1981 conference introducing recorded votes for the union and women's seats on the NEC. Activists began to insist on accountability: that their delegations report back to the membership. And they called for more democratic procedures for selection and the internal decision-making of the delegations.

A second consequence of the democracy debate and the Deputy Leadership campaign was to bring into the open political divisons which had previously been subterranean or informal. The atmosphere in many unions became more politically charged. The underlying causes of this lie more in the actions of the Conservative government. But events in the Labour Party and their repercussions in the unions opened up the channels for political expression. For instance, in several unions – ASTMS, APEX, the UCW, the EETPU – left groupings either came together or grew in numbers as a result of the Deputy Leadership campaign.

It is impossible to generalise about the form that these political divisions take. The AEU, for instance, has probably the most open 'party' system where left and right organise openly and campaign politically for union elections, though the position of the broad left is very weak at present. In the T&GWU political divisions have been (and in general still are) a very internal affair, and even then mainly between officials rather than being open to members. In the sixties and seventies the official broad left, mainly among full-time officials, dominated by the Communist

Party, focused almost exclusively on gaining positions: taking over or keeping control of the apparatus. The more unofficial left (there was movement and contact as well as tension between the two) was based on workplace activists organised around the problems they faced in their company (for instance the shop stewards' combined committees in Ford, ICI, Dunlop and other multi-plant companies) or in their industry (for instance the Docks Shop Stewards' Liaison Committee). The 'left' in the unions cannot always be equated with explicitly political organisations; in many unions it is more a matter of a broad alliance of socialist trade unionists, some in the Labour Party, some in other political organisations, some in none, pushing for a wider, more political perspective in their own workplace or locality.

A third significant feature of the democracy and Deputy Leadership campaigns was that for a brief period they strengthened, against considerable resistance, the channels and the legitimacy for the left of the party working directly and openly with the left in the unions.

The extent and the significance of these developments varied according to the structure, history and existing political leadership of each union. To provide a glimpse of these I have looked at the impact of the 1979–81 conflicts in the party on two unions of quite contrary character: the EETPU and NUPE. In many ways these two unions represent most sharply the two directions into which British trade unionism seems to be diverging.

The EETPU

For the left in the Electrical, Electronic Telecommunications and Plumbing Union (EETPU) events in the Labour Party were of tremendous significance. According to Steve Stevenson, an electrician from Swansea, 'Without a doubt this was when we felt we could become open and confident in our campaign for democracy in EETPU.' The 'we' to whom Stevenson refers is a scattered network of dissidents who keep in touch through a newspaper called *Flashlight*. Their candidates in executive elections are the main – usually the only – challenge to the leadership. In the most recent election (1982) for general secretary, their candidate, John Aitken, polled 32,000 against Eric Hammond's 80,000, pushing Roy Sanderson, a national official, into third place with 20,000. They are the main focus for left-wing opposition to the present leadership of the union.

Since the impact of events in the Labour Party on the EETPU directly concerned its own internal regime, it is necessary to explain the character of this regime and the nature of *Flashlight*'s criticism.

The EETPU has a media reputation for being a democratic union. For instance, a writer in *Management Today* said: 'Now all appointments and key decisions are made by postal balloting of members.'[12] Robert Taylor, the Labour correspondent of the *Observer*, argued in 1976 that 'the EETPU is more democratic than most.'[13] Two factors have been important in establishing this reputation. First, and most powerful, is the Communist ballot-rigging which took place twenty years ago, was brought to court and led to a transformation in the organisation of the union, under the leadership of ex-Communist Frank Chapple. Much of what the leadership has done since benefits from the reputations established by those who reformed the union in the aftermath of the ballot-rigging. The second factor is the high-profile support which the EETPU has given to balloting. The clumsiness and defensiveness of the TUC enabled the issue of ballots to appear the main issue at stake in trade-union opposition to Conservative legislation on trade unions.

After the ballot-rigging, there *was* a brief but genuine process of democratisation: regular conferences of shop stewards were organised; a rank-and-file appeals committee was set up and a proposal to extend the term of office for executive members was defeated. But from 1965 the union became progressively more centralised. Gradually all the plural sources of power at the base of the union, similar to those still surviving in the AEU, which help to make a union genuinely democratic, were progressively abolished. In 1965 the elected area committees of working members were replaced by meetings of advisory area industry groups whose composition is decided by the executive. The job of these committees is to advise the area officer who, since 1969, has been appointed by the national executive rather than elected by the area membership.

The power of the EETPU executive is now unique in the British trade-union movement. The EETPU rules state that 'the general management and control of the union and the handling

of the whole of its affairs shall be vested in the executive council.'
In most other unions such a sovereignty would lie in the hands
of the unions' annual or biannual conference. This central power
gives the executive overriding powers in relation to the union's
branches. For instance, the executive has the power to appoint
a full-time official to carry out the job of local branch secretary
and treasurer, 'if they consider it expedient'[14] – a power it has
used against its critics. Another power it has used widely to
disperse opposition is to close branches down. This has been
done to Swindon branch (1981); Birmingham branch (1979);
Cardiff branch (1977); the London Central branch, and the
London Contracting branch (1982–87).[15]

There in no check on the executive's power. The union's
biannual conference has no binding powers on the executive.
Even the elected Appeals Committee, introduced in 1961 as a
sacred last resort to protect ordinary members against any abuse
of power, has been abolished.[16]

The EETPU executive is made up of thirteen divisional representatives who are elected by secret ballot in their divisions,
plus the plumbing national officer and general secretary, who
are both elected by a national ballot. Out of 140 full-time officials
responsible for negotiations and organisation – as distinct from
employees responsible for research, educational and clerical work
– it is only these fifteen who are elected. In the past the thirteen
divisional representatives had to be working electricians and
plumbers. (In 1961, after the ballot-rigging, a rule had been
introduced by which only rank-and-file members could stand.)
In 1977 this was changed to allow full-time officials to stand
when the sitting EC member is retiring. Since then there have
been twelve replacements on the fourteen-person executive, and
ten out of these twelve were already full-time officials, initially
appointed by the executive.

Under the rules of the EETPU, full-time officials have a
huge advantage in getting elected. The union's rules forbid the
ordinary member from communicating with the branches and
the rest of the membership. No member may solicit nominations
and no branch may invite a candidate to attend its meetings.[17]
If a member manages, in spite of these restrictions, to get the
three branch nominations required to stand, he gets a list of
branch meetings which he may visit to present his case, if, that

is, the chair agrees. He is not given the chairperson's address. He cannot visit workplaces. He cannot send supporters on his behalf. He cannot produce circulars or leaflets beyond a manifesto approved by the executive. He cannot give media interviews. Full-time officials, by contrast, are regularly in touch with branches and workplaces through their work. The union journal, *Contact*, carries their photos and gets their names known.

The executive's control over the election manifesto also seems to put the critical member at a disadvantage: in two recent cases the executive has deleted specific criticisms made by candidates – Harold Best for the Yorkshire Division, and Ian Brown for the Plumbing Division – of action taken by the leadership. Yet it allowed Harold Best's opponent to call Best 'a self-avowed Marxist with a half-baked vision of a communist utopia'. Ian Brown's opponent was able to describe Brown – then convenor of the shop stewards' committee at Shell Carrington – as part of 'the "Wild Men" of the, left . . .' with their 'extremist solutions' (both Brown and Best are in fact long-standing Labour Party members).

Frank Chapple and Eric Hammond speak proudly of their secret ballots on important matters of policy. However, the executive is highly selective about what it considers important. On the issue of the Deputy Leadership of the Labour Party, for instance, there was no ballot or wider consultation, even though Chapple had argued passionately for 'one man, one vote' to be the basis of electing the party Leader.[18] The executive took the decision.

And even when the executive does decide to have a ballot it does not feel itself to be bound by it. On the EEC for instance, despite the leadership's strong support for British membership, the membership voted against. The executive, however, continued to promote a policy in favour of entry. In none of these ballots can members who hold a different view to that of the leadership put forward such a view.

This was, and is, the regime which described itelf as democratic.

A *Guardian* report in 1980 described how 'opposition elements within the union operate in a cloak-and-dagger atmosphere inevitably reminscent of the Iron Curtain politics Frank Chapple so often decries.'[19] One aspect of this atmosphere was the abuse of the criticisms that the leadership received from its own members. Every criticism was labelled 'pro-Communist', much as they are labelled 'pro-capitalist' in much of Eastern Europe. In this atmosphere the opposition had to work underground.[20] They often despaired of change.

The highly publicised debate about democracy in the Labour Party provided an outside stimulus to change inside the union. For a start it provided a legitimate way of talking about democracy in terms other than Frank Chapple's. Steve Stevenson describes the impact:

It gave us some levers to open up the debate about democracy in our own union. For instance when Chapple started putting forward the 'one man, one vote' argument we'd say 'Why doesn't he apply it to area and national officers in the EETPU?' The same goes for the manifesto. The debate around NEC control of the manifesto enabled us to raise the issue of who controls policy in our union.

Until the democracy debate in the Labour Party, these critics, most of whom were active Labour Party members – some were councillors and constituency officers – had been isolated, not only in their own union but also, as EETPU members, from the rest of the trade unions and the Labour Party. Labour politicians, even those on the left, shied away from any involvement in EETPU politics.

The repercussions of the party's constitutional reforms within the EETPU, in particular the close association of Chapple and others in the leadership with the SDP, made public the question of the political future of the EETPU. This provided an opportunity for *Flashlight*, because it stimulated political debate, at least among union activists, in a way which was difficult to suppress. At its 1981 conference, several members of the EETPU leadership who were concerned by Chapple's connections with the SDP arranged the first political fringe meeting for over twenty years. They believed that it was possible for the right to regain control over the party. It was organised through Solidarity, the right-wing caucus – pressure group created by Roy Hattersley and others in 1981 in reaction to the successes of the left. Unintentionally, this provided *Flashlight* supporters with their first legitimate occasion on which to address, from the floor, a meeting of EETPU members and put their case for union democracy, as part of the argument for party democracy. As it was a public meeting for conference delegates, no one could easily stop them from putting their case, especially at a meeting that was supposed to be about democracy.

The next year, for the first time, *Flashlight* had its own fringe meeting, the evening before the conference. Half an hour before the meeting they were not too hopeful about its success:

We thought Stan Thorne [MP for Preston], the main speaker, might not turn up. In the past politicians were frightened to come anywhere near the EETPU, in case they got smeared. But Stan turned up and we've had eve-of-conference rallies ever since. The union's drift towards the SDP was the catalyst. It meant we got support when we argued in defence of what was going on in the Labour Party.

These were the comments of Tommy Lyons, the EETPU convenor at the Port Talbot steel works. Tommy saw the power struggle in the union over its political future almost first-hand. He sits on the National Political Advisory Committee as the South Wales representative; though this is not where the real decisions take place. The decisions take place on the executive and its political subcommittee. However, at the National Political Advisory Committee Lyons found himself being one of Eric Hammond's strongest supporters in putting the case for the Labour Party against several national officials who were floating the idea of disaffiliation and closer association with the SDP.

The campaign during the political fund ballot was another time when *Flashlight* supporters found a ready response to criticism of the political direction in which Chapple's political leadership was heading. The vote in favour of a political fund was 84 per cent, which was one of the highest of all unions.

These experiences inspired several shifts of emphasis by *Flashlight* and dissidents in the EETPU. First, they felt confident enough to work in a more open campaigning way. Second, they decided to direct that campaigning as much towards public exposure of the EETPU, especially to other trade unionists and Labour Party supporters, as towards their own members. 'We know ultimately that we can only change the union from the inside,' said Ian Brown, 'but with all the restrictions placed on us it is sometimes easier to reach many of the membership through using more public platforms and convincing the rest of the labour movement.'

This approach has been strengthened since Wapping. The EETPU's collaboration with News International, its lies about its involvement with Rupert Murdoch in preparing to recruit EETPU members in place of the existing print workforce, have set it apart, even from unions on the right of the TUC like APEX.[21]

At the 1986 Trade Union Congress, the majority of delegates voted to discipline the EETPU. The general council subsequently found – only by two votes – a procedure for inertia. But the repercussions of the feelings represented in that majority vote at Brighton will not disappear. Moreover, they have an effect on EETPU members themselves.[22] In many workplaces EETPU members and shop stewards work closely with members and representatives from other unions. The growing confidence and openness of dissidents like those in *Flashlight* has meant that criticisms and pressures from outside the union have a focus on the inside. The movement for constitutional reforms in the Labour Party and the debates this opened up in the union helped to establish this open opposition.

The National Union of Public Employees (NUPE)

While the EETPU condemned the constitutional reforms, NUPE were quick to support them and campaigned to carry them through. And while the impact of debates in the party in the EETPU was to politicise the internal regime of a union which projects an apolitical business image, in NUPE the impact was to crystallise a shift at all levels towards an explicitly political trade union.

The arguments for making the Parliamentary Party accountable accorded precisely with the lessons which NUPE leaders and activists were drawing from the experience of recent Labour governments. The Winter of Discontent, the discontent of millions of low-paid workers, was the watershed. For Tom Sawyer, appointed in 1981, as deputy to NUPE's General Secretary, Rodney Bickerstaffe, this was because:

it marked the end of a period in Labour politics: the Wilson–Callaghan years during which politics was handed down from the top and the membership of the unions and the party, let alone people beyond, were not involved in any kind of democratic development of policy, strategy or tactics.

The lesson which Sawyer draws from his explanation for the Winter of Discontent sums up the reason why many trade unions supported constitutional reform:

The unions and the Labour Party were not talking to each other. There was a certain arrogance on the part of the parliamentary leadership, who failed to listen to what the unions were saying. Every conference was saying, 'Don't push the 5 per cent on us.' But Callaghan ignored us. So the lesson is to ensure that the Labour leadership cannot again disregard what the trade unions have to say and to make certain that this gulf of understanding does not open up again.

He draws a further lesson, specifically for NUPE:

The lesson for NUPE was that in the future we had to be much more involved in the Labour Party. We had to be more of a political union than we had been in the past. This was not a matter of us in the leadership having to say, 'Come on now, we've got a completely new strategy.' Everybody in NUPE was saying, 'Look, this cannot happen again. We're going to have to have a much bigger influence on the Labour Party if we're going to get anything like the kind of things we need.'

NUPE has always been a relatively militant union since its formation as one side of a split in the Municipal Employees' Association in 1908. The other side merged with other unions to form the General and Municipal Workers' Union, now the GMB. Throughout the seventies, NUPE led strikes and other kinds of direct action against low pay, in defence of the NHS and against cuts in public spending. It made its name through strong stands over groups of workers, mainly women, who did not figure in the priorities of Congress House. Until recently its militancy has been almost exclusively industrial. It has rarely had wider political objectives and has never involved paying much attention to the Labour Party. This was largely a product of the apolitical tradition of public-sector trade unionism of which NUPE – 'the dirty jobs side of NALGO' – was part.

Gradually, since the public-spending cuts of 1976, and most dramatically after 1979, NUPE has become increasingly active in the Labour Party. In the last six years NUPE has increased its affiliation from 500,000 to 600,000 (its total membership is nearly 700,000), and the number of NUPE members standing for Parliament has grown from seven to forty – including twenty-five safe or easily winnable seats. There has been a general drive to encourage NUPE members to become more active in the party.

The motivation behind this is very different from that of the EETPU when it encourages members to become involved in the party. The EETPU stresses internal party issues, arguing for EETPU delegates in order to change the political balance in the party towards, as they put it, 'the people who are best able to interpret, and more importantly, *represent* working-class aspirations.'[23] John Spellar, the EETPU's National Political Officer, is quoted in the *Financial Times* as saying that these delegates 'do not need to attend meetings month after month; two or three times a year will be enough.'[24] By contrast, NUPE's emphasis is on the issues facing its members at work and is much more activist: 'How could you work together with your local Labour Party in a campaign against privatisation? And how could you ensure that the Labour Party's decision-makers took notice of your campaign?' These are the kind of questions that NUPE encourages its workplace 'discussion leaders' to raise on privatisation. The stress is on taking issues and ideas into the party, on making the party work for NUPE, and with NUPE.

In many ways NUPE's campaigning literature is more political than the Labour Party's! The contrast is accurate: on many issues NUPE *is* more radical than the Labour Party leadership. After all, the Labour Party is a coalition with unions like the AEU, EETPU and APEX. Sawyer expresses this contrast when he compares his role as Deputy General Secretary of NUPE with his role on the NEC of the Labour Party. On the NEC he tends to support Kinnock against left-wingers such as Tony Benn and Jo Richardson:

Certainly, the movement as a whole is more conservative than NUPE. [Being on the NEC] is a difficult responsibility because it's part of a very broad coalition, including unions led by people as diverse as Eric Hammond and Arthur Scargill. And so it involves me in making compromises. There are tensions because there are areas where your members don't want you to compromise.

He went on to give an example, low pay, on which he pushed for two-thirds of the national average (NUPE policy) to be a manifesto commitment as the figure for the national minimum wage (the national minimum wage itself has been party policy since 1981). But he was defeated. Roy Hattersley argued that it was too expensive and the majority of the NEC, including David Blunkett, voted against it. Since then Hattersley has been arguing that the minimum wage is itself no longer a priority.[25]

It is not only the Labour Party NEC that can be to the right of NUPE's national leadership. On some issues, notably the Deputy Leadership, it has also been NUPE's members. During the Deputy Leadership campaign, NUPE's leadership arranged a branch consultation. Most of the executive were in favour of Benn but they did not make a recommendation. The members voted in favour of Healey. This and other experiences of a gap between the members and the leadership on political issues has led to a strong emphasis on education and membership involvement in the union's campaigns and policy discussions.

Steven Walmsley, the elected Secretary of the Sheffield local government branch of NUPE, was in the middle of preparing for a weekend school in Scarborough about political organisation, when I went to talk to him. There are similar NUPE weekend schools throughout the country every year. Each region is responsible for organising the kind of school appropriate to local circumstances. What did 'education about political organisation' involve? Steve described some of the work that participants would (or should) be doing before and during the weekend:

Before they come they've been given a fairly simple task, to go and find out who their councillors are, what party, which ward they live in, who their MP is and what party he represents.

I will be giving them a session on the Sunday afternoon about the structure of the party, and then I'll say to them: 'Look, the council has representatives on the health authority and there's going to be a debate in three months at the health authority about privatisation; how would you set about influencing the decisions of these councillors? Think about that.'

One of the intentions behind these weekend schools is that the members who attend will be able to go back and act as teachers, in the literal meaning of 'teaching', as 'guiding', other members of their own branch. In 1986 they had around 1,300 'discussion leaders', that is people other than branch officers who would lead small discussions at work about issues that might not come up in the normal business of the branch.

This has proved vital to building support for industrial action on political issues such as privatisation and the job losses and deterioration of conditions that goes with it. In the north-east, NUPE members have helped to lead a forceful and imaginative campaign against the privatisation of cleaning, laundry and catering services. Guerrilla strikes, occupations of district health authority meetings and careful attention to explaining the arguments to the public have all been part of a generally successful campaign to keep private contractors out of the hospitals of Northumberland, Tyneside, Newcastle, Durham and Sunderland. It began with weekend schools for hospital branch officers – mainly women – with full-time NUPE officers explaining government policy, exploring with the branch officers what it would mean in their workplaces and discussing what could be done. The women then went back to their branches. Jean Ferguson, Branch Secretary at the Royal Victoria Infirmary, Newcastle, takes up the story:

For six months we had regular meetings where we'd explain with flip charts how the contractors would be brought in, who they were, how jobs had gone and conditions were disgraceful in hospitals wherever they'd come in. We showed the video prepared by ancillary staff on strike at Addenbrookes Hospital [Cambridge] which showed they'd brought in a fourteen-year-old to work . . . We had no already-worked-out strategy. There was none. The members had taken it out of our hands. They understood enough to know it had to be stopped, and stopped before the tendering took place.

The men and women at the RVI went on a series of guerrilla strikes,[26] and that was a few weeks after the miners' strike. They were soon joined by workers from St Nicholas's and other Newcastle hospitals. It was a highly political strike, against the district health authority and the government as much as their own management.

One result is that the women who led it are raring to join the Labour Party: 'I applied to join three weeks ago, and thought I'd get an application form back immediately. It's in hand now because I complained, but it's dead frustrating,' remarked Joyce Wilson, a branch officer and representative on the NUPE area committee. For Jean Ferguson, it was a matter of rejoining.

She'd let her membership lapse. 'The people at the meetings were all in their sixties and seventies. The ward had no go in it.' But she is joining again because she will be going as a NUPE delegate, with her branch supporting her and with a clear idea of what she wants the party to do:

For a start we've got to get the right people from the council onto the health authority. At present the Labour people are no good at all. I don't know whether they are elected. It seems as if there are all these committees floating around and whoever volunteers is allowed to go on. They don't even put party policy forward. They discuss closing hospitals and wards for about two minutes and then: 'Oh, that's right, we'll close that ward down.' They just go on what the district manager recommends. They are so remote. They haven't got a clue about the health service. You just feel like getting up and . . .

The political logic among the Tyneside health workers was exemplary: NUPE–Labour Party policy discussed and developed at weekend schools, taken by shop stewards to meetings of the members, the members deciding to take action which leads them to see the positions of power, or at least influence, held, but not used by Labour representatives, and then, finally, to add to their trade-union muscle by pressing for union policies in the Labour Party. In many ways this brings a new radical force into some of the Tyneside parties, dominated, as they were, by 'the old (right wing) guard'.

In Sheffield, a city whose Labour parties, as we have seen, have a stronger socialist tradition than on Tyneside, partly under Communist influence, NUPE delegates also represent a new force, especially in the district Labour Party. As the representation of engineering workers and steel workers falls away with industrial decline, NUPE branches often provide the largest delegation of manual workers:

If you take most average district delegate meetings, NUPE's attendance, not just from our branch but the other four in the city, the health service branches, we don't do bad really compared to most affiliated unions, especially those representing mainly manual workers. I've been to delegate meetings of around 100 and counted around thirteen NUPE delegates. Which isn't bad. Nearly half of them are women.

NUPE officials always make a point of highlighting the role of their women members. Women make up 66 per cent of their membership and the majority of their potential membership, so promoting women is a wise move. Does it have any wider political implications beyond its benefits for the women concerned – and by example, for women throughout the trade unions? In Newcastle it was certainly the women who were most energetic. Jean Ferguson talks from her experience:

In this branch, it's the women who are the most active, the leadership. It's our branch really. We've got time, after all we've only got three jobs, kids, husbands! . . . But in this union, though the women are in the majority of members, we have the least places on the important committees.

In the Northern Region there are eleven women on the Divisional Council of twenty-six. And if the women in Newcastle are anything to judge by, they will be making full use of these seats and gaining more: Joyce again:

Another thing about women. If you feel strongly about something you're more likely to just go ahead and do it. While men sort of sit back and talk themselves out of it, women just jump in with both feet.

It takes confidence before women discover and express these skills and abilities. And in general, confidence is the last thing that most trade-union meetings and procedures provide. Usually it is the experience of taking action, organising a strike or a campaign, which builds up workers' confidence. NUPE's education method, as Keith Hodgson, the Education Organiser for the north-east, put it, is 'action-based: we start from an issue that's hitting people and hope to end up discussing what can be done. Usually by that time the members have taken over the discussion.' By all accounts, women members in particular have thrived on this. Tom Sawyer comments from his experience:

Women in the union scream out, 'Don't tell us what we want, give us the space to tell you.' So what we try to do, especially through our schools, is try to make more time, make more space for members to draw up their own agenda.

The starting-point of this discussion was NUPE's decision to become a more political union. For NUPE, being a more political union does not mean simply wielding the bargaining power of its block vote to win resolutions and positions in the NEC and the general council – though with Rodney Bickerstaffe chairing the TUC Economic Committee and Tom Sawyer the Labour Party's Home Policy Committee they haven't done too badly in this. It also means encouraging and supporting the political activity of the members, particularly by developing the political and social ideas that are implicit in most trade-union action. This combination of political education and trade-union action, Bickerstaffe and Sawyer believe, is ultimately the only way to make the Parliamentary Party accountable to the trade unions and the party. One aspect of this has been the creation of a base, a source of pressure around policies agreed in opposition. Sawyer draws the lesson from the failure of the trade unions under the last Labour government to exert pressure:

The Social Contract was a deal struck by leaders; the radical side of it did not have any roots among the people. For instance the arguments for planning agreements had not really been put over to the people who worked in the industries. What I'm sure of is that you've got to really try and build your base as strongly as you can for the policies you want to implement. Unless you do that you won't be able to stand up to hostile forces.

Clearly, on health matters, a base is being built. After experience of the campaign against privatisation, Jean Ferguson believes that:

people are waiting for radical changes, and if they're not seeing them they're just not going to be fobbed off with wishy-washy policies. They want radical changes like democracy in the health service. The workers need a statutory minimum wage. They're talking of, what, £85 a week. Well, that's no good. It needs to be more like £120 a week.

And their own struggles have made the women leading the hospital branch in Newcastle cynical of Labour leaders, on the alert:

They can't take NUPE's support for granted. I mean it's a big block vote they get off NUPE. We should be putting pressure on now before the election, to let them see that if we don't get the policies we want . . . This is why we are getting the branch to affiliate. There are a lot of women like us now and we've got allies all over.

Steve Walmsley would agree with this:

What worries me is that a future Labour government will not be open. We might get into the old ball game of corporatism, beer and sandwiches

for the leaders but no delivery of policies. I hope we're learning from
the mistakes of the beer-and-sandwiches brigade.

If one of NUPE's intentions is to generate the pressure that
will overtake the tired corporatism of the TUC, then the signs
are that in several areas they are succeeding – in ways that
sometimes overtake NUPE's own leadership. However, the old
brigade are still there in Congress House and Westminster wishing they could get back with the beer and sandwiches.[27]

Two directions for trade unionism

The EETPU and NUPE represent entirely different responses to
the breakdown of corporatism: on the one hand a business
unionism going with the grain of the market, on the other
a social unionism encouraging in many areas a new kind of
working-class politics. The leadership of the EETPU takes the
existing structure of society as given, NUPE seek to change it.
The first represents workers whose wages have increased under
Thatcherism, the latter is one of several unions organising the
growing underclass of the low-paid.

The debate on low pay at the 1986 Trade Union Congress
illustrated well one aspect of this difference: their divergent
views on the relation between collective bargaining and political
action. Eric Hammond treated the debate about the statutory
minimum wage as a kind of trade-union virility test, implying
that the advocates of the statutory minimum wage were just
covering up their own impotence.[28] For the EETPU leadership,
trade unionism is a collective law of the jungle: 'We're in a free
market for trade unionism,' said one of their officers. The
fittest survive; the weak can go to the wall. And like all good
entrepreneurs they have a flexible approach to their product
range: strike-free deals to woo the multinationals to give them a
single-union agreement; free collective bargaining and militant
threats against the public sector and the older established employers; private health insurance and other individual services
to attract the new technocrats in industries and localities that
lack a trade-union tradition.

NUPE's trade unionism is in many ways more traditional: it
is explicitly about the strong helping the weak (they represent
mostly the weak but they have made a conscious effort to build

links with unions which represent the strong); it is about political action to back up industrial action and it is about defending collective services such as the health service, local government and education.

Some would call these latter principles old-fashioned. A notion has grown up, or rather been built up, that the EETPU represents newness, modernism, 'coming to terms with contemporary reality' in the trade-union movement. By this view everyone else is seen as either following the pace set by the EETPU or fast becoming a dinosaur of a bygone age. But NUPE illustrates that there are alternative ways of becoming 'modern'; there are political and industrial choices in how to respond to monetarism's restructuring of the economy. There are alternative principles by which to adapt recruitment and bargaining strategies to changes in the workforce; there are different objectives in responding to the manifest evidence that trade unions have in many areas lost touch with their members; and there are different political values in responding to the breakdown of the corporatist relations between the TUC, the government and the CBI.

Alternative responses to economic change

First consider responses to changes in the composition of the workforce. These changes vary according to the sector of the economy. In the private manufacturing sector, the labour market trends are away from the specialist craftsman and towards multi-skilled workers. There is a premium on flexibility. The only areas of growth are: first, of well-paid technical workers employed in non-union high-tech companies often situated in localities – new, or non-industrial towns – without a trade-union tradition; and secondly, of employment in plants of American or Japanese multinational corporations. In the public sector there has been a long-term upward trend in women's employment and in part-time jobs. In the last six years, with privatisation and cuts in spending, this employment has become increasingly insecure and low-paid. In private services and retailing, part-time and casual work for women has for long been the pattern. But these latter sectors are growing, in relation to both manufacturing and the public services.

The EETPU's recruitment strategy towards its new constituency rests heavily on making a deal with the employers by proving that the union can improve industrial relations and encourage co-operation. Their appeal is first to employers, to whom they offer an industrial relations package. Hammond puts it like this: 'We co-operate readily with fair employers. Many managements have good cause to be grateful for our efficiency, expertise and effort.' NUPE, on the other hand, makes direct appeals to its potential membership. It does so with campaigns, like the low-pay campaign, which demonstrate how they will take up their interests; or by spreading the word about effective action, including industrial action, taken with NUPE's backing by workers in related circumstances. The anti-privatisation strikes in the north-east, for instance, combined with astute publicity, gave a considerable boost to NUPE's recruitment in the area.

The differences in the approach of the two kinds of trade unionism in their communication with their memberships are along similar lines. The EETPU maintains contact and strengthens loyalty to the union through an extensive range of services: the notorious deal with BUPA, the health insurance company, enabling EETPU members to get reduced rates for private health care; advantageous rates for unit trusts; help for vehicle breakdown and recovery; special arrangements for mortgages; employer insurance for members who set up their own businesses, and so on. In these ways it treats the membership primarily as *clients* for whom the union provides a service, whereas NUPE's emphasis, as we have seen from the examples of Sheffield and Newcastle, is on providing the encouragement and support for membership participation in the union. NUPE, like most unions, also provides individual services, but the union's main communication with the members is through strengthening involvement in the branch, spreading education and teaching to every workplace and initiating regular campaigns, often on issues raised by the membership.

Through its involvement with its members – predominantly female – NUPE's leadership, although predominantly male, has a more 'modern' and more egalitarian understanding of sexual politics. While Eric Hammond can attack London Labour parties for containing 'terrorists, lesbians and other queer people',[29] NUPE, along with several other unions, has affiliated to gay and lesbian rights campaigns and produces leaflets attacking discrimination against gays and lesbians.

Corporatism under attack

A fundamental difference, which leads back to the relationships between the unions and the Labour Party, concerns the unions' responses to the breakdown of (at least formally) close relations with government. Since the Second World War, British trade unions, through the TUC, had become increasingly part of a consultation process in the state's management of the economy (with a brief interruption between 1970 and 1973). One historian of this corporatist bias in the British state, Keith Middlemas, went so far as to argue that:

The extension of economic management in postwar years . . . has only been possible because of the existing nature of the triangular (trade unions, employers and the government) system, and the power, inherent in corporate bias, of governing institutions (the trade-union leaderships, CBI, and government) to convey popular consent by means other than political parties.[30]

Just at the moment when this triangular system was in collapse – the height of the strikes against the Labour government in the winter of 1978–79 – the TUC produced a classic statement of the ethos behind it and, as the TUC optimistically believed, the role of the TUC within it:

There is no answer in confrontation. Solutions to our problems have to be found in agreement. But agreement will only be possible if our people all recognise that we are part of a community of interest . . .

The government, business, financial institutions, and the trade unions, by their action help to decide how the economy performs . . . it imposes on the TUC, with its broad and undisputed representative capacity, the need to accept that its expanding role carries with it wider responsibilities.[31]

Thatcher's radicalism was aimed precisely at this form of government: 'socialist mediocrity' she called it. She saw no use for 'representational means of winning popular consent'; Labour's representative institutions anyway, she claimed, no longer had the credibility to win consent. Insofar as the unions had credibility, it was dangerous for a government to build up their status. She has preferred to achieve endorsement, or at least acquiescence, through her own person. She challenged the representative character of the unions, aiming to reveal, as she saw it, their true sectional character by throwing them out of the institutions that gave them social and political status. (They were still allowed to stay, indeed were positively encouraged to remain in lesser institutions of state, where the government *did* need their visible co-operation: for instance the Manpower Services Commission and the National Economic Development Council).

The trade unions responded to being thrown out of the corridors of Whitehall in three different ways.

The EETPU represented one kind of response: to go along with the Thatcherite industrial revolution and be the union best placed to benefit. Its policy is to co-operate with management, to equate the interests of trade-union members with the competitive success of the firm, and to base trade-union bargaining on this strictly commercial, business view. Not surprisingly, this kind of trade unionism is held out as a model by Conservatism politicians. 'This, to me, is what good trade unionism should be about,' remarked Kenneth Clarke, talking of the EETPU at the 1985 Party Conference. Norman Tebbit, opening the EETPU's high-tech training centre at Cudham in Kent, praised its 'progressive approach'.[32] It is the EETPU's commercial rather than social or political approach to negotiations with employers, and also the client relationship to its members, which wins the praise of the 'party of business' – in fact both parties of business, for the Alliance approves too – and makes the term 'business unionism' an appropriate description of what the EETPU represents. But, as we shall see, this does not rule out an instrumental but nevertheless influential commitment to the Labour Party.

The opposite response to the breakdown of corporatism is evident in NUPE's development since the 'Winter of Discontent' and the collapse of the Social Contract. Throughout the corporatist years, NUPE had always been something of an outsider to the beer-and-sandwiches brigade,' maintaining a militant syndicalism and a stroppy independence from government, other than as an employer. With the collapse of corporatism NUPE, increasingly along with COHSE, USDAW, leading sections of the GMB and the T&GWU, in its own way the NUM, and others, became themselves, as unions, more directly political. This has had two aspects: greater involvement at all levels in the Labour

Party and more novel attempts to highlight and take action around the political implications of its campaigns and its disputes. NUPE's anti-privatisation strikes in the north-east, with their campaigns to reach the public and their pressure on the district health authorities, are a good example.

Bickerstaffe and Sawyer say they learnt two main things from the 'Winter of Discontent'. First, the importance of legislation to back up trade-union action. Sawyer's support for the leadership of the Labour Party is motivated above all by the determination to achieve a statutory minimum wage. Second, they believe they learnt the importance of reaching out to the majority of the public and winning their support for the services in NUPE members' work. Their literature constantly stresses the case for the services and the link between providing good services and the wages and conditions of those who provide them.

A comparison between NUPE and the NUM indicates different kinds of political and social trade unionism arising from different traditions and circumstances. Like NUPE, the majority of the NUM leadership have for some time seen the need for a more political trade unionism. However, as a union they are far less geared up for public political campaigning on the wider issues of the future of the coal industry, the needs of mining communities and the alternative directions for government energy policy. This is not because they do not take these wider issues seriously. On the contrary they devoted huge resources to presenting their case against nuclear power to the inquiry into Sizewell B.[33] And in most areas they were extremely responsive to the campaigns of others on these issues during the recent strike.

The reasons for the difference of emphasis lie in the force of habitual thinking, customary responses and deeply established institutions. In the NUM, all these bearers of tradition and continuity are premised on industrial strength. And on such a premise popular political campaigning tends to become a low priority – at least as far as the day-to-day routine is concerned. NUPE by contrast has never been able to rely on such strength. For them a new emphasis on political campaigning is an obvious building of their strength. The weight of a contrary tradition does not bear down on them.

The NUM has yet to adapt to the decline of its industrial strength. This does not mean turning its back on industrial action. It means adopting as its own the kind of popular campaigning carried out on its behalf during the strike.

There is a third response to Thatcher's abrupt end to the tripartism to which members of the TUC General Council had grown so accustomed. This involved believing that in spite of all the Conservative bravado, the government would in the end invite them round the negotiating table. If not, it would not be long before the Labour Party would be in the chair and invitations would be automatic. The government's ban on the unions at GCHQ was something of a blow to these hopes and led the TUC to withdraw temporarily from the NEDC. But in the TUC the expectations remain of a return to business as normal. In this respect some members of the TUC, Norman Willis naturally being the prime example, are like rather complacent civil servants, confident in their own immortality, knowing that politicians act ephemerally and that their time will come once more. Ultimately, tripartite agreements – the holy trinity of employers, trade-union leaders and the state – are the way they have always been; that is the way to which everyone will return, 'in the fulness of time'.[34, 35]

Some unions contain all three kinds of response. The GMB is an example of doing all at once. For instance in their Northern Region (perhaps a mark of the desperate plight of any union in the north-east) they make single-union, pendulum arbitration agreements[36] with multinationals; but they also organise large open educational and campaigning conferences on energy policy, on the MSC, against the Fowler social security proposals, and they support the left-dominated Trades Council's Centre for the Unemployed, working with a variety of campaigning groups outside the official channels. The old ways have not worked; any new avenue is worth trying, but they keep their hand in with the old ways too, just in case . . .

Nationally, the GMB has made a dramatic turn towards organising women and other low-paid and part-time workers. In part it is a survival strategy at a time when the union has lost 23 per cent of its members (discounting its merger with the Boilermakers' Union) in six years, and when there are few prospects for union growth in the more male-dominated manufacturing industries. But it is also one of several outcomes of the political shake-up in the GMB to which I referred earlier in this chapter.

It is not an easy turn for the GMB to make. And there is a certain amount of passive resistance to it from an old guard of full-time officials. Traditionally the strength of these officials and the union apparatus has been in negotiating with their employers not in organising their membership. The General Secretary, John Edmonds, admits the problem:

The new approach is very much against the tradition of the union. We are a union where we train officers to be good negotiators. We have some of the best people for administering joint trade-union agreements in the business. But what we are not good at is organising, campaigning and recruiting. We do not have, as a stock-in-trade of the GMB official, that ability to go out. We have to learn it or relearn it and it's very, very hard. We have to lever people out of committee rooms into the outside world.

The other union which is levering its officers out of the committee rooms and into the streets and the unorganised work-places is the Transport and General Workers' Union. By contrast with the GMB, the T&GWU does have a tradition of organising, established at shop-floor and local level in, for instance, organising the growing motor industry in the forties and fifties and, for a time, reflected and encouraged in the national apparatus by Frank Cousins and Jack Jones. Much of the vitality of this tradition was lost during the period of the Social Contract, followed by the somewhat passive incapacitated leadership of Moss Evans. The present divisions within the T&GWU and the emergence of a pragmatic right wing are a consequence of this decline in the union's campaigning and organising activity. The background to this decline is the body-blow that the union has suffered from unemployment: a 29 per cent drop in membership in the last six years and an immeasurable loss of bargaining strength. But it is also the result of over-confidence and complacency amongst those on the left in official positions. As some of them recognise, once they had won control of the union they did not work concertedly to maintain and renew their popular base.

Ron Todd and his deputy, Bill Morris, have taken the initiative to put right some of these omissions of the past by launching a massive campaign called 'Link Up' to organise the low-paid and the unorganised, which particularly means women and black people.[37] It is combined with attempts to encourage political debate and awareness throughout the union. The *T&GWU Record* now tries to stimulate debate and controversy on sensitive political issues such as nuclear power and defence, where before the paper, for instance the letters page, was strictly non-controversial. The union's political education scheme has been stepped up so that last year over 20,000 branch and workplace representatives attended at least one of its weekend courses, led mainly by tutors and officers on the left of the union.

The political positions of the T&GWU, or at least its most recent conference, are very similar to NUPE except that it does not support the proposal for a statutory minimum wage. But building the T&GWU into a campaigning political union is a far more difficult task than it is with NUPE, even if its leadership were united. NUPE is a relatively compact and homogeneous union whose resources are not tied down on hundreds of different negotiations. It covers five main areas of the public sector – health, education, water and gas. The T&GWU by contrast is a vast sprawling organisation, whose members face very different conditions. It contains many centres of power: eleven powerful regional organisations and fourteen trade groups of varying weight. And continuously it involves its officials in a large number of negotiations. The full-time officials in strategic positions throughout this sprawling structure vary considerably in their political and trade-union approach. There are some who perpetuate right-wing machine politics which have not been entirely rooted out since Arthur Deakin's days (the West Midlands Region is such a case). There are others following in the early Jack Jones tradition: supporting shop-floor initiative and emphasising political education (the South-East Region contains several officers in this tradition).

If the T&GWU were won fully to the side of left-wing political and campaigning trade unionism it would cause waves throughout the trade-union movement, further isolating the EETPU. Whether it will be or not depends not only on the abilities of the left among the leadership but on the extent to which a new surge of confidence and militancy develops in the workplaces.

The miners' strike: phantom negotiations

The miners' strike showed business unionism, political unionism and the corporatist fantasy all at work and in conflict. The EETPU, accepting the new dominance of (politically led) market forces was aggressively hostile to the miners' case, treating it as a sectional interest opposed to that of their members elsewhere in the energy industry. It went through the formality of balloting its members in the electricity supply industry. But with the ballot form, Fred Franks, the union's national officer for the electricity supply industry, sent an aggressive open letter saying why he thought the TUC was wrong to support the miners. It also said:

The NUM, often through misinformation, opposes the use of nuclear power. It promotes an energy policy that would leave coal as the sole fuel for power stations, at a price decided by the NUM. This is a frightening prospect for our distribution members, already facing major problems in competing with gas. Spiralling costs will also assist the growth of private generation in areas where competition is not currently viable.

For the EETPU the NCB was just another business, and the miners' leaders were using the dispute to further their own political objectives.

The NUM's perception of the end of corporatism was essentially similar to that of NUPE, in spite of the difference in the character of their membership, their traditions and their style of leadership.

The NUM, like NUPE, recognised the concerted political attack which the government was making on centres of trade-union strength and the corporatist institutions, such as their own employer, the Coal Board. The NUM saw their conflict with the government, both the overtime ban and the 1984 strike, as both industrial and political: their members' needs were industrial but the obstacle to meeting these needs was political.

Some commentators on the strike have inferred from Scargill's talk of the strike as 'political' that he had insurrectionary intentions. Martin Adeney and John Lloyd put this view most explicitly.[38] They go on to argue that because of this revolutionary objective he greatly prolonged the strike, preventing a partial victory and 'a decent end'. This was also the view of those in the trade-union and party leadership who clung to the notion that corporatism was alive and waiting, and it was a crucial factor in the thinking of Neil Kinnock. I would argue that this view is based on an underestimation of Thatcher's determination to eliminate trade-union resistance to monetarist policies and MacGregor's equally single-minded obsession to achieve this goal for the coal industry.

It assumes that there *was* the chance of partial victory and a 'decent end'. From statements by Conservative politicians, from Ian MacGregor and Ned Smith, the director-general of industrial relations at the NCB (who along with Stan Orme tried to find the scope for a 'decent end') and from detailed analyses carried out by several journalists close to events, it seems clear that MacGregor and the government wanted nothing short of total victory and were prepared to pay the price of a long strike to achieve it. There is not the space here for a detailed analysis of each of the negotiations, but the issue at stake is important. Judgements about the character of the present leadership of the labour movement and of the left have depended on it. So I will summarise some vital evidence, skated over by the most influential commentators, and make particular use of the judgement of Ned Smith, who made his views known only after several of the major studies of the strike were complete.

There were three moments when serious negotiations seemed to be under way: July 1984, October 1984 and January 1985. Ned Smith was involved in all of them. An ex-union official, he stood for exactly the ordered, 'decent' industrial relations that the TUC and Labour leaders thought could win the day. His judgement seems to be the closest one could get to an objective assessment of the good faith of the two sides in finding a settlement.

Ned Smith resigned from his job on October 19 1984, half-way through the strike, because he disagreed with Ian MacGregor's conduct of the strike, in particular MacGregor's refusal to seriously search for a settlement. As he put it later in Philip Whitehead's Channel 4 series on Cabinet government: 'It became clear, as the strike went on . . . that there was no intention of settling with the NUM. I mean they were asked to subscribe to things that no trade union would have subscribed to, unnecessarily.' However, Smith returned for the negotiations at ACAS on

October 23, and again in January 1985, when he initiated talks, with, so he thought, MacGregor's approval. Mark Hollingsworth, a freelance journalist who carried out much of the research for the *Mirror*'s industrial editor Geoffrey Goodman's book on the strike, went to interview Smith in November 1984. Smith made it clear to Hollingsworth that MacGregor was determined that the Coal Board should not settle: the main block to a settlement was not Scargill's intransigence, but the NCB and, behind them, Thatcher. Smith told Hollingsworth that he was convinced there could be a settlement with the NUM, if only the Board was willing to make it.[39] This was why he returned on January 21 to have one last try with the NUM. Hollingsworth's description of the events of this day, based on his conversation with Smith, gives a vivid impression of Smith's sense of the betrayal of the proper industrial relations that he had always practised at the Coal Board:

On the afternoon of Monday January 21 1985, Ned Smith, the National Coal Board's Director-General of Industrial Relations, and Peter Heathfield, the NUM's General Secretary, met for talks to try to resolve the miners' strike. They met in some secrecy (at the NCB's pension-fund office in Cavendish Square) as it was the first meeting between management and the unions for three months. In order to prevent any premature disclosure, the Coal Board issued only a brief statement at 1 p.m. confirming the meeting: Michael Eaton, the Board's chief spokesman, cancelled all his briefings for the day.

The talks went extremely well. Smith produced a draft agreement, which the NUM Executive later agreed was a basis for a negotiated settlement. However, as Heathfield left the meeting at 3.15 p.m. to report back to Congress House, he bought a copy of the *Evening Standard* – and was amazed to read the front-page banner headline: 'Peace talks collapse'. Smith also saw the story and went to the NCB headquarters to ask Eaton how the *Standard* had managed to produce a verdict on the talks while they were still going on. Eaton reassured him that the story was completely untrue and that a settlement was still a possibility. But when Smith returned to his home in Kent that evening he was astonished to see Eaton on Channel Four News confirming that the talks had collapsed and that there was no prospect of further negotiations with the NUM.

The possibility of a negotiated settlement had, in fact, not been torpedoed by the Coal Board but by Mrs Thatcher. As soon as the government knew that the Smith–Heathfield talks were happening (from about noon) Bernard Ingham, the Prime Minister's press secretary, began briefing political correspondents that the meeting had failed. By 3 p.m. most members of the lobby had been told by Downing Street that the initiative had got nowhere. This was *while* the talks were still taking place – the meeting didn't end until *3.15 p.m.*[40]

The belief that a partial victory could have been achieved if it had not been for the revolutionary motives of Arthur Scargill underestimates the extent to which Thatcher meant what she said when she insisted that there could be no compromise. Her motives were not simply revenge for 1974 and a determination to show that she could win where Heath could not, nor hatred for Scargill as the symbol of all that she most feared from the working class as an organised force. These motives were no doubt at work, but her determination was more firmly, and materially, based. It flowed from an objective fundamental to her premiership: the cutting back of union power to submit to market pressures. Any negotiation which left the NUM with a lever against market forces would destroy her whole strategy; it would have been a submission to the same forces that imposed a U-turn on Edward Heath. Francis Pym provides further corroboration for this assessment:

There is a myth about the miners' strike, usually propagated by the Labour Party, that a ready compromise lurks somewhere in the wings. It is hinted that only the government's intransigence prevents a solution, and that others more flexible . . . would end the strike in no time. This is nonsense. However it is dressed up, the final outcome will be a defeat for one side or the other . . .[41]

Throughout the strike Roy Hattersley and Neil Kinnock kept warning against insurrection and revolution, and by implication imputed such motives to the NUM leadership. In fact, although the consequences of its success would have massively weakened the government, as the miners' strike did in 1972 and 1974, the 1984–5 strike was no more revolutionary than NUPE's anti-privatisation strikes, or the miners' strikes of the seventies. All involved defensive industrial action against a determined political attack. They became political strikes because their industrial demands faced political resistance. They were political without being revolutionary.

This distinction could not be grasped by many TUC and

party leaders. They did not want to grasp it. These men talked constantly as if the NUM's claim, or as I would argue, recognition of a fact, that the strike was political implied that it was revolutionary. This suited Thatcher very well. It is part of the explanation for why the Parliamentary Labour Party did not consistently scrutinise the *political* conduct of the Coal Board.[42] It never even insisted on a parliamentary debate. It left the NUM to fight an essentially political strike by the only means, trade-union means, at their disposal. In effect an *ad hoc* party formed to fill the vacuum: Women Against Pit Closures and the informal national network of Miners' Support Groups.[43] But without a national, parliamentary lead, challenging the government's definition of the issues, the strike was ultimately isolated from the popular support it needed to win.[44]

The absence of this parliamentary political lead requires an explanation. This has several aspects. The most obvious involves the persistence of the defensive approach to electoral strategy which I analysed in Chapter 2. Everything done by Scargill and the NUM was seen as a 'hostage to fortune'. Every eye was on the short-term polls. There was no understanding of the longer-term impact the government's behaviour might have on its popularity;[45] no willingness to take risks and attack, rather than respond. But this needs further explanation. Why was a strategy that went on the political offensive such anathema? I would suggest that the answer lies in the deeply rooted assumption, described above, that public-sector industrial relations are ultimately corporatist, so that an assertion by the strikers of the political character of their strike appeared as a challenge to what was, in fact, a phantom framework of corporatist government, overthrowing the imagined negotiating tables. It therefore appeared to be revolutionary, the biggest 'hostage to fortune' of all.

The final impossibility of a negotiated settlement was not only a defeat for the miners, it was also a defeat for the last remaining corporatists, leaving the powerless figure of Norman Willis standing by bewildered, pinning everything on the return of a Labour government and the restoration of the TUC to its proper negotiating position. The EETPU gloated and exploited the disarray in the TUC to do a deal with Murdoch. The politically minded unions licked their wounds and learnt some lessons. The lessons learnt by NUPE and the left of the T&GWU and activists through-out the trade unions led them back to the basic tasks of organis-ing, educating and agitating. I have described this trend earlier. Many experiences have fed into it too. The miners' strike was one of them because it revealed how deeply workers' responses to the idea of solidarity action had changed since the early seventies – not only as a result of Conservative legislation – and therefore how the basis for solidarity had to be rebuilt.

Polarisation

The trade-union movement is thus becoming increasingly polar-ised, with the corporatist trend disintegrating in favour of trends in two quite opposite directions. In the private sector, the obvious first base for business unionism, the EETPU has not been having it all its own way, in spite of the hype. Its membership has continued to decline, by over 100,000 in the last eight years. It faces a continued threat from the declining demand for craft-workers and the fact that an increasing number of craftworkers are gaining the status of technician (because of the flexible skills involved) for whom the EETPU has no negotiating rights. This is made worse by the creation of a technician's 'super-union' through the merger of ASTMS and TASS. The final details of this new union, including its name, have yet to be settled, but it poses a serious threat to the EETPU at a time when the craftworker is giving way to the technician.

Neither are its plans for growth through merger going accord-ing to plan. The National Council of the AEU voted in 1987 that the election of officers would be a condition of any merger it entered into. It should be clear from my earlier description of the EETPU's rules that this would be a very difficult condition for the EETPU to meet. The EETPU's attempts at a loose alliance of the right have also come to nothing. In 1985 it floated the idea to representatives of the AEU, UCATT and APEX, under the heading of 'Project 2000'. But the executives of UCATT and APEX decided to have nothing to do with it.

The EETPU's co-operation with News International has, as I have already mentioned, reinforced this isolation. So has its all-out war for members, in the course of which it ignores TUC agreements (notably the Bridlington agreement) against unions poaching each other's members. Neither have its distinctive strategies for the private sector gathered the expected momentum; its no-strike agreements cover only 25 per cent of the total workforce in manufacturing.

In the public sector, at least, the moves towards a political unionism are stronger. Here union strength has not declined to the same extent as in the private sector. Between 1979 and 1985 the EETPU lost 20 per cent of its membership, the T&GWU a staggering 29 per cent, the AUEW 24 per cent, and ASTMS 21 per cent, whereas NUPE lost only 3 per cent and NALGO actually gained 2 per cent. The confidence to fight is still there, when given a lead.

The nature of the government's attacks has provoked an increasingly political response, including reactions from unions not affiliated to the Labour Party, for example NALGO's £1.2 million advertising campaign against privatisation. The highly successful campaign to defend the unions' political funds, for instance, led to the creation of political funds by unions who had never previously had them (the Inland Revenue Staff Federation, the clinical section of the National Communication Union and the Broadcasting and Entertainments Trade Alliance). It also led several unions to suddenly discover the skills of campaigning and communication with their members and workplace representatives; although in many cases the unions' relationship with their members went back to normal as soon as it was over.

The example set by NUPE and NALGO, the campaign around the political funds ballot and, perhaps most important, the attacks from the government, have been a catalyst to a more political and campaigning approach among other unions, especially those responsible for the lower-paid and those in the public sector.

This polarisation will find expression within the Labour Party too. So far it has remained latent because of the priority of unity around the Leader until the election. But the role of the two kinds of trade unionism within the party will be decisive to the party's future. Let us consider each in more detail.

Some political journalists (such as Peter Jenkins of the *Independent* and Peter Kellner of the *New Statesman*)[46] imply that the logic of the EETPU's business unionism is towards disaffiliation from the Labour Party. While the EETPU and the AEU are likely to reduce their affiliation fee to the Labour Party – partly because of their financial difficulties due to membership decline – the idea that they might disaffiliate overestimates the ideological nature of the trade union–party links and underestimates the power that the business union wing has within the party. It also takes insufficient account of the support for the Labour Party amongst EETPU members, which is indicated indirectly by the size of the vote in favour of the political ballot.

For the EETPU, as for most unions the party–union links are fundamentally instrumental: they add another weapon to the armoury for trade-union advancement and so will not be given up lightly, even though Labour has lost its monopoly as the alternative party of government. The fact that a union becomes 'apolitical' and market-oriented in its industrial bargaining strategy does not necessarily mean that it will spurn influence within a political party that could help to create – even in a pact with other parties – more favourable conditions for its industrial negotiations. The Alliance cannot offer such influence. It wants nothing to do with trade-union affiliations, and the SDP leadership are not even keen to talk to trade-union leaders who have any Labour attachment. The 1987 election result has further reduced the attraction of the Alliance to right-wing unions.

The brief flirtation of the EETPU leadership with the SDP was a distinctively Frank Chapple initiative, produced by his anger at the strength of the left in the party and the inability of the right and centre to get organised. He recruited John Grant, an SDP member and ex-Labour MP to head the union's Press and Publicity Department. But the present leadership, Eric Hammond and John Spellar, are firmly – though still instrumentally – pro-Labour, without any of Chapple's political instability. Some of them are pro-coalition as well, but this does not necessarily imply a weakening of links with Labour; it is rather an adaptation of the use of these links to the circumstances of a three-party system.

Since the early eighties the union's apparatus has become increasingly politicised in terms of a commitment to the right wing of the Labour Party. That is, it has become a very well-oiled machine for rebuilding the Labour Party as the party of right Labourism. Along with APEX and the AUEW, the EETPU supports Solidarity, the organisation of the right and centre, and uses its apparatus to promote Solidarity's objectives on policy and organisation. The party's organisation is the priority. A periodical, *Political Bulletin*, put out by John Spellar, the national officer and parliamentary candidate for Northfield, gives a flavour of their priorities. This goes to all EETPU branches and EETPU members who are individual members of the Labour Party. In the September 1986 issue the lead article, headed 'The NEC – Let's Get It Right', urged Labour Party delegates to vote for the Solidarity slate, and attacked the left in an unrestrained manner as 'generals of gesture' and 'out for self-publicity'. The impression given is of a determined and confident campaign to mobilise the EETPU to drive out, or at least subordinate, the left and reconstruct the party. There is no balanced presentation or assessment of debate within the party; no information about the left to allow the readers to judge for themselves. It is explicitly and unashamedly the bulletin of a faction.

Moreover, it reads like the bulletin of a faction which is there to stay. It implies that the EETPU has a long-term view which will persist through even a third election defeat for Labour. It is confident that electoral logic will draw other trade unions towards its approach. The prize is a return to a party rebuilt in its image, over which it has influence.

This then is the political logic of *one* of the attempts to develop new trade-union strategies for the problems presented by the Thatcherite economy: business unionism is one description, aggressive sectionalism would be another. It has all the elements of a collectivist Thatcherism. As we have seen, the EETPU is not alone, even though it has become isolated recently. Besides the AEU it often gains the support of APEX. It is a determined and potentially powerful block: it represents modern Labourism and is as determined as the Labourism of Bevin and Citrine to have a *labour* rather than a socialist party, let alone a radical socialist party with all its 'feminists, trendies, blacks and gays'.

For business unionism most of the activity described earlier in constituency parties, in local councils, in women's sections and black sections is a huge and damaging diversion. When other feminists refer to the 'men's movement' I interpret the phrase selectively. Many (if not most) gatherings of trade-union men, as of most men, exclude women in all kinds of explicit and tacit ways. But it is to this grouping in the trade-union movement –

proudly sectional, narrowly economic, and, in the case of the
EETPU, ruthlessly centralised – that the phrase most accurately
applies. It assumes a remarkably homogeneous working class for
which it claims to speak, not only in its negotiating strategies
but in all its cultural and political opinions too. And it wants a
party which will speak with the same voice.

It intends to achieve this, first, by defending trade-union
power within the party and, second, by diluting the political life
of the constituency parties. As far as defending trade-union
power is concerned, this section of unions is likely to oppose
proposals to reduce the voting proportion of the trade unions at
conference. These proposals, likely to be considered along with
other options after the general election, involves allocating voting
strengths according to financial contributions. Trade-union
'affiliated' members theoretically pay an annual subscription of
75p, whereas constituency party members pay £10 (unwaged
£3). When this is calculated together with the members of each
(there are 6 million affiliated members and 250,000 individual
members) it works out that CLPs should have around 20 per
cent of the vote rather than the present 10 per cent. Other groups
argue for voting parity. Still others point to the electoral college
for the Leader and Deputy Leader as a model. These proposals
weaken Labourism and create the conditions for radical socialism. They will be resolutely opposed by the business unions, as
will such proposals as women's seats on the NEC being directly
elected by the Women's Conference. They are not a high priority
for the party leadership – except insofar as they are part of the
realpolitik which determines present constitutional disputes.

The other indication of its move against socialism is its desire
to introduce one member one vote through postal ballots at
constituency level for the selection and reselection of MPs. Postal
ballots would open the way for absentee politics; they would
sanctify a non-participatory party and devalue party meetings
and collective debate. They would be an important step towards
the depoliticising and what some have called 'Americanisation'
of the Labour Party – though with the important difference
from the US Democrats that it would remain, at least formally,
trade-union based. Thus the dream of modern Labourism is to
see the dead souls of Labour providing the 'base' of the constituency parties as well as the trade unions.

246 LABOUR: A TALE OF TWO PARTIES

Political unionism and Labour

Political unionism takes a different view. Rather than depoliticising the constituency parties they favour strengthening their position and increasing the active participation of unions within them. For instance, NUPE and the left in the T&GWU support the idea that the constituency parties should have more voting power at conference. They are more sympathetic to the proposals from the Women's Conference. And though they have mixed views on 'one person, one vote' and the different forms it could take, they oppose the secret ballots. At a leadership level, however, attitudes to party reform are hedged with caution, especially in the wake of an election defeat. In some cases, as we saw with NUPE, they are more confident about taking radical stands as a union than within the party. The gap between campaigning trade unionism and defensive politics within the party is also a result of the new, post–1983, electoral circumstances. This gap could grow wider. It could lead trade-union leaders who are on the left as far as trade-union and policy issues are concerned into allying with the trade-union right to marginalise the left in the party, in the interests, as they see it, of electoral success. This prospect springs from the pervasive view discussed in Chapter 2, that the left is the cause of Labour's electoral decline, a view which is influential even when it is not simplistically held. Left-inclined trade-union leaders face a direct clash between the kind of political trade unionism necessary to resist government policies and the Labour leadership's timid attempts to court electoral popularity.

The likely political future of the new, more political trade unions does not depend entirely on their leaderships. More fundamental will be the extent to which trade-union resistance reasserts itself after the election. Among those still at work the organisational strength of the unions is still sufficiently intact for this to be possible.[47] Rising profits in the private sector and sustained attacks on working conditions in the public sector make it likely: there are plenty of dammed-up expectations, and much suppressed anger. In the public sector, low pay and bad conditions have already led to a new surge of militancy among groups such as teachers and civil servants who have never previously taken sustained industrial action. Such militancy among further groups, for instance local government or health workers faced with privatisation, will have significant political repercussions.

As we have seen, the distinctive feature of the Labour Party, a source of its radicalism and a pressure for its conservatism, is its direct links with the unions. The party's founding constitution sought to establish a dignified distance between Labour's parliamentary representatives and the demands of the industrially organised working class. It sought to have the best of both worlds: parliamentary respectability and trade-union loyalty. Nevertheless the character of trade-union militancy or the lack of it underlies the political direction of the party. Trade-union quiescence gave a free rein to the political right and centre, for instance in the 1950s. Trade-union militancy creates an awareness and collective self-confidence which responds to the political lead of the left as it did in the 1970s, after Labour's parliamentary leadership had disappointed trade-union hopes.

Until the seventies and the divisions in Labour's transformative tradition, the Labour left was not inclined to become as involved as political activists with trade-union initiatives. Its faith in Westminster gave it little reason to see the significance of workers' self-organisation beyond its defensive trade-union role. It wanted left-wing leaders to be elected, because that would swing the block votes their way. But that was an internal matter for the unions, with a few informal nudges here and there. The new Labour left, by contrast, as we have seen, has a different view. Workers' organisation and initiative became for it part of a challenge to the elite character of the British state. Consequently the new left, from the Campaign Group through to the left of the Labour Co-ordinating Committee, responds positively to workers' actions, turning the formal trade union–party links into an active relationship.

This is particularly noticeable at a constituency level. I found evidence of this in the survey I carried out of a random sample of constituency delegates at the 1986 conference. Fifty four per cent of the sample answered yes to the question 'Have your party's links with the unions become more active over the last ten years?' Thirty-seven per cent said a lot. Sixteen and a half per cent said a little. When I asked what form this increase in activity had taken, eighty-four per cent said 'active party support for trade-union disputes', sixty per cent said 'joint initiatives and campaigns'. Forty per cent had elected a trade-union liaison officer.

The new relationship is also reflected in the activities of the Campaign Group of MPs. The initiators of the Campaign Group, after the 1979 election, saw their role as parliamentary campaigners for the movements and struggles based in the workplace, the community and the streets. Their wholehearted involvement in building support for the miners, inside and outside Parliament, illustrated this most forcefully. They are now exploring how to consolidate their links with the left in the unions into some lasting organisation.

There is still however an uneasy tension between a continuation of the old Labour left tradition, where the only contact between politicians and the left in the unions was through left-inclined general secretaries, and the more workplace and local focus of the new left. Working through left general secretaries appears to offer a tempting short cut, especially to winning votes at conference. But the experience of the last ten years, the shift to the right in the AEU, the votes for Healey in unions led by the left, the precarious position of the left in the T&GWU, have been among the factors leading the Campaign Group to work with the active membership as much as with leadership. The tensions unavoidably remain, but members of the Campaign Group seem willing to face them as they arise.

The new left's attempts to overcome Labourist and parliamentarist taboos on a political relationship with trade-union activists also raise the fundamental issue of the unions' corporate, or block, power within the party. It is this power which makes the Labour Party ultimately a trade-union party rather than a socialist party. Trade unions are not socialist; as we have seen there will always be a limit on the radicalism of the most political unionism as far as the union as a whole is concerned. On the other hand there are significant minorities of socialists amongst the individual members which could grow as a result of argument, debate and experience. The block vote is such that these minorities are not reflected in the decision-making of the party.

Historically the Labour left has evaded this problem in various ways: their labourism meant they would not mount any sustained attempt to transform the constitution. Bevan for instance spoke as if he assumed that the mass of trade-union members were socialists but simply were not represented by their right wing leaders: 'I represent your membership as much as you do,' he said in frustration as the block votes swung to the right at conference after conference. But as over a third of affiliated trade unionists vote Conservative or Alliance any such assumptions have become even more blatantly untenable than they were in Bevan's day. In fact the whole basis of the block vote no longer bears much relation to real flesh-and-blood affiliated members. Unions affiliate more on the basis of what they can afford than on the basis of actual affiliated members. Yet at the same time it is more and more urgent for party members to organise as party members within the union, to win the political arguments against Thatcherism.

This points to the need to reform the unions' constitutional position within the party. Such reform would have two objectives. The first would be to retain the trade-union link. The need for political action to further the interests of the trade unions, as unions, will continue as long as we live in a class society. The second objective would be to establish a political base for the Labour Party amongst individual trade unionists in the workplace.

In the early eighties the left proposed and won the party's approval for workplace branches as one means of achieving this. Interestingly, such branches have only really gathered lasting momentum in unions like NALGO and NATFE which are not affiliated to the party. One explanation for this is that such a structure of individual party members, organised within the union, cannot successfully be sustained alongside a corporate relationship. A more radical proposal would be to change the character of the union's corporate relation to the party: to separate the issue of financial support for the party, which should remain a matter for the union as a whole, from the issue of decision-making power within the party which should be based on individual members of the party organised through a workplace/union party branch as well as the local branches which exist at present.

Now is not the occasion to discuss details but the essential points are these: the union as a whole would decide as it does now to allocate a part of its political fund – which would be gathered as it is now through a political levy – to the Labour Party as the party most likely to defend its interests as a union. As a result of this financial support it would have *de facto* influence, because the party would still depend in part on the funds. However, its financial support would not buy voting power as it does at present. Neither would payment of the political levy imply automatic affiliation to the party. Individual trade unionists would have to be positively recruited to the party and would be encouraged to organise as *Labour party members* within the union and/or workplace. They would also have voting power within the party as union delegates or at a national level as delegates from the union's Labour Party section. These members who join through their workplace or union branch might initially pay a lower subscription as part of a process of turning affiliated members into individual members, but the aim would be an equal subscription and an equal vote. There would no doubt be an element of double voting to sort out in having workplace/union branches as well as local branches and, at conference, constituency delegates as well as trade-union section delegates. But these problems are resolvable. The decisive benefit would be that the power of the trade-union section in the party would be based on a real political commitment. Moreover it would be a commitment of a two-way kind: the political generalisation of trade-union and workplace experience and expertise into the party and the campaigning energies and political thinking of the party into the union. Yet at the same time the union would continue to make a corporate financial and political commitment to the party.

The prospects for such a transformation are long term. Trade-union barons, even of a left inclination, are not going to give up their corporate power in the party unless pushed by events and by their members. In the meantime the prospect of such a reform depends not on constitutional manoeuvres but on the left establishing organisations of socialist trade unionists – in effect filling and more than filling the vacuum left by the decline of the Communist Party – throughout the unions, recruiting members to political activity rather than simply seeking to sway the block vote. In the end it will require unions themselves giving up corporate voting power within the party in favour of corporate influence and the voting power of those of their members who are also members of the party. Until they do this the party contains an inbuilt source of conservatism and political corruption which makes its claims to be building a democratic campaigning party entirely hollow.

6 A Party in Waiting?

A democratic revolution

Prime-Ministerial power is both the jugular and the rib-cage of the British state. It is a vital part of the state, while it also acts as a protection of its secrecy and its sanctity. The Labour left lunged, cracked a few ribs but missed the jugular. Too much depended on getting the right man, Tony Benn, into the leadership. He would no doubt have committed himself to the election of the Cabinet, he would have stripped himself of his powers of patronage and done a lot more besides. Whether he would have become Prime Minister is another matter. It would certainly not have been a calm and orderly process: in Britain his programme of democratic reforms was tantamount to revolution. Even the plans that he, with the support of the majority of the party, intended to introduce at the Department of Industry, were considered too radical. The president of the CBI was prepared to take action, including illegal action, to block them.[1] Perhaps this provides a clue as to why Benn and the left lost; the radicalism of their demands far outstripped the political organisation and strategy they had fashioned to promote them. The left, as it has often been tempted to do, was using the alleyways of the Labour Party as a short cut to the kind of change which needs a movement down the High Street.

Many MPs on the right of the party mutter darkly about the well-resourced and powerful organisation behind the constitutional reforms and the Benn campaign in 1981. But as I suggested in the Introduction, the institutions of the Labour Party exaggerate the strength and the weakness of the left. This is partly a function of the position of the trade unions in the party: if the left gains support from several large unions, for whatever reasons, it quickly seems to be a mass movement, and if the issue is one that can unite the unions and they see something in it for them, then victory is almost assured.

So it was with the constitutional reforms. After Callaghan's

5 per cent pay policy and the 1978–79 'Winter of Discontent', several key unions were responsive to proposals for reforms that would give them more leverage over the Leader. The CLPD – an extremely *under*-resourced organisation, as anyone who goes to its 'office', the home of Vladimir and Vera Dierer, can tell – was an energetic lobby and had a shrewd sense of the pace at which different unions could be won over and which proposals they could be won to. The electoral college had its attractions to trade unions, left and right: men like David Basnett and Clive Jenkins rather fancied themselves as king makers. But making Tony Benn the king was a different matter. There was not much, if anything, in that for the majority of trade-union leaders. Benn stood for the aspirations of the workplace leaders and the active members. As we have seen, trade-union support for Benn came in several cases in spite of trade-union leaders.

For the brief moment in 1981 of the campaign for his candidacy the left really *was* a movement.[2] And it was a movement that reached far beyond the Labour Party; for the ideas that Benn stood for represented much more than those of a strand in an inner-party struggle. But the motor for this movement was a small, rather *ad hoc* group of organisers and a persuasive leader. There was no organisation with roots in the trade unions and with the programmatic depth to sustain and build on its impact.

So when the new leader, Michael Foot, was elected and the trade-union leaders (loyalists as by nature they usually are) were rounded up to rally round, the left suddenly seemed extremely small and the leadership increasingly powerful. Since then, and reinforced by the election of Neil Kinnock, the effect of the electoral college has been to immensely strengthen the position of the Leader.[3] One problem meanwhile for the left is that nationally there has been little cumulative process of organisation to develop ideas, let alone a 'cadre' of activists, and win popular support. Though far more serious has been the sustained assault on the left – hard and soft – by the Thatcher government.

The character of the new left

There has however been a more diffuse process of continued organisation and initiative. One of the aims of this book has been to describe at least some of the important elements in this movement (because these developments *are* so scattered, I would not pretend that my description could be anywhere near comprehensive). A second aim is to place us in a better position to assess the future of the new left and, for those of us who share many of its ideals, to see ways in which this radical left can reach out and establish lasting, cumulative popular support.

It is to this second purpose I now turn. 'The radical left' is not homogeneous. It is influenced by different regional political traditions, as we saw with the municipal left in just five English cities, let alone Scotland, Wales or smaller English towns. Its priorities are shaped by a variety of different and sometimes conflicting interests combining gender, class and race in ways that cannot be simplistically categorised or polarised. It is affected by the kind of alliances it makes to achieve power or influence in its union or constituency party. Finally, it is fed by a variety of socialist traditions that have expressed the revolutionary or transforming ideal. And although I have focused on its expression within the Labour Party, there are many socialists outside who share similar outlooks. In spite of these diverse influences and origins it tends in the same direction, a direction expressed at different times only in symbolic individuals or events: Tony Benn, the GLC, support for the miners, CND. How can this direction be characterised?

Tony Benn talked in 1981 about the socialist movement as a 'mosaic'; the GLC is said to have mobilised a 'rainbow coalition'; the miners' strike is described as having been a symbol of hope for people of 'many hues'. Critics, especially in Fleet Street, have dismissed this motley crew as single-interest groups, as if these critics had a class analysis. Certainly politicians – and writers! – often reel off lists of oppressed groups and campaigning causes in a way which can appear naïve. Certainly, too, it would be misleading to convey the impression that there is a coherent socialist coalition into which movements arising from different oppressions have merged. None of these diffuse movements share an explicit common political ideology. But the judgement that there is no bond between the *socialists* who support and are influenced by them – that is, that there is not a distinct kind of socialism influenced by these movements – is a superficial one.

There is a socialism emerging which is more than the sum of these movements, though it has been influenced and in part produced by each one of them – feminism, peace and ecology, black organisations, militant and political workplace trade unionism and a multitude of community and cultural campaigns.

I argued earlier that this socialism represented a split in the transformative tradition of the Labour Party, a split which has emerged from practical political problems, in particular the failure of Labour governments to carry out the changes to which the Labour Party has long been committed. I cannot fully theorise this split but will instead point out the directions in which it is developing on the central issues of the economy and the state, from experiences with which I am familiar.

An economics of need

The views of the new Labour left on economics were shaped first by the collapse of Keynesian demand management as a strategy for full employment. This led in the 1973 programme to a confident and detailed reassertion of the need to intervene in production, for the state and the trade unions to own and control the profitable as well as the infrastructural sectors of the economy. Since then the debate, off-stage, in local government, among a minority of trade unionists, among socialist feminists and in socialist wings of the peace and ecology movements has gone much further. It focuses on the *purpose* and social relations which could be achieved through social control of production.[4] The traditional socialist case against the capitalist economy has been its periodic crises and the mass unemployment and waste which these bring about, and the failure of Keynesianism to overcome this tendency has revived the traditional socialist notion of planning production on the basis of a full use of resources to meet social need. The distinctive new influence of recent social movements is to reinforce and expand the scope and diversity involved in the notion of need among workers and consumers.

The focus on the purposes of production has led in several directions. First, it has involved a concern with the nature of the commodities or services themselves and their technology, whether they are weapons, pollutants, unsafe deodorants, unhealthy food or unresponsive public services.[5] Second, it has stimulated a greater emphasis on the quality of working conditions, on health and safety, the uses and design of technology and the control of labour's time – time for education, for child-care, for recreation.[6] Related to these concerns is a scrutiny of the division of labour, its sexual and racial roots as well as its basis in class power. And third, the influence of the new socialism has stressed the relationship between the workplace and its surrounding community.[7]

In contrast to Labourism, this socialism is interested in a lot more than how wealth is distributed and by whom it is owned: it is concerned with the principles and details of how it is produced. As Robin Murray, once economic adviser to the GLC, now working with Labour local authorities in the south-east, put it: 'The factory, office or enterprise is no longer seen as a black box with the value of labour power going in one end, and surplus value coming out of the other. It is the site of a whole politics of production . . .'[8] Again, on the nature of class conflict, this politics of production goes further than Labourism's assumption of a confrontation between sectional interests. It embodies a clash of principles for organising the economy: the principle of accumulation for private or, at any rate, unaccountable profit, versus the belief in production for democratically decided need. This has become clear in recent trade-union struggles against unemployment and in the debates about the investment strategies of the new municipal enterprise boards.[9]

The driving forces of democracy

'Democratically decided' is a phrase which begs many questions and leads me into the minefields of the state and the market. One reason why these *are* minefields for socialists is because we have tended to accept the dichotomy of the market and the state. That in fact has been the historic divide between the ideologies of Labourism and Conservatism: both claim to espouse a democratic ideal; Labour has tended to equate democracy with party control of the state and the Conservatives have equated democracy with the market. Given the way that the state and the market have in fact developed (under Labour as well as Conservative governments) we end up with an impossible choice between extending the bureaucracy of the existing state and deepening the inequality of the capitalist market. The growth in the postwar period, as in any period of economic prosperity, of relatively independent workplace trade-union organisations and a dense network of movements and initiatives in the community among groups with diverse needs enables us to imagine and take steps in another direction. This direction is towards an economy in which the main drive comes from democratic organisations in the workplace, in the neighbourhood and region which would be co-ordinated through new institutions – an economic parliament for instance – nationally and internationally. In other words, an economy in which democratic organisation in the enterprise and across enterprises is itself an economic mechanism.

The market in its place

What is the role of the market in such an economy? Can anything be read into recent local and trade-union initiatives on this question?

Labourism has long shared the commitment of Fabians and progressive liberals alike that the basic material conditions of human agency – health, housing, education and a basic income – should be provided independently of the market, as of right. But it has not questioned the workings of the capitalist market in production itself. In fact, a defensive reaction to the success of Thatcherism has weakened Labour's will to develop non-market criteria for investment and other economic decisions. Again we encounter the debilitating consequences of seeing economic alternatives in terms only of the existing market and state. Moreover, this defensive response to the success of pro-market ideology allows a number of distinct problems to blur into one misleadingly abstract issue of 'the market'.

There are at least three distinct aspects to the problem of the market. First, the usefulness, justice and democracy or otherwise of market mechanisms in different conditions of ownership and income distribution in particular, as a means of allocation and distribution. Second, the constraints of working within a world market, whatever kind of economy exists in Britain or Europe – constraints which must weigh heavily on any discussion of economic strategy today. Third, the reality of economic organisation under modern capitalism. I will begin with the last, since it is the starting-point for most of the initiatives upon whose ideas I will draw.

There are two outstanding facts about the operation of the market in the kind of capitalist economy we presently live under. First, for many of the corporations that most powerfully shape this economy, the market – usually the international market – is only a final constraint – there are many *different* ways in which the company can operate within that constraint. These corporations engage in an immense amount of planning, in the course of which numerous choices are made, not on the basis of the 'impersonal' workings of the market, but on the basis of a variety of personal and bureaucratic judgements within a hierarchy of power and income. Moreover, corporations frequently co-operate and plan between each other, agreeing, for instance, to divide up markets where they might otherwise compete. The choice in these circumstances is not simply market versus plan, but rather, whose plan? Who does the planning, and to whom are the planners accountable?

The response of a minority of workers and local authorities in such circumstances has been to argue that where there is planning, whether in the public or private sector, then the struggle must be to make it transparent, accountable and answerable by the workers, communities and consumers affected by the plans. Workers defending their jobs in British Telecom, in Lucas Aerospace, in Fords, Kodak and other corporations have been resisting undemocratic planning decisions as much as the pressures of the market.[10] Their demands have been for information, for consultation, for the right to negotiate over investment and technology. In other words, they have been demands for economic democracy as well as material security.

The crucial point is that these initiatives demonstrate that we are not limited by the choice of bureaucratic state planning versus the market. They illustrate elements of a third option, based on democratic organisation and negotiation as themselves economic mechanisms.[11] Democratic organisation can perform many of the functions of the market, but in a way which consciously calculates and acts upon the social as well as narrowly commercial, economic costs and benefits. Flexible and responsive forms of democracy are a more fruitful incentive to innovate than the rewards of a traditional hierarchy because they release the creativity of workers at all levels; they are a more effective form of economic discipline because the moral and social basis for efficiency is transparently and collectively arrived at and, finally, a democratic enterprise is more likely to provide work satisfaction and scope for the ability of the majority of workers. Of course democratic planning would not be free of conflict. Like 'the market' it would have to handle the tensions between consumers and producers, between short- and long-term interests, between innovation and protection.

The second outstanding feature of the market as it actually exists in the British economy is that it acts to discipline labour. Under a capitalist market, labour power is a commodity. If it is in surplus – if there is unemployment – employers, that is purchasers of labour power, are in a strong position to bargain down its price: workers' livelihoods. That has been the underlying purpose of the Conservatives' policy of 'freeing', that is strengthening, the forces of the private market. Thus, in an economy where production is based on private accumulation and unregulated competition, the market is not an innocent bystander to the clash of class interests.

The furniture industry in London is a good example of where the market has operated very directly to discipline labour (in contrast to industries like engineering or motor manufacture dominated by large multi-plant corporations where the market operates indirectly, through the planning decisions of the corporation). Furniture is a visibly cut-throat operation between medium-sized companies, geographically concentrated. The pressure of international competition is so intense and, due to lack of investment in the years of the boom, the British manufacturers are in such a weak position, all bunched together in the low value-added end of the market, that one company can only make a profit if another goes out of business. 'They delight, literally, in seeing their cousin going out of business,' was how one furniture worker described the attitude of his employers. Furniture workers feel totally demoralised, unable to advance their standard of living, seeing colleagues made redundant every week.

This extreme example of the role of the market in disciplining and weakening labour illustrates how any socialist strategy, even for a consumer sector like furniture, where the market would play an important role, would need to take account both of how best to respond to individual consumer taste (the democratic aspect of the market), and at the same time, the needs of the workers. The distinct feature of the market in a capitalist economy is that it separates workers and consumers and reinforces their conflicting interests.

In the case of the furniture industry in London, the GLC, through its Enterprise Board, GLEB, tried to overcome, or rather indicate how to overcome, the conflict of interest between consumers and producers in the furniture industry. It tackled the power of the international market in the furniture industry by aiming for co-ordination and planning across the industry. GLEB staff drew up plans for improving the position of the London-based industry as a whole, its design capacity, its marketing and so on. Eventually, faced with resistance and suspicion from the employers, it drew in the shop stewards and paid their lost wages to enable them to take time off to discuss and amend the plans and consider what pressure they could put on their employers, through collective bargaining.[12]

In the end, the crisis in the industry was too deep and the international circumstances too unfavourable for either the GLC, GLEB or the trade unions to have much impact. But the experience, generalised to the national economy, does provide us with another kind of model of state support for a planning process based on workers' organisations and ideas. A market would be part of this in two ways, both different from the role of the capitalist market. On the one hand, within the London industry there would still be competing enterprises, though the planning process would have to make these enterprises as complementary as possible on a national or regional scale. This would enhance the position of the British industry on the international market. However, this market would have a different effect on production because the enterprises would be taken into some form of social ownership and co-operative control, so the market's effects on production would be mediated by democratic decision-making in the enterprise. Moreover, the enterprises would be co-ordinated through a state body – regional or national depending on the geography of the industry – which would regulate the effects of the market across the industry on employment and working conditions. If demand drops in one enterprise, a productive one would be required to take on any workers made redundant, or some part of the state would find them useful employment. There would be a guaranteed right to work.[13]

At the same time, in international terms the aim of the planning would be to so improve the position of the industry by design, new technology, product co-ordination and innovation, that the industry could hold its own in the world market.

No one industry or service provides the basis for a blueprint of institutions of a democratic economy. They would vary from sector to sector and region to region. I will illustrate this further by tracing the steps implicit in recent workers' struggles in some of the most powerful centres of economic power: the multinationals. Passing a resolution calling on the Parliamentary Labour Party to nationalise these top companies has *not* been the first step that sprang to mind. The politically minded stewards in these corporations know better than anybody that nationalisation of the UK branch of a large multinational, for instance Ford UK or the photographic corporation Kodak, without a fuller international strategy would mean that all that the government would have would be some factory buildings, an assembly line or processing plant starved of key inputs (which would come from other European plants outside the UK), and components which would be largely useless unless European centres of these two firms co-operated, which would be unlikely.

As I mentioned above, politically minded shop stewards working for such corporations are calculating on more radical and more practical strategies for social control. These are based on a combination of industrial action, that is, a power over which they, the shop-floor representatives, have some control, and state action. Workers' action combined with political action offers a far more effective lever than state intervention on its own, especially if they can achieve international trade-union co-operation. But trade-union power still needs to be supported by state action, for instance through public purchasing and tariff bargaining power and public takeover.

This implies a new kind of relationship between workers' organisations in industry and services, and socialist representatives with some elected power within the state. It recognises that on their own neither group have, or could have, sufficient power to direct production: the trade-union organisations potentially

have the detailed knowledge and bargaining strength to plan and
exert accountable control within production itself, and the state
has the complementary power to exert democratic controls over
the external economic environment – trade, finance and ownership. Work by the GLC and other left local authorities with shop
stewards in, for instance, the motor industry, illustrates that such
a relationship can support, and positively encourage, workers'
solidarity and association – in some cases on an international
scale.[14] This partnership is a much more active and positive
relationship than the traditional one between governments and
trade unions. For it is based on a recognition of workers not
simply as wage earners – Labourism's assumption – but as
producers and citizens with the knowledge, social concern and
potential power to play a part in controlling the way in which
their industry or service should be run.

A brief story of the T&GWU and the motor industry will
illustrate the contrast of this approach with Labourism's traditional approach to economics. A member of the rank-and-file
combine committee in Ford described to me, with despair, a
discussion of officers in the T&GWU Motor Trade Group:

The meeting was meant to be discussing the union's strategy for the
industry. It considered a motion on nationalisation of the industry which
probably comes up every year. The chair commented that he did not
really think this matter was his responsibility; 'We should leave this
kind of thing to the Labour Party', he said. 'Then he asked for
discussion. Not a word. The motion was passed on the nod.

There will be some ritual meetings with Labour's front-bench
spokesman who will promise import controls and several other
measures, possibly even some degree of further state takeover,
which he is almost certainly not going to carry out, even if he
were in a position to do so. The cynicism will grow.

Meanwhile the steward who reported this meeting was about
to leave for the Philippines on a trip, paid for by his region and
by the World Council of Churches, for a week-long 'think
tank' with trade-union representatives from Ford plants in other
countries and sympathetic economists. Ideally, the results will
feed back into a joint trade-union and political strategy. But
the political channels are clogged and the trade-union policy
procedures are fragmented and under-resourced.

Workers and the state

A small minority of politically active trade unionists – the motor stewards who travel to the Philippines and elsewhere, Telecom workers who meet their European colleagues in Amsterdam and London, the health workers who come together across Britain – are putting an economic and political argument to Labour. They are saying: 'We can guide your intervention in industry, your mangement of the services; we can tell you where the state can make a decisive intervention that will change things, and we have the power and knowledge to follow up and back up this intervention. Why not combine this power and knowledge with your political overview, your powers of finance, purchasing and expropriation? You need an ally on the inside, but if we are your ally you must listen first to us. Trust us not simply as trade-union supporters and Labour voters, but as people who know how our service or industry should be managed in a socially responsible way. We have a vested interest in change; the present directors or senior administrators have an interest in maintaining things as they are.'

An empowering state

If the Labour Party were to accept this message, what would be the implications for government? First, it requires such a Labour government to work with the trade unions and other non-parliamentary democratic organisations concerned with the economy – either economic needs or economic resources – to establish the conditions for democratic planning and association. This involves breaking up the present centres of unaccountable power, both within the state and outside: the banks and financial institutions, major multi-plant corporations, the Treasury, and so on. This negative action is a necessary function of a genuinely empowering political order. By empowering, I mean encouraging sources of power other than its own. Thatcher has led an empowering state for private capital. Labour should lead an empowering state for the organisations of working people. Without this, the democratic economy would exist precariously and for a minority in the crevices of an increasingly undemocratic economy.[15] On a small scale, the GLC's use of this negative power was a precondition of its more positive forms of 'empowering'.

Consider the example of the GLC's 'Community Areas' policy described in Chapter 3. The aim was to achieve the control of certain valuable pieces of land in London by community and trade-union groups. For this, not only did the GLC provide political encouragement and sometimes grants to community groups, it also used its planning and compulsory purchase powers to take the land away from private property developers. Thus Labour's elected representatives were centralist and interventionist in their dealings with the powerful, so that those previously excluded from power could have democratic control over their future. Transferring this approach to the national level will mean a strong state in relation to the powerful institutions I have just listed, and a supportive, decentralised state as regards popular associations and individuals.

There will always be a tension between these two sides of the state and the party or parties leading it. The pressures of popular organisations and parties will need to be powerful to keep under control the tendency of state bodies, even state bodies undergoing a process of transformation, to dominate everything. But then a socialist government of the sort I am describing would never come into being unless there was already massive popular pressure. Party democracy, through the accountability of MPs and the Cabinet, then becomes a crucial way in which the pressure on the government to honour its commitments is carried to where it counts. The rapid dismantling of the entrenched mandarin Civil Service and its security services would be a precondition for this democracy to prevail.

A central part of the dismantling and democratising of the present state apparatus would be a break-up of its geographical concentration. In other words, any attempt to make private and public corporations accountable would need many different levels of public ownership, funding and other kinds of intervention: in different localities, in different regions, in different industrial and service sectors. These would need to have some autonomy from national government, though working to nationally negotiated targets as far as capital goods and infrastructural industries are concerned. This applies not only to the economy, but to other aspects of the kind of participatory democracy which socialism clearly requires.

At all these levels of the state, the role of political representatives will be first and foremost to enable and empower these social associations. This will mean providing a means of co-ordination and, at different levels, a framework of industrial and economic strategy. Part of this framework will include legislation for minimum standards for pay, hours, working conditions, leave, training and equality of opportunity.

Stronger local and regional government, perhaps in the long run a federal system as part of a federation of Europe, would be its logical development, with certain infrastructural and capital goods industries that benefit from economies of scale – steel, coal, aerospace – planned on a European basis.

Europe

When we explore political structures which such a political economy would imply beyond Britain, we hit upon a difference with the new left. The difference tends to reflect the two distinct origins of this left. Those whose origins lie within the Labour Party and parliamentary politics have tended until recently to see socialism in national terms.[16] In this sense Labourism has lingered on. In the campaign to vote 'no' in the EEC referendum Tony Benn shared the same platform and spoke a similar language to Michael Foot. Benn more than Foot recognised the overwhelmingly international character of modern capitalism but nevertheless seemed over-optimistic about the ability of the British left to go it alone.[17]

As we have seen, the attitudes of Foot and Benn towards Parliament developed in fundamentally different directions. Unlike Foot, Benn believed that Parliament on its own could not stand up to the pressures of capital and the non-elected apparatus of the state. However, like Foot he still believed that it was control or transformation of the nation-state that mattered and that this could be achieved through national action. Membership of the EEC would only add a further *external* obstacle. The idea of *European* rather than national initiatives for socialism and democracy against the present Treaty of Rome and the undemo-cratic institutions of the EEC was outside his thinking at that time, though he has recently become involved in such initiatives.

By contrast the new left organising around the issues – peace, nuclear power, unemployment, feminism – rather than around

Parliament, was drawn in an inevitably international direction by the international character of the institutions it was up against. Thus the peace movement protesting against Cruise missiles and Pershing SS 20s increasingly began to ally directly with peace movements in other NATO and Warsaw Pact countries. Similarly the anti-nuclear movement started to make common cause with anti-nuclear protesters in Germany and Italy against a common technology. In both cases the alliance is material, not just rhetorical: joint action leading to marches, direct action, political pressure and joint study and debate through conferences, publications and research. In more particular ways trade unionists, especially those working for multinationals, are increasingly establishing contact as we have just described, with trade unionists in Europe and beyond. Their managements are restructuring on an international scale and cannot be resisted effectively by merely national action.

A new kind of party

A vision of socialism based on power built up from below, but without a party able to encourage and sustain that power, is wishful thinking. I believe that the elements of such a party have existed for some time now, all over the country, inside and outside the Labour Party. Some of those inside the party I have described in earlier chapters. Occasionally momentous issues or struggles, such as the siting of Cruise missiles and the miners' strike, bring them together and with socialists outside the party. The priorities and structures of the national Labour Party, in particular the leadership of the Parliamentary Party, however, do not give them expression or power. On what criteria can I say this? What are the elements of the kind of party which those who believe in a democratic economy and an empowering state need?

Parties reflect strategies for political power and the purposes for which that power is used. A party, like the Labour Party, which aims for the power to steer the existing state in the interests of working people, is organised first and foremost to win government power. That is, it is organised to win elections and to develop policy for Labour governments or councils to try to implement. Because of the party's origins, the trade unions have heavy representation within its structures, but their position does not formally alter the electoral character of the party. The purpose of their presence is to contribute to the party's electoral efforts and to influence the party's policies for government.

For the membership, the party's activities and structures have two centres of gravity – the first is around election activities: choosing the candidate, getting in the votes; the second is around policy-making through conference and passing resolutions up the structure to the NEC. These two activities also set the terms of the party's relationships: its relationship to the mass of people outside the party and its internal relationships. As far as electoral activity is concerned the relationship is one of a machine to its product; the language of electoralism is of 'electoral machines' 'bringing in the votes' like a combine harvester bringing in the corn. The people, the voters, are seen as essentially passive.

Bernard Shaw summed it up during the early days of the party when its structures were beginning to set:

The people want a policy (at least one out of 100 of them do), but they can't make one, they must go to the thinker and tactician for it . . . In offering them the Fabian make of shoe I don't question their capacity or their loyalty, I only assume what everybody knows as a plain matter of fact, namely that they can't make the shoe themselves.[18]

This view of the voter is unconscious and deeply ingrained in the party's structures. It manifests itself in both Labour's traditional electoral methods and its new image-conscious methods. It underpins the predominant view of policy: it is almost exclusively a party matter. There is virtually no process of involving or consulting non-party progressive organisations except, in a formal manner, the unions. As far as the members are concerned, their main political activity is within the party. Political progress for party members, except at election time, is measured in terms of the policy resolutions or positions which are won by themselves or their political comrades.

Many individual members, and increasingly whole sections, break out of these relationships, but even then, as we saw with women's sections and black sections, the electoral and 'resolutionary' imperatives of the inherited structures press hard. It requires immense counter-pressure and will, often from the outside as well as the inside, to sustain a different way of organising.

In order to be in a good position to answer the practical question 'What is to be done?' it would be useful first to imagine the kind of party (or parties) needed to work towards a political economy based on democratic association. Such a party would need to be much less of a machine to bring in voters and more of a political nervous system to stimulate, sustain and co-ordinate a collective self-organisation and initiative.

Its relationship to the mass of people outside the party would be governed by the idea that these people have the capacity, potentially, to control or have a direct influence over many of the institutions which govern their lives. Potentially they *do* have policies. On matters close to them they usually have more suitable ideas than the experts so beloved of the Fabian drafters of the party's constitution. The base of its members' activity would therefore not be the party itself, but organisations building the potential for democratic control in the workplace and community: trade-union organisations, including the professions such as teaching; community campaigns; women's groups; black organisations; the peace movement. The priority of its members would be to strengthen these organisations, encourage their political self-confidence and self-education, work with them to make wider connections and provide support in their struggles against the existing state and other unaccountable centres of power. The party itself would be a source of ideas, political resources and support for such involvement; it would be a base for testing and clarifying priorities and making links between desired objectives.

The party would also be a means by which members learn and generalise from the experiences and ideas of different movements and organisations. Policy, strategy, ideas: the development of these would not be a sealed-off process. A party provides a way in which the process can be cumulative and framed by definite principles, but each new advance is the product of close, and sometimes critical, involvement with popular organisations.

Such a party would also be a platform, a means of political expression, and, where it has political control, a source of executive power, for organisations outside the conventional definition of 'political' – women's groups, community groups, single-issue campaigns. The party's relationship with these organisations would begin to prefigure the relationship which a new kind of state would have with democratic associations. The party would respect their autonomy but be responsive to their initiative and ideas.

The other side of the relationship between the party and the 'non-parliamentary' organisations will be the party's work of persuasion and campaigning. Clearly, it will be rare for a trade-union organisation or community group to agree fully with the principles and ideas of the party. More often than not they will have a rather sectional response to party policies, agreeing with the ones that take up their interests and being uninterested, or even outright hostile, to ones outside their experience.

A classic example comes to mind from my own experience. While at the GLC I worked with a group of skilled furniture craftsmen. All of them were white, two of them were explicitly racist. So at the same time as working with them on their ideas about the furniture industry and trade-union organisation I and several of the furniture workers themselves tried to challenge their racism. The same situation crops up in trade-union and tenants' groups everywhere. The kind of party I am describing would constantly need to be explaining and winning support for its policies among the people on whom, after all, it depends to carry them out. It is not enough for a party to win power and then assume it can administer radical policies. It must have popular support for these policies. As we saw with several local councils, this lesson took a long time to be learnt, partly because the Labour Party thought that it was enough to have the right policies and to be in charge.

Persuading and campaigning will be the party's daily routine, the activities around which much of its structure is built. But it will also need structures for representation in the existing state. These will need a greater capacity for disciplined and united action; for such representatives will find rapidly themselves against the state as well as in it. They will need both to be accountable and to have support to follow up the limited openings that electoral success can bring.

In such a party there will be a constant tension between the independence and scope for debate and diversity which its branches and members will need in order to establish creative relationships with popular organisations, and the discipline which the party will need in its interventions in and against the state and the private market and electorally. It is a tension between the flexibility and diversity of prefiguring the future which you are working for and the tautness and unity that you need against the enemies of such a future. Such a tension is built into organisations and movements seeking to transform society; the problem is that all too often they cannot hold the tension. They slip into one or other side of it: becoming too loose and diffuse to survive the battery of hostile forces, or tightening up to an extent that cuts them off from popular initiatives.

A party in waiting

Many of the activities of Labour Party members already involve these tensions. Many party members are already, in their own political work, trying to create a party of the sort I have just described. From the evidence of earlier chapters, this seems more likely where the members have some independence from the existing structure: women's sections, black sections and some local parties all fall into this category. But even there, the influence of the old structure still runs deep – with all its parliamentary arrogance and inward-looking sense of its own importance.

For instance the left in several London borough councils have enthusiastically combined the kind of policies that we described in the GLC, particularly equal opportunities. But all too often they have done so in a way which assumes that resolutions in the Labour Group and instructions from the Council Chamber can change society. Similarly, the leadership of the black sections and the Women's Action Committee sometimes end up engaged in negotations and manoeuvres over structure and position when their base is narrow and in need of repair. The old structure, with all its short cuts and illusions of power, still has a magnetic effect on even these more independent spirits.

In the miners' strike

Between 1984 and 1985 there was a powerful magnetic pull in the opposite direction: the pull of the pit villages and their extraordinarily resolute fight for survival. The normal routine of many constituency parties was thoroughly disrupted by their involvement in the strike. For the most part this was welcomed: 'The party came to life: we had something practical to work on, we had a cause,' said a member of the Woking CLP. 'We reached out to people in a way we never have before,' came the report from Hull. 'It brought us into contact with organisations we've never worked in before' (Rugby and Kenilworth). 'Many inactive members got involved in our collections and started coming to meetings again, and new members joined' (Brighton).[19] 'We built up personal and political connections across the country from which we learnt so much. We are really *grateful* to the miners. We felt they were fighting for us. That's why we had to get involved.' Alison New, from the Cambridge Constituency Party, expressed a feeling that was widely shared.

'They were fighting for us' first and foremost because they were standing up to Thatcher. Also they were fighting for jobs, for community, for industrial democracy, for a natural resource, for a safe energy policy: all central to Labour's alternative. Perhaps most important of all, the struggle in the pit villages symbolised what socialism at its best was about, combining old traditions of mutual support from the working class with a new recognition of distinct interests within that class and of diverse allies outside. And it provided a *practical* expression of these traditions.[20] The practical and positive character of the support for the strike is important. The quickness with which many parties set up support groups, made contact with particular pits, organised an imaginative range of activities, illustrates that inside many a 'resolutionary' Labour Party delegate there is a practical socialist trying to get out.

The aftermath of defeat

The defeat of the strike reduced the likelihood of such opportunities arising from national trade-union action. The defeat meant also that most of the good intentions to keep support groups going after the strike were unfulfilled. There were exceptions, especially in the first year after the strike, when twenty or so groups continued to organise in support of the miners who had been sacked or jailed. In a few towns, Oxford, for instance, a well-supported coalition of trade unions, Labour parties and other organisations has continued to provide a a focus for campaigning activity.

Moreover, even where support groups no longer exist, local Labour parties have not fallen back entirely into their conventional routines. Look at Sheffield Brightside: before the miners' strike, even though it was a 'left-wing' CLP – measured by the MP it selected or the conference resolutions it supported – it never got involved in industrial disputes, beyond occasionally inviting a speaker to a party meeting and giving a donation from party funds. Soon after the miners' strike, workers at the engineering firm, Firth Brown, went on strike over management's consultation procedures which bypassed the elected shop stewards. The strike lasted sixteen weeks, during which time party members did a lot more than they had ever done before for an industrial dispute: 'People actually went out doing street collections, producing leaflets, explaining the case. It was a new thing that, since the miners' strike,' said Steven Walmsley, secretary of one of the party branches.

The survey I carried out at the 1986 party conference indicates that the impact of the strike on the Sheffield Brightside constituency was typical of many. 68 per cent of the delegates interviewed said that the party had become involved in more public campaigning since the strike. 60 per cent said that party membership had increased during the strike. 90 per cent said that the miners' strike created an increase in the political involvement of existing members, and 61 per cent reported that this involvement had continued since the strike. 96 per cent said that the strike had increased debate and awareness within the party and 75 per cent said that this had been sustained. In their general comments, many delegates stressed the ways in which it had unified the local party for the first time in years, bringing together the younger 'white-collar' left and the older manual trade unionists.

'You have to go out and do stalls on a windy day'

Another lasting impact can be seen in an area such as Durham, where the local parties, as parties, never became actively involved in the strike: 'They did their bit, giving the levy, but that was it,' said Ann Suddick, who was Secretary of the Durham support groups (the circumstances in Easington, described by Heather Woods in Chapter 4, were typical of CLPs in Durham County; Durham City CLP was more active). It was only individual party members who were active. They came together with miners' wives and campaigning organisations such as CND and Anti-Apartheid to create a county-side support group. It formally disbanded after the strike, but the contacts and the memory of something new remained.

For Ann Suddick in particular, the memory was powerful. As for many women – and men – in the mining communities, the experience of the strike had been an exciting period of self-discovery, simultaneously with political discovery. Before the strike she was not involved in any kind of political acitivity: 'I was just passive Labour, like most people round here.' She had worked for eighteen years as a secretary in the office of the Durham Mechanics, a section of the NUM, but it was only during the strike, at the age of thirty-eight, that her tremendous organising and speaking abilities came out. The kind of organisation she had helped to create during the miners' strike inspired her and others in the north-east of England to create a new, more permanent organisation: Links. Its initial focus was nuclear power. It organised leafleting and petitioning across the country in the aftermath of Chernobyl. Ann Suddick explains:

The Labour Party is practising a conservative philosophy; so we had to start Links, to bring people campaigning on different, connected issues together across party boundaries. We began by linking our campaign for the coal industry with the issues of nuclear power and the campaign against the Druridge Bay Power Station. The Labour Party isn't pre-pared for this kind of thing. You have to go out and do stalls on a windy day.

This kind of spread of the skills and energies released during the strike defies the expectations of many commentators and politicians. They have assumed that because the strike was defeated, the memories of its participants and supporters are little more than nostalgia, without political efficacy. Some have willed it to be so, believing that the strike's defeat vindicates their hostility to the leadership of the NUM. For the vast majority of those involved, however, defeat has not led to doubts about their decision to strike or to support the strike. Without rhetoric, they believe it was an achievement to have resisted. Among them the memories, the arguments and the lessons are very much alive. This has produced a political imagination which sees beyond the traditional divisions within the Labour Party, to a different kind of party. Ann Suddick describes the kind of party she would like the Labour Party to become:

A party with open debate; less manipulative and without the issues clouded by factionalism; an open, challenging party with a *real commitment to change*. Campaigning on personalities isn't going to bring that about.

Locally there needs to be time to develop friendships and political ideas. I've yet to discover when they discuss policies. In Langley Park for instance, where there is eighty-four per cent unemployment among the youth and fifty-four per cent among the adults, all that the branch discusses is litter bins and committees. No young kid wants to go to a meeting to discuss litter bins.

Given the character of the local party, Ann Suddick keeps her party membership but puts most of her energies into campaigning that is based outside, like Links:

At present I think that campaigning outside is a more effective way of getting the Labur Party to do things. If you can engender support outside then they've got to recognise the issue; that's what happened over CND and nuclear power.

If you just work inside, you get compartmentalised and labelled and then when you've got an issue to bring up there's a predictable line-up and people don't debate the moral issues involved. Some issues are far bigger than factionalism. They call me a militant. But I'm not. I want change and that upsets their equilibrium, their cosy equilibrium.

Upsetting their cosy equilibrium

One independent movement which has upset the Labour Party's equilibrium is the peace movement. The peace movement's opposition to the Cold War states, east and west, is paralleled by a scepticism about the parties which run those states. Of all the social movements discussed in this book, the peace movement shows the strongest, most confident belief in the political power of mobilisation independent of political parties and the state. It has much in common with other movements in terms of the kind of change to which it is aspiring, but it is determinedly independent of the Labour Party.

'We're "for" but not "of" the Labour Party,' was how Anna-Joy David, ex-vice chairperson of Youth CND, now aged twenty-two, an organiser of Red Wedge, described the relationship that many younger members of CND, and now Red Wedge, have with the Labour Party.[21] The peace movement's active membership has in recent times probably been larger than that of the Labour Party. The old CND, closely allied to the Labour left and the Communist Party, has been transformed by a massive influx of young people and women. The majority of its members are now under thirty. On its National Council women outnumber men two to one. The young recruits feel little of the historic association – tense though it might have been – that the middle-aged stalwarts feel with the Labour Party. Anna-Joy again:

We haven't been brought up in or with the Labour Party. We've been brought up under the Thatcher government. My generation have been involved in single issues, not political parties. The growth of CND, for example, is the success of my generation.

They feel that through CND they were part of something new:

We saw when we did Brockwell Park [a political youth festival] in 1983 that we were the stepping-stone for a whole new way of campaigning; it has inspired not simply other single-issue movements to grow, but a whole new mechanism of young people understanding they can do things in practical steps – through music and other arts, with youth clubs and the more radical local authorities. What we're seeing is not simply a reaction to Thatcherism, but young people setting their alternative agendas.

Another source of the peace movement's confidence and independence has been the action led by women at the Cruise bases, Greenham Common and Molesworth. Their direct action – embracing the base, cutting the wires – had political reverberations nationally and internationally more powerful than any number of Labour Party resolutions.

The international character of the peace movement gives it an autonomy and strength from which it can appeal directly to governments. Unlike most of the rest of the left it can speak with a European – increasingly east and west – voice. It is the peace movement, based as it is, massively, in civil society rather than political parties, which has contributed to the pressures that lie behind recent moves towards disarmament. Of course the peace movement has its allies within the Labour Party, and the Liberal Party, but the base from which it has reached and persuaded public opinion has by and large been outside party politics.

An important feature of much of the left described in this book is that its scepticism about parliamentary politics has meant increasingly less dependence on a national leader. In the past, the Labour left has always organised around a leader in waiting, mirroring the existing structure of the party: Cripps, Bevan, Benn. This is to some extent unavoidable. The leadership of the left has become at once more fragmented, representing a greater diversity of constituencies – constituencies of region or city, gender or race, movement or union – and to some degree more collective (through, for instance, loose relationships between the Campaign Group, women's and black sections, parts of CND, the left of the trade unions). This left has a certain distance from the existing structure of the party.

It has a certain 'do-it-yourself' air about it. This was apparent during the miners' strike. The activities of the Chesterfield Constituency Party illustrate this well. The Chesterfield Party organises as a federation of workplace and community organisations, regularly mounting local campaigns, arranging public meetings, organising internal political education, even establishing an international committee which has followed up the international contacts made during the miners' strike. Tony Benn, Chesterfield's MP, explains the motivation:

We do not believe that the party in Chesterfield is any different from other constituencies . . . But at a time when the establishment is trying so desperately to obliterate socialism, and when the use of public-relations techniques seems, to be taking precedence over hard policy commitments in party propaganda, we think our work at the grass roots is much more in tune with the needs of society.

In order to identify these needs and to advance solutions, the Chesterfield Party produced a statement of aims and objectives, the outcome of discussion in party wards, trade-union branches, the women's group and the black section: 'We have decided "to do it ourselves" without waiting for permission, and to develop a "manifesto of demands" instead of the old idea of waiting for a "manifesto of promises" from on top.'

A crisis of political representation

It may sound presumptuous of me to describe these diverse developments as elements of 'a party in waiting' – they express many principles in common but they contain differences of emphasis and of interest. I use this phrase, 'a party in waiting', to highlight a problem facing them all: a crisis of political representation. It is a problem for the left inside the Labour Party because its ideas too have no direct platform; and it has no direct communication to its potential supporters outside Labour. However hard they try, whatever truce they have made with the leadership on internal issues, the left in the party sees its arguments refracted and diverted as if through a prism, by internal party conflicts. The refracted view is then enlarged by the more powerful prisms of the media, so that the original ideas survive only in a sub-culture of left newspapers, public meetings of the converted, and the occasional late-night programme on Channel 4. Earlier chapters illustrate how the left's programme of democratic reform, its ideas on industry and the economy, its experiments and achievements in local government have all suffered this fate. As Labour's electoral position has become more precarious and the Labour leadership has become more centralised, the process has become more intense.

In their own areas, left majorities in local government have proved to be exceptions – exceptions that illustrate the rule. In Manchester and the GLC, left policies and personalities similar to those marginalised nationally have been popular. A vital condition for this is that they have had their own platform, a direct means of communication to the public. They were able to mobilise the latent support which, as I argued in Chapter 2, exists for radical democratic politics, if not yet for socialist politics. A leading article in the *Financial Times* commented on this at the time of Labour's 1987 Local Government Conference: 'There is in the regions, and in parts of London, a new Labour Party trying to break out.' And the article added, 'It seems a pity that the front bench should be seen trying to stifle it.'[22]

Radical movements or struggles outside the party are clearly affected by the fate of the Labour left's arguments – after all, they share most of them – but they face other problems as well. One problem is that of following their successes through. Take the peace movement, for instance: through a massive presence at every level of society, it has achieved major shifts in the positions of political leaders. But in Britain it has not been able to turn that popular support into a means of sustained pressure and detailed vigilance on the politicians who, from expediency or genuine commitment, have adopted its cause. In Germany, Denmark and Holland, by contrast, radical left parties with political representation have performed this function to some effect,[23] acting virtually as the parliamentary wing of the peace movement, amongst others, relatively unimpeded by the considerations of party unity and discipline which inhibit or distort the activities of the parliamentary left in Britain.

Another problem is that which faced the miners during their strike against pit closures: without positive political representation of their case they were easily ghettoised, at times criminalised, by the government and the press. The Labour leadership was on the defensive, echoing many of the attacks of the government; and the Labour left's expressions of support were translated into conflicts within the party. As a result, the positive social, moral and economic case for the miners – for their jobs, for coal, and for communities – was rarely clearly heard. It is not a case which a trade union running a strike can put on its own. The same applies to the issues raised by Murdoch's attack on trade unionism at Wapping. And the teachers' action over the past two years. Without positive political representation, trade-union disputes appear exclusively sectional.

Proportional representation and a party on the left

The crisis of political representation goes deeper than the injustice of Britain's electoral system. But Britain's electoral system *is* unjust. Socialists should be in the forefront of attempts to make it fair, whether or not it is to our immediate advantage. The last three Conservative governments have been elected on minority votes. If the 1979, 1983 and 1987 elections had been conducted under proportional representation there would have been large parliamentary majorities against the Conservatives. It is not surprising that the majority of voters would like electoral reform – over 70 per cent in a recent Gallup poll. Our electoral system is one of the many reasons for the widespread disaffection with existing political institutions. Not the most important one, but significant none the less. If, when proportional representation becomes an issue for parliamentary debate and action, Labour continues to defend the status quo, then it will itself become even more of an object of this general disaffection than at present. In the long run, socialism needs the active support of the overwhelming majority of people; we have nothing to fear from an electoral system which requires us to win such support.[24]

Support for proportional representation among the new left is growing, not only among leading figures such as Ken Livingstone and Arthur Scargill but, perhaps more significantly, among constituency activists. In the survey that I carried out at the 1986 conference, I found that 61 per cent of the delegates interviewed supported 'a change in the electoral system to introduce some form of proportional representation'.

It is significant that support for proportional representation comes far more from people who represent the new transformative tradition than the old. Among the constituency activists interviewed in my survey, there was a significant overlap between those supporting PR and those (77 per cent) who agreed that 'the power of Parliament is limited, therefore the Labour Party must help to build extra-parliamentary movements to achieve change', and also those (74 per cent) who felt that the Labour Party 'does not give sufficient priority to extra-parliamentary movements'. Two explanations of this are relevant here. First, the new left is more critical in every way of Britain's parliamentary institutions. Westminster is not for them the hallmark of the democracy that it is for the Labourist left; all its institutions, including its electoral system, are open to question to an extent previously unthinkable. Second, the new left, with its experiences of campaigning in close co-operation with other organisations on the left, is far less protective of the Labour Party's monopoly of working-class politics – defence of this monopoly is a strong instinct behind Labour's resistance to proportional representation. Through CND, in the Anti-Nazi League and Anti Apartheid, in local trades councils, in support campaigns like that for the miners, the new left has for some time worked in alliances where the Labour Party is one amongst several organisations on the left. So the prospect of electoral competition from the left, which could be one of the consequences of proportional representation, does not appear as a threat.

Some would argue that if proportional representation is introduced it would provide the opportunity for some part of the left, from inside and as well as outside the party, to establish an electoral competitor to the Labour Party. Paradoxically, judging from the German experience, this would not necessarily be a disadvantage to the left inside the Labour Party. It could even assist them, just as the electoral presence of the Greens in Germany – an alliance rather than a unified party – has strengthened the left under the leadership of Oskar Lafontaine, within the SPD. At present, in a situation where Labour's electoral competition is from the right and the centre, the all-powerful pressure within the party is to silence the left in the mad rush for the centre. An electoral competitor on the left would be able, again like the Greens in Germany or the Socialist People's Party in Denmark, to turn popular feeling, for instance, against nuclear power and nuclear weapons into an electoral threat. This would be no substitute for the popular movements themselves but it would enhance their political impact, and it would improve the cultural conditions for the left throughout society. Such electoral pressure on the Labour Party would be only one form of pressure, secondary to movements in society. But such a party could provide a beacon spreading light on needs, initiatives and ideas that up till now have existed only in Labour's shadow.

In many ways it is an attractive option. However, without a significant split from the Labour left, it would probably not establish a significant enough electoral presence (and I am here assuming the introduction of PR). The red-green-feminist coalition is far more associated with the Labour left than ever it was with the left of the SPD in Germany. This is partly because socialist, working-class traditions have a greater weight in postwar Britain than in postwar Germany; and partly because of the attraction of the reform movement in the Labour Party for many members of these wider radical movements. Although, as the limits to these reforms have become apparent, the party has lost much of its potential attraction.

The left and Labour

There are however two very strong factors inhibiting any option involving a left split from the Labour Party, whatever the frustrations of the left's present position.

First, the 'party' section of the federation that makes up the Labour Party, that is the constituency parties, tends to support the left and is likely to continue to do so.[25] Its recent conference voting reflects tactical differences within the left, especially since 1983, on how far to go along with the leadership's electoral strategy. But on policy issues the vast majority has remained consistently on the left. Moreover, although there is much press talk of unrepresentative constituency activists, detailed case studies and reports of membership voting in the selection of MPs shows that the majority views of GMC delegates reflect the views of party members. This gives the left strong grounds for believing that the party is *their* party.

The second reason concerns the unions. For the new left, even more than the old parliamentary left, the party's organisational base in the unions is potentially vital. Socialists with a vision of socialist production based on workers' control are not likely to throw away an institutional bond with workers' organisations. Of course, the problem has always been, and still largely is, that the nature of this bond is not such as to encourage the political participation of trade-union members. On the contrary, the party–union bond has historically acted as a passive substitute for a genuine working-class political party. But during the last ten years or so trade-union members have begun to throw off this passivity and demand a greater say in the union's party activities.

The conditions for unity

In the second part of my Introduction, concerning the unity in the Labour Party of the ameliorative and transformative traditions (and therefore the impossibility of a separate left-wing party), I suggested three conditions for this unity. These were, first, the unity of the trade-union movement, second, the first-past-the-post electoral system, and third, the faith in the existing state shared by both traditions. In Chapters 1 and 3 I have aimed to show the growth of a new transformative tradition – bits of the shell of the old still clinging to its back – which has in practice lost many of its illusions in the existing state, even if it has not fully developed its theory of an alternative. In Chapter 5 I gave an indication of deep divisions within the unions which have their roots not simply in the ebb and flow of industrial militancy, but in the profound restructuring of the economy taking place throughout the capitalist world. And the third condition, the electoral system, is now being questioned from all sides, including the left of the Labour Party.

A fourth condition might be added though it is derived from the other three: Labour's electoral position as an alternative party of government.

The three initial conditions are weaker now than they have ever been. Even the fourth looks a little shaky though the difficulties facing the Alliance in the wake of the 1987 election give it, for the time being, a renewed resilience. The party is not on the verge of a split. However the divisions between Labourism – left and right – and the radical left are deeper than the divisions within Labourism ever were. For the time being, and for the foreseeable future, the radical left has lost the battle for the party's structure. Whether it can ever win this battle is open to question given the roots of that structure in the corporate institutions of the unions and in Parliament. What is certain however is that its long term success depends on the growth of socialist and radical democratic aspirations amongst millions of working people. And this cannot be achieved through the crossfire within the fortified walls of the Labour Party.

It requires the left in the Labour Party to reach out and work with socialists, the unions and the radical social movements. It will also depend on the left's confidence to publicly set an agenda for political and economic change. Finally, it will depend on the extent to which the left shifts the emphasis of its political routine, as it did during the miners' strike, from internal party life to involvement in local and workplace initiatives and movements.

This is not merely an organisational matter, it is also a matter of strategy and identity: a strategy based on popular initiative and organisation, supported by Parliament; an identity based not on British nationalism but on new identities of region and race with international as much as national connections.

For the left to achieve this, it will need to establish a positive independence it has never, except momentarily, had before. First, consider the question of political agenda and ideas. The left has to regain the policy and intellectual initiative it had in the seventies, particularly on the economy and on the state. At that time the new Labour left, in close collaboration with the left outside the party, generated ideas that began to explain the crisis of the British economy, that identified the forces behind the arms race, that exposed the character of the British state and that traced the multiple structures producing women's subordination. The foundations were created for new policies and strategies distinct from Labourism. But when the left lost control of the NEC in 1982, and with it lost the momentum of its struggle for power, these ideas lost a national political base.

The Labour left did not place any priority on the need to go beyond the existing party programmes. The problem was to implement them, and to the Labour left that was a matter of power within the party. The defeat of its struggle for power led it intellectually and programmatically to stand still, for fear of losing the benchmarks of its advance. As a result it did not consolidate or generalise radical developments made in practice in the late seventies, but not explained in theory. These include the questions of democracy and the state which, as shown in Chapter 1, were raised by the party's constitutional reforms. They also include the issues of industrial and financial strategy debated in the aftermath of the IMF crisis.

Practice almost always moves ahead of theory, but if there is no determined effort to improve the theory in the light of practice, the practice loses its way. This became clear in the dramatic decline of the left in the anticlimax after the Deputy Leadership campaign.

Away from national politics there *has* been further development of the theory, as I have tried to show earlier in this chapter. But this has yet to be integrated and expressed with a confident political voice as an alternative to Thatcherism and to the Alliance. For this the left needs to step away from the sterile arguments within the party – sterile, because the right and centre of the party have no new ideas. The 'new' policies they have produced are in general a rehash of the policies of the seventies, with some concessions to the left mixed in. The 1986 statement on social ownership is the best illustration of this magpie approach to policy.

The left needs to consciously set itself an intellectual and programmatic objective, rather as the Thatcherites did in the seventies with Keith Joseph's Centre for Policy Studies and the Institute of Economic Affairs. But with an important difference. The agency for the policies of the IEA, the existing state, was there to be taken over and reshaped from above. For us the agency and the policies need to be created simultaneously, challenging the existing state and establishing new kinds of democratic power from below. This involves an approach to intellectual and policy work that is part of a political movement. But it must be a distinct and conscious part which is given time, resources and support.

In the last ten years or so, networks and centres of such an approach have been established in different towns: trade-union research and resource centres; parts of the Workers' Educational Assocation; the various branches of the History Workshop; centres of trade-union education, such as Northern College in Barnsley; groups of socialist, feminist and peace-movement intellectuals such as the *Feminist Review*, the *Journal of the Campaign for European Nuclear Disarmament*, the Conference of Socialist Economics, and the Socialist Society. But until recently this kind of policy, intellectual and educational work, has been badly undervalued by the organised left in the Labour Party. The imperatives of the inner-party struggle leave little time for such concerns, ultimately to the left's cost.

The second direction in which the Labour left's independence will mean a wrench from these inner-party pressures is towards 'non-political' movements in the locality and workplace. To give an example from London's dockland communities, which bulldozers, property developers, City financiers and a non-elected development corporation quango are turning into a business people's paradise: ever since 1981, when the London Dockland Development Corporation took over the land and overrode the power of elected local councils, dockland people have been fighting for their communities. Between 1983 and 1985 some of the strongest protest came from North Woolwich, a community surrounding the Royal Docks where developers were intending to build an inner-city airport. Tenants' leaders organised a determined and ingenious campaign which gained real popular support, with street parties, sporting events in the dockside sheds and meetings in every part of the community. It turned the local Labour council against the airport (they were initially going to support it), it won political and financial support from the Labour GLC. But with the exception of one or two individual councillors, the Labour *Party* was nowhere to be seen. It passed resolutions in support, for sure. It was its active involvement in spreading support for the campaign that was missing. 'We went to them,' says Connie Hunt, one of the women organising the campaign, 'but they weren't really part of us.'

Without being 'part of us', the left will never have the active popular support that is necessary for its participatory vision of socialism. The problem might seem at first to be simply one of time and priorities: 'How can we maintain our position on the GMC or select left councillors *and* be involved in local campaigns?' But the fact that the Labour left is faced so starkly with this choice between inner-party priorities and local working-class concerns indicates a deeper problem. This is the Labour Party's lack of an active popular base.

There is nothing new about this. Academics have been documenting it for years. But there are deeply rooted attitudes in the Labour left which either ignore the problem or presume that it can be solved *after* the left has won control of the party. The experiences of the seventies and early eighties indicate that such procrastination is based on wishful thinking. The left can gain control of key positions within the existing structures and win formal support for its resolutions. But it cannot hold on to these positions, nor turn the formal commitments into action, because the content of the party's structures, in particular the weight within them of the trade-union and parliamentary leadership, is heavily biased against change. Only when the Labour left has briefly become a focus for a popular force that can counter this weight – the peace movement, trade-union militancy – has it had a real impact.

Such moments have been short-lived, because the left has not found a way of making itself a direct voice for such popular forces. Instead, reinvigorated by the popular movement, it scuttles back into its hole in the Labour Party, leaving most of the movement behind, bemused and suspicious. The Labour left's only chance of lasting change is if, in the process of winning control, it positively creates a different kind of party both inside and outside the existing structures, a party which is the natural political voice for the anger of those like the people of Docklands.

Realising this potential would involve, in some form or other, a process of refounding the left – establishing its ideas and structures independently of its conflict with the Labour Party leadership. Its dealings with the leadership would need to be on the basis of ideas and initiatives worked out through its own structures; the relationship would be one of negotiation, on the basis of an open independence. In a sense, the left would be part of two coalitions: the coalition of Labour and the coalition of radical socialism which reaches beyond Labour. In this way its ideas and strategies would flourish without being perpetually clouded by tactical considerations. It would establish its own involvement with the unions, encouraging the process of political debate and democratisation which began during the consti-tutional reforms. Its MPs would be one part of a wider movement, rather than the minor royalty they have traditionally been. Women and black people would have the right to independent organisation. Close working alliances would be formed with other socialist organisations and with socialists among Scottish nationalists and Plaid Cymru, and in the peace movement, the CND and anti-nuclear supporters among the Liberals. The loose network of cultural and intellectual groups that have existed in the half-light since the late sixties would gain political expression. Only through this kind of independence will the left be able to give a powerful political voice to the social and industrial resistance likely to grow under a third term of Thatcherite Conservatism.

Such an alliance will be scorned, satirised and pilloried. Its inevitable blunders will be amplified by a gleeful press. But the hatred that motivates the ridicule stems from a real fear on the part of the establishment. Its members know that Britain is not a democracy, and they know how much they stand to lose should it become one.

7 After 1987:
Just an Electoral Machine?

Labour's campaign for the next election started on June 12, 1987. Neil Kinnock declared this to be so. Many politicians make declarations of this sort, but Kinnock, for once, was not indulging in rhetoric. He made a similar remark when he first became leader. And on both occasions he meant something very specific: that everything the party did must be geared to winning election. And there was only one way of winning. What was that way? Why did it fail? How will it change? How should it change? What does the independence of the left now imply?

At first sight the Kinnock way to win is about modernising the party image, ridding it of extremist and old-fashioned associations, streamlining its central organisation, and building an energetic mass membership. A dynamic party, a young leader – of the people – fit to govern. But the effect of his strategy, the labourist tradition within which he thinks and the alliances he makes, has been to encourage a regime of centralised conservatism geared more to avoiding risks than to grasping opportunities, to controlling initiative rather than releasing it. It has different manifestations. I witnessed a minor but telling one behind the scenes of Labour's campaign.

It was at the 'Family Funday' on the Sunday before polling; children covered with 'Vote Labour' stickers were milling around the entrance to the Islington Business Centre, paper sellers were offering their wares, stewards with bleepers were cheerily checking the tickets of those wishing to go in. Inside the fun was well organised, nothing left to chance. There were cartoon characters on stilts, huge nets full of balloons, party streamers with accompanying notes telling you to throw them 'when the balloons come down', stewards encouraging you to sit down 'to show the cameras that it's full'. The afternoon promised entertainment and inspiration: Lenny Henry, Glenda Jackson, the Gospel Inspirational Choir, and then Neil Kinnock himself. Kinnock's earlier speeches in the campaign had provided a powerful attack on Thatcherism – more powerful than any he had made since becoming leader. The effect of the three-party competition had been to strengthen Labour's campaign in its need to clearly outflank and distinguish itself from the SDP. In response, party activists were sinking their differences to see him succeed. 'We've given up nearly everything,' said a member from Haringey, as the event became more and more like a Democratic Party convention, 'It must succeed mustn't it'?

A friend then told me of something else that participants in the 'Funday' had to give up. Like everyone she had been searched. (I had assumed it was a routine security.) As her belongings wee being looked through, one steward had turned to another and asked, 'Is the *Listener* all right?' Astounded, she asked what would have happened if she had brought in a copy of *Socialist Worker*. 'You'd have been interviewed by a higher authority,' came the reply, without a smile. Not being able to believe my ears I went outside with a colleague and bought a single copy of *Socialist Worker*. Slipping it under my arm I returned to the hall. When I came to be searched, an earnest young man asked me 'Please could you leave the paper on one side and pick it up afterwards.' Don't be ridiculous,' I replied laughing, 'Why should I do that?' 'Please,' he pleaded, 'it will embarrass Neil Kinnock.'

A steward, Carmel Bedford, later provided the full explanation. At the official briefing stewards were told that the only political paper anyone was allowed to bring into the building was *Labour Weekly*. A case of over-assiduous stewarding perhaps.

The language of vengeance

It seems however that a similar drive to exclude underlies the attitude of leading members of the party towards independent voices from a wide spectrum of the left. We have already seen some of this in action over black sections and the demands of the women's conference. It surfaced again after the election. Around the time of the Shadow Cabinet elections talk was of 'how to marginalise the Campaign Group'. Labour MPs spoke to journalists off the record about 'plans to crush the hard left'. The 'hard left' is a moving target and no doubt there are subtle distinctions between the 'loony' and the 'hard', though in the minds of most right and centre MPs they blur conveniently into one. After the election this target has moved from Liverpool (where left as well as right gained some of the largest swings in the country) to London. 'One Northern MP described the London Labour Party as "a cess pit"', reported the *Independent*. Ken Livingstone cannot do a thing right in the eyes of such Honourable Members. Soon after he had embarrassed the Prime Minister – surely something an opposition is meant to do? – and enraged the Tories with his revelations about the role of MI5 in Northern Ireland, one complained, 'Here we are not three weeks from losing the election and the bugger stirs things up over Ireland . . . Ugh . . . It's outrageous.'

There is no conspiracy, just a license to close ranks against anyone perceived as a threat by the dominant sections of the centre or right. In Birmingham, for instance, it has been feminists and blacks. Before the election the Leader of the Council disbanded the Women's Committee, withdrew the whip from a black councillor, Phil Murphy, who was involved in the movement for black sections, and removed senior councillors such as Teresa Stewart, the long-standing campaigner on social service issues, from their committee posts.

Kinnock has given attacks such as these a wider legitimacy. He set the example with his dramatic defeat of Militant at Bournemouth in 1985. This he made the symbol of his leadership, rather as the 'victory' of the Falklands' task force became the symbol of Thatcher's. Both wars were escalated to demonstrate the prowess of the leader. Both political machines used their symbolic value to the maximum, Labour Party propaganda evoking its emotion during the 1987 campaign in the same way as Tory propaganda evoked the symbolism of the Falklands during 1983. Since then defeats of the dissident left, regardless of their distance from the politics of Militant, have gained a certain heroic aura, as if somehow they will help the party to win. (The recent election results have not borne this out. The centre and right candidates in the West Midlands did relatively badly compared to candidates of all political persuasions further north. The results do not indicate that the left does significantly better than the right or centre, but they do demonstrate that candidates on the left – including supports of Militant – are not, other things being equal, vote losers.)

Conservative centralism

Exclusion is one aspect of conservative centralism; another is the avoidance of risk, uncertainty and unpredictability. It is this which appears to have governed the policy-making process. The mentality at the core of this seems to have been that of the production-line – though facing numerous breakdowns – rather than of the laboratory, which would test new ideas, build on successful experiements and generalise from practical experiences.

Peter Mandelson, the man recruited to streamline the party's publicity and communications, talks approvingly of Kinnock as a 'walking quality controller'. In Kinnock's office the miners' strike, an immense social struggle, was known as 'the lost year', rather in the same way as managers talk of 'lost days in production'. It was viewed as a year of risks. Rather than build the 'Jobs and Industry' campaign around the issues raised by the strike (the management of nationalised industries, the shorter working week, energy policy and employment), and take the high ground away from Thatcher on the economy at a time when opinion polls showed she was slipping, Labour postponed the launch of the campaign until after the strike was over.

Labour local authorities provided another example of innovative policies on which the national party could have built. Many of them really were experimenting, as we have seen, with all the problems involved in venturing onto new ground in unpropitious circumstances. Moreover they were experimenting with ideas which contain at least the elements of a radical and socialist alternative to Thatcherism; ideas which, as I have tried to show, emerged prior to or in parallel with Thatcherism, and, like the Thatcherite revolution, as a reaction to the collapse of the Keynesian consensus. Potentially, many of them answer Thatcher's siren calls to both the material and democratic desires of the skilled employed working class by offering a possibility of economic democracy, community democracy and flexible state provision.

In general the leadership did not build on these – too many hostages to fortune. One result of the party's suspicion of most of the innovating local authorities, particularly those within a taxi ride from Fleet Street, was the devastating campaign against the 'loony left' which Norman Tebbit launched in November 1986. Although the bulk of it was based on what Goldsmith's College Department of Communications has shown to be fabrications, or on blowing up what many of the councillors responsible themselves regard as mistakes, it undoubtedly had an impact on the election result. Martin Linton, political correspondent on the *Guardian*, helps to explain the success of this campaign: 'the key to it was that the Tories created the impression of a pattern of behaviour. They would link every little thing they could dig out about a Labour local council to the theme of "loony left" so that incidents that would never normally be reported, or were taken out of context, would all become newsworthy because they had the "loony left" tag. Labour did not sufficiently project an alternative pattern of the good things Labour councils had done. If they had I think it would have been much more difficult to sustain the campaign.'

Jack Cunningham, Labour's front-bench spokesman on local government, echoed rather than challenged the Tory attack. Only after Kinnock had seen the Goldsmith's College report in May 1987 did the leadership project a positive counter campaign, and by then it was too late.

There was one policy area, employment, where the Shadow Cabinet minister responsible, John Prescott, did take up the ideas of local authorities and seek to spread them. Although this too was weakened by Shadow Cabinet hostility, it was sufficiently developed to illustrate what might have been possible. Initially four councils put forward their plans for creating useful jobs. The press response was positive, even to the plan put forward by the 'loony' Southwark. When other councils started drawing up their plans the movement gathered momentum. A powerful wing of the Shadow Cabinet, however, objected to the plans to increase the powers and resources of local authorities. Moreover they were against any initiative which raised expectations. Prescott persisted, and produced a pamphlet summarising the four plans and their wider national implications. But as official party policy it slipped into the background and with it slipped a way of illustrating alternatives to unemployment, and Prescott was demoted for his pains.

Policy making or packaging?

The caution of the Shadow Cabinet is built into the new policy-making process. In 1984 the NEC created ten Joint Policy Committees, on Kinnock's proposal, to streamline (and no doubt enable the leader to exert some 'quality control' over) what had been a plethora of NEC policy committees and subcommittees.

The new system consolidates effective power over the details of policy in the hands of the parliamentary spokespeople. In fact this has always been where power ultimately lay, even when the NEC and the PLP leadership were in conflict. The present system is more directly based on the real balance of power, whereas the old system, with its numerous nooks and crannies and small subcommittees allowed all kinds of radical policy discussions to take place and statements to be produced. These may not have been well co-ordinated, but at least they produced new ideas, which the present system does not.[1]

The conservative character of the Joint Committee System is illustrated by the fate of imaginative plans such as the GLC's Community Areas Policy, a scheme which would have been attractive to those well-off workers in places like Harlow, whom Labour needs to persuade. This policy would have increased community control over the local environment, developing plans in concert with the council, to counter the forces of the predatory property market. Despite the efforts of George Nicholson, Chair of the GLC Planning Committee, 'Public Action Zones' met with inertia from the PLP and resistance from the right, in the person of then Shadow Environment Minister John Cunningham. Formal party committment was soon hedged around with talk of tight criteria and pilot projects. This hesitancy about a policy for extending public rights contrasts markedly with the confident tone of the Conservative Party when they reassert their enthusiasm for the market, with bold and detailed policies.

The dilemma for the more aware and progressive amongst the Labour leadership who realised that they needed innovative thinking was that the majority of such ideas were generated by the radical left out of experiments which the leadership found an embarrassment. Some of these ideas slipped on board the policy statements through people like Nicholson but they were regarded as risks, treated like stowaways, and hidden in verbiage.

As a result the main policies on which Labour fought the election were, with the exception of defence, policies which in effect simply defended the post-war settlement. This meant – given the desire of the Alliance leaders to return to the old consensus – that Thatcher's programme for promoting the private market and centralising public power was the only radical programme on offer.

Swathing it in consensus

This is more than a failure of imagination. As far as Kinnock is concerned there is already a consensus out there; it is just a matter of hooking onto it and pulling it in like some giant fishing net. There is little sense in his speeches prior to the election campaign that the problem might be to *create* a consensus around Labour's politics. His method of seeking support for ideas that are at any one time unpopular is to show how they are consistent with the existing consensus, Thatcher's consensus.

Take defence for example. The party's original commitment to decommissioning Polaris and Trident and sending back Cruise missiles also contained a new foreign policy which made these defence policies coherent. This was to be a foreign policy based on Britain's position as a medium-sized European power; it involved the beginnings of a reassessment of the special relationship with the United States, the cornerstone of Labour's acceptance of a bipartisan foreign policy since 1945. Moreover it talked confidently about the economic benefits of nuclear disarmament, of releasing the vast resources, including most of the country's most skilled technologists, locked up in the arms industry. These were the arguments agreed by Conference and made public in a policy statement in 1984. They were radical arguments providing the foundations for a radical policy; and arguments for which it would take time to win the support of even half the British public. An ideal case for a campaign, building on the popular awareness built by CND and the Greenham Women.

No campaign took place, however, until November 1986. By then the arguments had been changed. The commitment to nuclear disarmament had stayed but the foreign policy, like a camouflage, was essentially the bipartisan approach of the past. Britain would still behave like a major power; Atlanticism was preserved. Not only this, but the country's technical resources would remain in the hands of the military. Conventional defence would be massively built up as nuclear defence was dismantled. The campaign had been prepared partly with the guidance of qualitative market research which had indicated that the basic premises of Labour's new defence policy were not at all popular. The only chance of the anti-nuclear commitment being electorally acceptable was if it was wrapped in the old assumptions of Britain's greatness and a strong defence against an implied Soviet threat. And thus a new defence statement was prepared. It did not go to the NEC because it was 'campaign material'. The purpose of launching 'the campaign' in November 1986 was not to have time to win the argument – by then it was too late – but to take the sting out of press comment before the election.

In this process, the Labour leadership gave up, or rather failed even to start, a process of creating a new consensus. Instead they sought to steal a share of Thatcher's. Labour's defence policy had been transformed from a policy for peace to a panegyric on Britain's conventional military might. Moreover, Kinnock's stance in Parliament was to demonstrate his devotion to the state rather than to represent the people. In his attempt to outdo Thatcher in protecting 'national security' over the Zircon spy satellite, he seemed virtually to bow at its altar. His acceptance of Thatcher's definition of national security (in circumstances when the threat to security, as distinct from a threat to the government's relations with the US and the government's own parliamentary standing, never existed) drew him into her definition of the nation itself: a definition in which Labour plays a subordinate role.

The limits of Labourism

And so on June 11 it proved to be. In his four-year leadership Kinnock's skill at quality control had put a new shine on Labourism. The campaign remedied all the technical, organisational and leadership flaws of 1983. But as we have shown, Labourism is a subordinate ideology, lacking its own positive perspective for reorganising the economy and transforming the state. Thatcherism has cruelly exposed the truth of this; it taunted Labour for its socialism yet benefited from its timidity. Against Thatcher's attempts to redirect the whole economy, Labour appeared to be concerned only with problems of distribution. True to its origins as an ideology of trade unionism it concentrated on distribution and took for granted production and the generation of wealth. As far as the state was concerned, whether nationally or locally, in services or in industry, Labour stood for little more (and sometimes a little less) than a return to the status quo before Thatcher. Its election campaign used the techniques of the eighties, but its ideas went little beyond the achievements of 1945. The image makers might project a strong leader but their efforts could not disguise the absence of a strong vision for society.

The party fought the 1987 campaign as a united party (one reason for this was that the left, unlike the right in 1983, accepted the discipline of party unity). But the source of the party's divisions – the failure of Labour governments and the issues of state and economy which these failures exposed – had not been addressed. Yet these are the very issues at the centre of the new conservatism. Those in the Labour Party who sacrifice everything for unity are in danger of sacrificing the independence necessary to develop a convincing ideological alternative to Thatcherism.

Pragmatic voting

Who does such an alternative have to convince? One answer can be found by looking at the voters in Harlow, a new town in the south-east, which Labour lost to the Conservatives in 1983. The largest group amongst these voters are semi-skilled or skilled workers. It is the kind of seat Labour has to win if it is to win a general election. As the *Almanac of British Politics*, published in 1986, commented:

If there is no way back for Labour in the hypermodern town of Harlow, it would surely offer a frightening face of the future for the party.

But in 1987 the Conservatives increased their majority from 3,674 to 5,877, and little of this can be accounted for by the middle-class voters who live in surrounding villages. The local Labour party calculate that at least 3,000 skilled or semi-skilled workers in employment voted Conservative for the first or second time. Carol Haslan, the Constituency Women's Officer, describes the response of such converts to Labour canvassers: 'They saw our policies more as a threat than a benefit, they thought that if others were going to gain through more money spent on services, they would lose out.'

Insecurity as much as prosperity explains this view. All the major firms in Harlow: STC, United Glass, Cossors and International Distillers, had cut back on jobs. New jobs had come in retailing and in warehousing, but not many and mostly part-time. The point was, however, that workers felt they had something to hold on to and did not trust Labour to offer anything better. Judging from national opinion polls this was not something that good advertising could overcome: according to one opinion poll in the run-up to the election the Labour Party rated only half as high as the Conservatives as a party which keeps its promises in government.[2] Labour's past, it seems, lives on even under a leader whose hands are clean.

All this points to a pragmatic shift to the Conservatives amongst the voters whose support Labour needs to win, rather than a deep ideological attachment to Thatcherism. (In local elections, throughout the eighties, many of these same people in Harlow have voted for a Labour council, indeed one influenced by the radical left.) This does not make the future of the national Labour Party if it remains as it is any less frightening. But it does indicate that the problem is a tractable one rather than one of reversing some mysterious transformation of the southern working-class psyche. Nonetheless, that it is a problem which cannot be solved with the tools of Labourism.

A new image for Labourism?

While defending Labourist politics, the party leadership has however been concerned about its image. First has been the problem of Labourism's inappropriateness to the changed character of labour itself, particularly the increased proportion of both the workforce and the unemployed who are women and blacks. In the rhetoric of the party, 'working people' is increasingly understood as including women and blacks. And women have found it possible to prise open some space for policies which would have been unthinkable five years ago; in particular the proposals for a Ministry for Women. As we saw in Chapter 4 however, the old caution stops the process short at women members' rights for direct representation at the centre of the party's power structure or recognition of black members' rights to self-organisation.

Labourism and individualism

The second issue is that of individualism. Thatcherism has been able to exploit a fundamental weakness in the collectivism on which Labourism is based: its tendency to treat the collectives to which it is loyal, the trade unions and the state in particular, as wholes (often idealised wholes), apart from the individuals who compose them. Because of this tendency to reify social structures – instead of recognising that while social structures do pre-exist individuals, they depend on individuals' agency and activity – Thatcher has been able to make great ideological capital out of trade-union and state bureaucracy. She has created a powerful dichotomy between the state which provides (or hands out) with all the connotations of uniformity, indignity and power-lessness, and the individual who buys and decides with positive associations of variety, choice and self-respect. By counterposing the self-interested individual to the alien collective she denies the existence of social relations which constrain and exploit individuals. Society becomes nothing more than individuals competing for their own self-interest. And success or failure lies solely with the individual.

Like sinners under the spell of a new priest, Labour leaders have turned to the religion of individualism, hoping it will provide the route to salvation. 'Being part of a collective is not as strong as it used to be,' confessed Mr Kinnock a few weeks after the election. 'Our initial approach has got to be from the party to the individual. They have got to be told that socialism is the answer for them because socialism looks after the individual.' And it seems in this new creed individuals are defined not in terms of the various social relations which define or constitute their social identities, but in terms of the property they own:

'We have to appeal to the individuals who own their own house, a car and perhaps £500 worth of shares,' concluded Bryan Gould, fresh from his job as Campaign Co-ordinator.

There are few signs of internal critique of Labourism amongst the leadership, of a process of asking *why* Thatcherism has been able to make such headway with a spurious philosophy. Rather, the approach seems to be that Labourism was appropriate to its times and circumstances and still has its uses – in the north (when do you hear Neil Kinnock or John Smith questioning the racism and sexism implicit in many of the attacks launched from the strongholds of Labourism on the 'London Left'?), in the trade-union block vote (now to be introduced in the process of reselection of MPs) and in macro-economic policy (the continued faith, against all experience from 1964 onwards, in the Holy Trinity of the CBI, the TUC and the government being able to run the economy). The result seems likely to be an amalgam: Labourism when they can get away with it and individualism where market research says they cannot – home ownership, share ownership, the image of the party's membership.

The new espousal of 'individualism' is likely to remain largely a matter of packaging, but packaging seems to have replaced most policy-making. Moreover, the uncritical adoption of the rhetoric of individualism signifies a deep lack of confidence in Labour's (or rather its leadership's) sense of direction. It would therefore be useful to make a brief philosophical detour into the assumptions concerning the individual and society which underly the contending politics.[3] Such a detour would also enable us to see more clearly the fundamental difference between Labourism and radical socialism. Unless these philosophical issues are clear, the radical left may end up defending Labourism as if none of the conflicts and innovations of the last ten years had happened.

Individuals and society

Radical socialism emerged as a reaction to the different bureau-cratic collectivisms of Labour and of the Soviet Union and their failures (the post-1956 critique of ex-members of the Communist Party and the critical impetus of Trotskyism have both been historical influences on the radical left). It also involved (cul-turally as much as politically) a rejection of the glorification of individualism which flourished during the consumer boom of the fifties. Its underlying model of society is neither as the sum of individual actions (individualism) nor as supra-individual wholes (collectivism), but as relatively enduring but transformable relations between individuals.

On this basis socialist transformation implies democracy, economic and political, which will bring social relations under public scrutiny, and it also demands resistance to those relations which are exploitative and oppressive and the creation of others through which individuals can achieve well-being.

Consider the contrasting views on nationalised industries for instance: a collectivist view would imply that state ownership and control was itself the social transformation needed to meet the needs of working-class people. An individualist view would advocate individual shareholdings as meeting people's individual self-interest. A 'relational' view would concern itself consciously with understanding and transforming the details of the relations between workers and managers, amongst workers, and between those who work in the industry and the community outside. The social ownership and control of an industry's capital would be a condition for changes in the relations between individuals.

The same contrasts could be made in relation to health, education and housing, where the collectivist relies on universal provision, the individualist on the market, and the relational view stresses the democracy of social provision and its responsiveness to varying needs. This is the view which, implicitly and often unevenly, runs through the activities of the radical left, whether Tony Benn's stress on democratising the nationalised industries in the early seventies or Manchester Council's attempt to establish Neighbourhood Forums to control its local services. It is a view which theoretically distinguishes this left not only from the Labourism – and now Labourism/individualism – of the leadership, but also from the tendency on the part of those on the left who reify and idealise 'the working class'.

Constitutional reform

The opportunistic amalgam of individualism and Labourism is evident in the debate about reforming the party's constitution. Here Neil Kinnock is introducing a selective stress on the democracy of the individual vote. This *is* selective however, geared more to a desired outcome (no more Pat Walls, Peter Tatchells or Deirdre Woods) than to the democracy of the process. The argument for one member one vote (so long as it is based on meetings rather than postal ballots) is in itself a strong one, especially if ways are found of involving the individual member in the accountability of the MP. But the implications of this argument – one shared in principle by many on the radical left though with a scepticism about the leadership's use of it – would imply a critical attitude towards the present character of the block vote.

On the criteria of a participatory party, the present form of block vote by which votes are cast by delegates on behalf of levy-paying trade-union members (many of whom are unaware that they are paying a levy and do not support the Labour Party) should be drastically reformed. The leadership however are reported to favour the block vote being introduced, as part of a local electoral college, into the reselection of MPs. So here is Neil Kinnock, the passionate advocate of the participation of the ordinary member and the elimination of procedures open to manipulation, introducing the procedure most open to abuse and least likely to foster participation. The only explanation for Kinnock's contradictory position is that he is more concerned with the outcome than the principles of the process.

Pressures from the right for a more consistent approach will not be strong. A consistent right-wing view would involve breaking the institutional links with unions and doing away with the block vote altogether. The party could still maintain an informal relationship with the unions and receive financial support. This is the position in Germany between the Social Democratic Party and the national unions and with the Democratic Party and the main unions in America. It would have been the ideal of the majority of those who formed the SDP (though they never had the courage to say it so long as the block vote went their way).

From the left too there is a strong case for reforming the block vote. In Chapter 5 I suggested, drawing from the ideas of Eric Heffer, a way of basing the trade union – party relationship on real, flesh-and-blood party members organised through their union and place of work. A block vote based on individual party members organised through the union would not automatically favour the left, but it would be more democratic than the present system, would make for a more genuinely participating party, and would in many cases strengthen the political culture of the unions. Now is not the time for a detailed discussion of this approach. The point of stating this proposal is to show that there are more democratic and more political means of sustaining the party's working-class roots than through the unions' corporate voting power.

The atmosphere in the party however is not one which fosters open debate in which proposals can be discussed on their democratic merits. The atmosphere is one of *realpolitik*.

Another example of a headlong rush from collectivism to individualism is in the party's methods of policy making. Market research is becoming the central focus of policy making. 'Market research will tell us what people want and then our job is to show that we are the party that can provide it,' is Bryan Gould's winning formula. 'We need market researchers more than we need philosophers,' agrees Austin Mitchell. They throw out collectivism because it no longer delivers them power, but because the only alternative they can see is individualism, they also throw out the Labour movement. For the method they have overlooked, or cannot conceive of, is a process – already going on – whereby the party, with union and community activists, themselves carry out from the bottom up the listening and arguing, learning and leading which is so clearly necessary. Through market research, which gauges individual opinions away from any social context, the leadership will further swathe what is left of party policies in Thatcher's consensus. By contrast a policy-making and campaigning process based on the listening and leading skills of trade-union and party activists like Jean Ferguson and Joyce Wilson at the Newcastle Infirmary, Ann Suddick in the Durham pit villages, Carol Haslan in the Harlow Town Council communities, Hassan Ahmed of the Nottingham black section or John Shiers in the Manchester Neighbourhood Forums would have a good chance of creating a new consensus. They have shown that they can do it in their own workplace or community. But Kinnock, who has final power over the policy-making, is politically afraid of such a process: as if transfixed by the hostile glare of Thatcherite forces, he dare not move except in their shadow.

The left's dilemma

The particularly taut electoralism of the present leadership poses the radical left in the Labour Party with a dilemma. It is not a new dilemma, but the collapse of the traditional electoral certainties make it more stark.

The radical left wants, and needs, to win elections, and indeed has had some success in doing so, both in the 1987 election and in local elections. It has different views, however, from the leadership as to how Thatcherism can most effectively be challenged. In addition it sees electoral changes as only one part of a socialist transformation. Since 1983 the space for the left to put forward these differences has become increasingly small within the national institutions of the party. Differences voiced on the NEC, for instance, will very quickly be presented as disloyal and as jeopardising Labour's electoral chances. Some on the left will simply go along with the leadership, in the faint hope of influencing the occasional policy; those who remain in opposition will find themselves in an increasingly defensive corner, unless they strike out on a more independent path.

There are two aspects of the politics of the radical left which it would be useful to think about in distinct ways, even though ultimately they must be connected. One side is electoral and parliamentary, the other is concerned with struggles and movements seeking change of a more fundamental kind.

I draw a distinction between the two because there is a subtle institutional pressure coming from the very fibres of the party for the left to present their politics as a whole, as a competing electoral strategy to that of the leadership. This can lead supporters to make patently unrealistic claims and assumptions about the extent of socialist consciousness amongst the electorate. It also strengthens a tendency to push for full socialist programmes on all occasions for fear of making compromises, rather than using the wider strategic view to identify more limited initiatives within electoral or parliamentary politics, while continuing extra-parliamentary activity.

Let us consider the problem of electoral strategy first. It is not the most fundamental but it is the one which dominates public political debate. The problem we face is that the extent of Labour's defeat, following a technically and organisationally competent campaign, indicates that we could face two more terms of Conservative rule unless there is a marked change in political or constitutional alignments. There are two kinds of response the left could make to this. One is to rely on shifts affecting other parties – the further collapse of the Alliance, for instance, or a split in the Conservatives – and to make sure that Labour is well placed to reap the benefits. This would let too much hang on wishful thinking. The other option is for the Labour Party itself to make a dramatic shift on political or constitutional issues.

Three kinds of moves would in theory be possible, two of which I have already mentioned. The first would be a leap from Labourism to the right, breaking the formal trade-union links, making an explicit commitment to the market, dropping unilateralism. The second would be a turn from Labourism to the left, towards the kind of radical alternative to Thatcherism sketched earlier. Moves towards the first option are likely to be tried, but Kinnock will resist most of them both for reasons of personal principle and because of his and the party's deep historical and financial dependence on the unions. The second option is unrealistic as an effective *electoral* proposal. Labourism runs too deep in the party's bones for the left to make a major impact of such a fundamental character within the present parliamentary term. Such an ideological shift would only be possible as a result of the independent pressures of the left working inside and outside the party backed by the force of wider social movements. This is the lesson of all previous major changes of position within the party. And such a movement will be a long haul, far longer than a single electoral term.

The left therefore needs to select or develop policies which directly challenge and expose the Conservative government – including its democratic illegitimacy – and which, while not necessarily being socialist in themselves, will open the way to socialism. This process needs considerable work and discussion. I would suggest that a central theme should be democratic reforms aimed at the main centres of power – about which there is widespread but unfocused discontent: the City, the Westminster/Whitehall establishment, the judiciary and big corporations. Some of the necessary measures would be democratic reforms of the constitution and the state. They should include:

the restoration of powers to local authorities and the extension of their economic powers; a Scottish and a Welsh Assembly with economic powers, a commitment to democratic regional government elsewhere; the withdrawal of troops from Northern Ireland and a constitutional assembly for Ireland, a Ministry for Women, a Freedom of Information Act, the accountability of the security services directly to Parliament rather than the Prime Minister, electoral reform, an elected second chamber and an opening up of the judiciary together with a Bill of Rights.

Others would be steps towards economic democracy, for example government action to establish a right to work so that no compulsory redundancies could take place without alternatives (including shorter working hours) being found – action which does not block technological advance but reduces its social and human costs. Another step would be industrial democracy based on the unions and elected regional authorities to run the re-nationalised industries. A final example would be action which imposed political and economic controls on the City, of the same ruthlessness as those Thatcher is imposing on local government. The aim of all these measures would quite explicitly be to break the concentrated power of the British establishment.

These reforms, modest though in fact they are by the standards of the left's long-term goals, involve a radical break from the assumption which is really at the heart of British Labourism. That the good old British way of doing things – from Whitehall to the local planning department – can produce equality and even socialism, because it is essentially democratic. Individual MPs such as Tony Benn, Dennis Skinner, Claire Short and Robin Cook, and now Ken Livingstone and forceful groups of women, blacks and Scots have been and will be alerting people to the elementary fact that the present way of doing things – under Labour as well as under the Conservatives – is a basic impediment to a more equal and free society, let alone socialism. These guerrilla forays by individual MPs could be built into an effective democratic programme for which the left could campaign in the party and in the unions as the central theme of the party's electoral strategy.[4]

Such a programme would not achieve socialism. But it would prepare the way. Socialist transformation is a far deeper process. Its foundations must be built into the institutions of daily life, especially material life. The Labour Party traditionally has not inhabited these institutions except as the union boss, as members of a governing body or as the employer. Given the endemic weakness of other working-class parties in Britain, there is at present virtually no sustained and nationally organised socialist presence in these spheres. As Steve Riley, the young secretary of the 3,000 strong T & G W U branch at Fords Dagenham declared, almost in despair, 'There's no party that workers can turn to, in a dispute or just to help make sense of things.' And that means a party that is present in every factory, design office, hospital, school and community. Only by filling this vacuum will the radical left, inside and outside the Labour Party, and its allies produce the impetus and confidence amongst people to create socialism, in the wake of defeating the present government.

Notes

Introduction

1 – For a detailed analysis of Bevanism see Mark Jenkins, *Bevanism: Labour's High Tide*, Spokesman, 1979

2 – H. A. Turner, 'The Trends of Strikes' in *Social Trends* (1970 edition)

3 – Aneurin Bevan, *In Place of Fear*, Heinemann, 1952, p.5

4 – Vic Allen, *Trade Union Leadership*, Longmans, 1957

5 – Peggy Duff, *Left, Left, Left*, Allison and Busby, 1971. Similar situations occurred locally during the same period. For instance in Leeds, the local Labour Party paper, *The Weekly Citizen*, then edited by a left-winger, put out a broadsheet in support of a textile workers' strike. The union's regional officials were not pleased and, with regional Labour Party officials, ensured that such party involvement with union affairs was not repeated.

6 – Sheila Rowbotham, Lynne Segal, Hilary Wainwright, *Beyond the Fragments*, Merlin Press, 1980. See critical comments by Elizabeth Wilson, 'Beyond the Ghetto: Thoughts on "Beyond the Fragments"', *Feminist Review*, 4, 1980, p. 38; Anna Paczuska, *Socialist Worker*, June 1980. For further development of some of the ideas see *Beyond the Fragments Bulletin* 1–4

7 – See Henry Phelps Brown, *The Origins of Trade Union Power*, Oxford University Press, 1986

8 – Tom Nairn, 'The Nature of the Labour Party' in *Towards Socialism*, Fontana/New Left Review, 1965; David Howell, *British Social Democracy*, Croom Helm, 1976; Geoffrey Foote, *The Political Thought of the Labour Party*, Croom Helm, 1985; Barry Jones and Michael Keating, *Labour and the British State*, Clarendon Press, Oxford, 1985; and Ralph Miliband, *Parliamentary Socialism*, Merlin Press, 1985, are good places to start.

9 – By no means the majority of those involved in this militancy developed in this direction. Some, frustrated by Labourism, and lacking any labour-movement alternative, ended up supporting Thatcher: see Doreen Massey, 'The Contours of Defeat', *Marxism Today*, September 1983; Anthony Barnett, 'How Mrs Thatcher Hijacked the Thrusting Class of '68', *The Guardian*, April 14, 1987.

Chapter 1   Reselection and the State

1 – Interpretations of the result are complicated by the existence at the previous election of a ratepayers' candidate while at the 1977 election the only third candidate was a representative of the National Front. However, the important point is that in spite of a Tory campaign whose main theme was the 'Marxist takeover of the party' the Labour vote went up.

2 – *Sunday Telegraph*, July 6, 1975

3–*Daily Telegraph*, February 24, 1978
4–*Daily Mirror*, July 18, 1975
5–*Guardian*, July 18, 1975
6–The full list of signatories is in *Tribune*, December 11, 1981
7–The detailed story of the campaign for the constitutional reforms is told in D. Kogan, M. Kogan, *The Battle for the Labour Party*, Fontana 1982. Leo Pantitch provides a far more analytic, and more profound, study of the background to these reforms in *Lions, Donkeys and Jackals*, Verso (forthcoming, 1988)
8–Edward Milne, *No Shining Armour*, John Calder, 1976
9–Quoted in Richard West, 'Find the Source of Power', *New Statesman*, February 23, 1973
10–The only public support Milne received in senior Labour–trade-union circles was from Joan Maynard, then a member of the party's NEC and a farmworkers' leader in Yorkshire. The story continued within the constituency. After the election at which Milne was narrowly defeated, the Labour agent, Peter Mortakis, was fined and barred from office for five years for fiddling election expenses.

The new MP, John Ryman, fox-hunting London-based barrister, was not a regular visitor to his constituency. In 1986 the Blyth Central branch of the constituency party passed a vote of censure on him for not holding advice surgeries and for not attending party meetings. This appeared on the agenda of the GMC. But in the meantime, Ryman announced that he was not going to contest the next election after all.

In December 1986 the constituency selected miners' leader Ronnie Campbell (by then unemployed, following the closure of Blyth pit). During 1986, Mortakis ran for chair of the constituency but was defeated. He and Ryman alleged Militant infiltration (incidentally, the one or two Militant supporters in the constituency had voted with Mortakis against Milne on the grounds that Milne was discrediting the party). Mortakis told journalists, without a smile, that Militant was in league with the Freemasons. They hoped to get the NEC to overturn Campbell's selection. The NEC did hold an inquiry, but found insufficient evidence of 'infiltration' and endorsed Campbell.

Mortakis and Ryman resigned from the party. Ryman is being investigated by the police over alleged irregularities over expenses claims at his London chambers.

In May 1987 the Alliance took control of Blyth Council and at the general election Ronnie Campbell held the seat for Labour with a reduced majority.
11–Patrick Seyd and Lewis Minkin, 'The Labour Party and its Members', *New Society*, September 20, 1979
12–'Disillusion in the Labour Party', *The Times*, February 21, 1968. 'The State of the Labour Party' by Paul Foot in the *Sunday Times*, September 29, 1968, reports a more complicated pattern whereby the state of collapse varies according to the political character of the party. The parties dominated by the left were nearest a state of collapse. Foot concludes: 'More and more the local parties are being run by what Transport House and the regional officers describe as "the right kind of people", by which they mean the younger middle-class, interested in efficiency rather than socialism.'

13–*Guardian*, March 6, 1968

14–Richard Crossman in his Introduction to *The English Constitution*, Fontana, 1963

15–Ken Livingstone explains in an interview with Tariq Ali in *Who's Afraid of Margaret Thatcher?*, Verso, 1984

16–For useful accounts of Wilson in government, see David Coates, *The Labour Party and the Struggle for Socialism*, Cambridge University Press, 1975; David Coates, *Labour in Power*, Longman, 1980; Paul Foot, *The Politics of Harold Wilson*, Penguin, 1968.

17–See *State Intervention in Industry; A Workers' Inquiry*, Spokesman, 1981. See Stuart Holland, *The Socialist Challenge*, Quartet, 1975, for the critique of Keynesian demand management and indicative planning which underlay the 1973 Manifesto.

18–The electoral college is based on 40 per cent trade unions, 30 per cent CLPs and 30 per cent MPs.

19–For the earlier figures, see Patrick Seyd and Lewis Minkin, *New Society*, *op. cit.* The later figures are more approximate, based on interviews with a sample of past and present branch secretaries in the case of Brixton, and on party records in Walworth Road in the case of Widnes.

20–Michael Foot and Shirley Williams, among others, went to speak on Sandelson's behalf.

21–For a full analysis of this historical legacy, see Ralph Miliband, *op. cit.*

22–Lewis Minkin, *The Labour Party Conference*, Manchester University Press, 1980, for a magnificently detailed analysis of this shifting balance.

23–I am grateful to Anthony Barnett for making this connection.

24–In Germany, the Green Party insist that no one is an MP for more than one consecutive session; see Fritjof Capra, *Green Politics – The Global Promise*, Paladin, 1985.

25–Solidarity was formed in 1981 after the collapse of CLV, when most of CLV's members joined the SDP.

26–J. A. Tidball, *A Study of Barnsley Constituency Party*, MA dissertation, Politics department, Sheffield University

27–Richard Rose, *The Problem of Party Government*, revised edition, Penguin, 1976

28–Letter from Roger Godsiff, an APEX official, to R. H. Nethercott, then South-West regional secretary of the T&GWU

29–John Golding is unrepentant: 'They pack, we pack but we pack better than they do.' Many similar episodes have occurred but such detailed documentation is not available.

30–Interviewed on *A Week in Politics*, February 12, 1983. See also E. Heffer, 'An Approach for Labour' in *New Left Review* 140, July–August 1983, and E. Heffer *Labour's Future* Verso 1985.

31–Tom Nairn, *The Glamour of Backwardness* (forthcoming)

32–Peregrine Worsthorne, *Sunday Telegraph*, March 15, 1987

33–Egon Wertheimer, *Portrait of the Labour Party*, Putnam and Sons, 1929

34–Neil Millward & Mark Stevens, *British Workplace Industrial Relations 1980–84*, Gower, 1986 and John Kelly, *Labour and the Unions* Verso 1987

35–*A Week in Politics*, April 10, 1987

36–D. & M. Kogan, *op. cit.*

37–Such developments are not restricted to these three councils: see Chapter 3.

38–Tony Benn is an exception to this, but his ideas on these wider issues are not developed by others on the Labour left. See his two books of edited speeches, *Arguments for Socialism* and *Arguments for Democracy*, Penguin, 1982, and an extended interview with him in *Parliament, People and Power*, Verso, 1982. Outside the Labour Party the work of Raymond Williams, *Parliamentary Democracy*, Socialist Society; 1983, and *Towards 2000*, Chatto & Windus, 1983, and Ralph Miliband, *Capitalist Democracy*, Oxford University Press, 1982, provide at least some of the tools for analysing these connections.

39–Coventry, Liverpool, Newcastle and North Tyneside Trades Councils, *op. cit.* Alan Freeman, *The Benn Heresy*, Pluto Press, 1982

40–Wilson's memo is under the Official Secrets Act.

41–See also *Arguments for Socialism* and *Arguments for Democracy*, *op. cit.*

42–Joe Haines, *The Politics of Power*, Hodder & Stoughton, 1978

43–Richard Crossman analyses 'the secret of Prime Ministerial government' applying the approach of Bagehot's analysis of the 'secret of Cabinet government' in his introduction to Bagehot *op. cit.* But he looked no further.

44–'We were living on borrowed time. But what of the bailiffs, in the shape of the international financial community, from cautious treasurers of international corporations, multi-nationals, to currency operators and money speculators? Would they give us time – to win the support of the miners and take all necessary corrective action?' Harold Wilson, *The Final Term: The Labour Government 1974–76*, Weidenfeld & Nicolson/Michael Joseph, 1979.

45–Vivian Hart, *Distrust and Democracy*, Cambridge University Press, 1978

Chapter 2   The Devil's Mark: Verdict on 1983

1–*Observer*, August 10, 1980

2–Reply to Ivor Crewe on *How Britain Votes*, *Political Studies*, 1987 (see footnote 3), 12, 18, 19

3–Ivor Crewe, 'On the Death of Class Voting: Some Comments on *How Britain Votes*', *Political Studies*, 34, 1986, 620–638. See also Chapter 8 of Särlink and Crewe, *Decade of Dealignment*, Cambridge University Press, 1983

4–Roger Jowell and Colin Airey (eds), *British Social Attitudes: the 1984 Report*, Gower/Social and Community Planning Research, 1984

5–Michael Leapman, *Kinnock*, Unwin Hyman, 1987, p. 57

6–Michael Leapman, *op. cit.*, p. 105

7–For details of the history of Militant and the conflict between it and the party leadership see Michael Crick, *The March of Militant*, Faber & Faber, 1985. Crick's description here and in his earlier book, *Militant*, Faber & Faber, 1982, is very informative. However, I think he takes Militant's grandiose claims and ambitions too seriously. Moreover he does not adequately explain the attraction of Militant, especially for young working-class people, which is, partly at any rate, that it provides sustained, albeit sometimes dogmatic, education in socialist and Labour history and theory which is otherwise almost completely lacking in the Labour Party.

8–See *Sunday Times*, April 12, 1987

9–Denis Healey, *Sunday Times*, September 11, 1983. This and other verdicts are summarised in David Butler and Dennis Kavanagh, *The British General Election of 1983*, Macmillan, 1984.

10–Quoted in Austin Mitchell, *Four Years in the Death of the Labour Party*, Methuen, 1984

11–Eric Hobsbawm, 'Labour's Lost Millions', *Marxism Today*, October 1983

12–'After the Landslide', pamphlet, LCC and 'Open letter to the Left' by Peter Hain of the LCC, available from 9 Poland Street, London, WI, 1983. Also, unpublished essay by Nigel Stanley, a leading member of the LCC, 'Picking Up the Pieces', 1983.

13–Speech by Susan Crosland at the Fabian Society's Crosland Memorial Lecture, March 1980

14–An example of Labour's failure to challenge the terms of public debate would be over defence – both in 1983 and since. Although the party is committed to unilateral disarmament, its leadership accepts, or certainly does not openly challenge, a central premise of the establishment's view of defence: namely, that there is a Soviet threat. Yet on the basis of this premise, Labour's defence policy is unconvincing. In the long run, therefore, Labour suffers from not challenging this premise and thereby failing to shift public opinion.

15–For instance, the priorities identified in the party's 1986 'Freedom and Fairness' campaign were decided upon partly through presenting a list of Labour's policies to a sample of 'floating' Alliance voters and asking them to rank them in order of priority.

16–Pergamon Press, 1984

17–Tony Benn, 'Spirit of Labour Reborn', *Guardian*, June 20, 1983

18–Front page of *Tribune*, with the headline, 'The Guilty Men', documenting the ways in which Shadow Cabinet members and Jim Callaghan had undermined Labour, June 10, 1983

19–See journals such as CND's *Sanity*, the *END Journal*, the publications of the British Society for Responsibility in Science, the Conference of Socialist Economists, the Socialist Society, trade-union and community resources centres, and women's centres throughout the country.

20–The editorial of the first issue declared the new journal to be against 'the politics of pragmatism', in favour of socialist analysis and a forum for the green, feminist, anti-militarist and democratic left. See 'A New Departure', *New Socialist*, 1, September–October 1981.

21–The exceptions to this were through individual researchers in Walworth Road who pushed for such contact; for instance, Roy Green made contact with the shop stewards and trade councils who conducted an inquiry into the industrial policies of the 1974–79 government. There was some desultory regional consultation on industrial policy.

22–A. Heath *et al*, *op. cit.*

23–See survey results reported in Heath *et al*, 'Reply to Ivor Crewe on *How Britain Votes*', *Political Studies*

24–*The New Hope for Britain*, Labour's 1983 Manifesto, p. 12

25–Cf Eric Hobsbawm, 'Labour's Lost Millions', *op. cit.*

26–See Marian Fitzgerald, *Political Parties and Black People*, Runnymede Trust, 1984

27-Opinion polls on GLC policies carried out by Harris on behalf of the GLC and published by Harris Research Centre 1987

28-See Ken Livingstone, *If Voting Changed Anything They Would Abolish It*, Collins, 1987, forthcoming

29-Ibid.

30-Harris Research Centre, *op. cit.*

31-See Geoffrey Foote, *The Political Thought of Labour*, Croom Helm, 1985

32-Frances Morrell, speech at a seminar of the Labour Party's Economic Strategy Group, January 1987

33-The alternative plans, demands and bargaining positions of the shop stewards at Lucas Aerospace, Chrysler, Vickers, Alfred Herberts Machine Tools, British Leyland, British Shipbuilders, C. A. Parsons and elsewhere.

34-See 'Economic Planning and Industrial Democracy', a document produced by the TUC/Labour Party Liaison Committee which contained emasculated proposals for industrial democracy.

35-Golding, one of the NEC members pushing hardest for the expulsion of the Militant editorial board in 1982, went on to say that he 'prefers Militant to the trendies. On our political committee [of the NCU] I must admit I sometimes side with Militant against the trendies always bringing up blacks and women.'

36-See Paul Gilroy, *There Ain't No Black in the Union Jack*, Hutchinson, 1980.

37-Quoted and analysed in Anthony Barnett, *Iron Britannia*, Allison and Busby, 1983 – one of the best studies of the significance of the Falklands War, and Parliament's conduct of it.

38-Gwyn Williams, 'Salvation was Ripe', *Guardian*, 1980

39-See Christopher Hitchens, for example, 'Empty Rhetoric', *New Statesman*, November 1981

40-*Tribune*, November 1980

41-Many of those who said this meant 'from Tony Benn'.

42-Peter Tatchell, *The Battle for Bermondsey*, Heritage Books, 1983

43-See Duncan Campbell, 'The Real Mafia Man', *New Statesman*, August 6, 1982

44-Interview in *New Left Review*, No 49, May–June 1968

45-Michael Foot, *Another Heart and Other Pulses*, Collins, 1984

Chapter 3   Local Experiences

1-I do not discuss the south-east in this book other than London. But there are several south-eastern towns – Basildon, Harlow, Stevenage and Brighton – which are represented in Parliament by Conservatives but have a Labour council. These councils are increasingly responsive to the kind of policies carried out, for instance, on the arts, on women and on employment policy by the GLC. They have joined together to form the South East Economic Development Society (SEEDS) to work on a regional strategy which draws from the GLC's approach.

2-For instance, since 1979 local councils have lost £17 billion in government grants. The government's political objective of destroying the autonomy of local government has enormously strengthened existing centralising pressures in Whitehall.

3-For useful summaries and discussions of recent developments in Labour's municipal politics, see Martin Boddy and Colin Fudge (eds), *Local Socialism*, Macmillan, 1984; John Gyford, *The Politics of Local Socialism*, Allen & Unwin, 1985. These are now somewhat out of date but provide useful background.

4–For a detailed history of the recent GLC administration, see John Carvel, *Citizen Ken*, Chatto & Windus, 1984, and Ken Livingstone, *op. cit.*

5–For a description and critical analysis of these attempts to share power, see Maureen Mackintosh and Hilary Wainwright (eds), *A Taste of Power*, Verso, 1987

6–See GLC Arts and Recreation Committee, *Campaign for a Popular Culture; a Record of Struggle and Achievement – the GLC's Community Arts programme*, William Hampton, 1986

7–Valerie Wise is working on a book which outlines the lessons, positive and negative, of the GLC Women's Committee.

8–For a study of Sheffield politics in the sixties see *Democracy and Community: A Study of the Politics of Sheffield*, Oxford University Press, 1970

9–Allison Young, *The Reselection of MPs*, Heinemann Educational Books, 1983, p. 86

10–In 1981, however, the newly established Employment Department had appointed one Equal Opportunities officer and later an Equal Opportunities Unit with two additional staff. Though their task was an uphill one, it led to the creation of a Women's Employment Forum and to a Women's Technology Workshop, both of which have given the needs and organisation of women an important base in the Department. See Sheffield Council, *The Women's Unit*, 1987

11–Val Stevens, 'The Labour Party in Manchester 1978–84: Policy and Practice', BA Thesis, Manchester Polytechnic.

12–*Sunday Times*, May 1984. Manchester was reported to be top of Norman Tebbit's list of loony left councils. See *Daily Telegraph*, December 15, 1985

13–Stephen Yeo, *Area Unionism*, a paper written in the hope that community associations of various sorts in Brighton would recognise this potential in themselves. At that time, and in that town, there was no chance of stimulus and support from the local council.

14–For further details on the financial background to the Liverpool crisis, see Michael Parkinson, *Liverpool on the Brink*, Policy Journals, 1985.

15–Full report discussed in Michael Parkinson, *op. cit.*, pp. 61–71

16–For a full documentation of this experience, see *The Racial Politics of Militant in Liverpool*, Liverpool Black Caucus. For further analysis of the politics of Militant, see Michael Crick, *The March of Militant*, Faber and Faber, 1986.

17–Amilcar Cabral, *Unity and Struggle*, Heinemann Educational Books, 1980

18–David Green, *Power and Party in an English City*, Allen and Unwin, 1980

19–Ferdinand Mount, *Sunday Telegraph*, June 1986

20–Henry Drucker, *Breakaway*, The Scottish Labour Party, Edinburgh, EUSB, 1978

21–For the history of the STUC, see Angela Tuckett, *The Scottish Trades Union Congress*, Mainstream Publishing, 1986

22–See *Radical Scotland* No. 25

23–The London Labour Party has never been a strong party, since Herbert

Morrison's days (1930s). One problem is the obvious lack of geographic cohesion. Another problem it faces is that, like the Scottish party, it does not directly employ its staff. They are appointed by Walworth Road, and once in post are there virtually for life. The present staff were appointed primarily as supervisor election agents. They have all the skills to organise a good canvass, to identify the Labour voters and bring them in on election day. But they have no experience of the kind of campaigning needed to explain and defend the policies of the GLC and the Labour London Boroughs. Up to 1986 the London Labour Party did not even have a press officer.

24 – London Edinburgh Weekend Return Group, *In and Against the State*, Pluto Press, 1980

25 – For a detailed analysis of the unions in the GLC between 1981 and 1986 see Paul Soto, 'The GLC as Employer', in Maureen Mackintosh and Hilary Wainwright (eds), *op . cit.*

26 – For a critical discussion of the left's experience of management see Dave Morley *et al*, *No Way to Run a Railroad*, Comedia, 1986

27 – For an inspiring and humorous description of the achievement of the Anti-Nazi League and the Rock Against Racism movement, see David Widgery, *Beating Time*, Chatto & Windus, 1985. The initiative and much of the organising drive came from the Socialist Workers' Party, but the new left of the Labour Party was extensively involved.

28 – Keith Bright, ex-managing director of United Biscuits. He was unsympathetic to the policy aims of the new GLC and eased the government transfer of control of London Transport from the GLC to the government. See Maureen Mackintosh's chapters on London Transport in Mackintosh and Wainwright, *op. cit.*

29 – Though the role of the gutter press in giving these councils a bad name should not be underestimated; see Goldsmith's College *Mediawatch*.

Chapter 4   Women and Blacks: What is All the Fuss About?

1 – This cultural and political weakness is more fully analysed by Raymond Williams in *New Socialist*, No. 2, November–December 1981, pp. 28–33.

2 – Sarah Perrigo, 'Socialist Feminism and the Labour Party: Some Experiences in Leeds', *Feminist Review*, No 23, Summer 1986

3 – This theorisation has been begun by Sheila Rowbotham in 'Feminism and Democracy', in *New Forms of Democracy*, ed D. Held, Polity Press, 1987

4 – Some of these arguments are contained in more detail in Sheila Rowbotham, Lynne Segal and Hilary Wainwright, *Beyond the Fragments*, Merlin Press, 1979, and in Lynne Segal, *Is the Future Female?*, Virago Press, 1987, and Anne Phillips, *Divided Loyalties*, Virago, 1986.

5 – This is a point implied by Audrey Wise in *Women and Workers Control*, Spokesman, 1972

6 – Melissa Benn, 'Sisters and Slogans', *Marxism Today*, April 1987

7 – Sarah Perrigo, *op. cit.*

8 – Raymond Williams in a talk to the Socialist Society in June 1981

9 – From Jean McCrindle and Sheila Rowbotham, *Dutiful Daughters*, quoted in Geoff Mulgan and Ken Worpole, *Saturday Night or Sunday Morning?*, Comedia Press, 1986

10–Jill Liddington, *The Life and Times of a Respectable Rebel: Selina Cooper 1864–1946*, Virago, 1984

11–Caroline Rowan, 'Women in the Labour Party', *Feminist Review*, No. 12, 1984

12–Other useful books on the 20th-century history of women and the labour and socialist movement include: Jill Liddington and Jill Norris, *One Hand Tied Behind Us: The Rise of the Women's Suffrage Movement*, Virago, 1978; Sheila Rowbotham, *A New World for Women: Stella Browne – Socialist Feminist*, Pluto Press, 1977

13–Sarah Perrigo, *op. cit.*

14–Judy Sadler, WAC pamphlet, 1981

15–Frances Morrell, 'A Programme for Labour Party Women' in *Why Women Demand Power*, WAC, May 1986

16–*Ibid.*

17–'The Women's Movement and the Labour Party', an interview with Labour Party feminists in *Feminist Review*, No. 16, April 1984.

18–Jenny Beale in *Getting it Together*, Pluto, 1982; Anne Phillips *op. cit.*; Helen Hague in 'Women and the Unions', *Marxism Today*, June 1986; John Edmonds, 'Uniting the Fragments', *New Socialist*, June 1986, all describe or reflect these developments in the unions.

19–The national organisation for black sections was formed in 1984. There are now (April 1987) about twenty black sections. For historical material see the *Black Section Newsletter*; also Trevor Carter, *Shattering Illusions*, Lawrence and Wishart, 1986.

20–Quoted in Paul Foot, *The Politics of Harold Wilson*, Penguin, 1968

21–Richard Crossman, *Diaries* (condensed version), Methuen, 1979, p. 132

22–Paul Foot, *op. cit.* p. 256

23–*Bandung File*, 'Roy Hattersley's Asians', 1985

24–See Marion Fitzgerald, *op. cit.*

25–Enoch Powell, *Guardian*, Agenda, March 11, 1985

26–Stuart Hall, 'The Gulf Between Labour and the Blacks', *Guardian*, Agenda, p. 15, July 1985, also Darcus Howe, *Race Today*.

27–*Sunday Times*, April 1987

Chapter 5   The Unions: Business or Politics?

1–Quoted in Anthony Fenley, 'Labour and the Trade Unions', in Chris Cook and Ian Taylor (eds), *The Labour Party*, Longman, 1980, p. 62

2–For a useful summary of the role of socialists in the formation of the Labour Party see John Lovell, 'Trade Unions and the Development of Independent Labour Politics 1889–1906', in Ben Pimlott and Chris Cook (eds), *Trade Unions in British Politics*, Longman, 1982.

3–Speaking at the 1937 Labour Conference. Quoted in Peter Hain, *Political Strikes*, Penguin, 1986, p. 259

4–See survey of the UCW by M. Moran, in which 50 per cent of them did not realise they were paying the political levy, reported in M. Moran, *The Union of Post Office Workers: a Study in Political Sociology*, Macmillan, 1974

5–Tom Nairn's description of the block vote in 'The Nature of the Labour

Party', in Perry Anderson and Robin Blackburn (eds), *Towards Socialism*, Fontana/New Left Review, 1965

6–See A. Glyn and B. Sutcliffe, *British Capitalism, Workers and the Profit Squeeze*, Penguin, 1972

7–Informal discussions of this kind took place after the 1983 election amongst a group of individuals mostly involved in the Labour Co-ordinating Committee.

8–For details of both these see Coventry, Liverpool, Newcastle and North Tyneside Trades Councils, *op. cit.*

9–Jack Jones was elected General Secretary of the T&GWU in 1968 and led the union for nine years. See his autobiography, *Union Man*, Collins, 1986

10–See Jack Jones, *op. cit.* Chapter 26

11–Clive Jenkins became joint general secretary of ASTMS following the merger of ASSET and ASCW. He had previously, by appointment, been general secretary of ASSET.

12–*Management Today*, May 1986

13–*Observer*, 1976

14–See EETPU rule book

15–See Patrick Wintour, *New Statesman*: Wintour's article provides a very useful summary of the background and recent history of the EETPU. Frank Chapple replied to Wintour's article in the *New Statesman*. A more recent article covering Eric Hammond's leadership of the EETPU is Bob Fryer, 'Why Hammond Mixes it', *New Socialist*, March 1986.

16–Since 1971 there has been a TUC-appointed appeals committee for major disciplinary matters against individuals.

17–This is how the executive committee interprets a rule circularised to branches in 1980.

18–In 1983 the executive decided to abstain in elections for Labour Party Leader and Deputy, as they oppose the electoral college.

19–*Guardian*, July 26, 1980

20–Between 1969, when the elected appeals committee was abolished, and 1971, when the TUC-appointed appeals committee was set up, a number of dissidents were disciplined or expelled.

21–See Linda Melvern, *The End of the Street*, Methuen 1986, Chapter 8

22–See Mark Hollingsworth, 'The Protests Rise within the EETPU', *New Statesman*, February 15 1986

23–EETPU, *Political Bulletin*, April 1981

24–*Financial Times* 10 February, 1981.

25–See report in the *Guardian*, 9 April, 1987. Ironically it is the issue of low pay and the high priority the union put on a statutory minimum wage which is one factor in the pragmatic alliance between Kinnock and Sawyer. For both almost everything is subordinate to winning the election.

26–The action of NUPE members in the north-east was inspired partly by action against privatisation in hospitals elsewhere, in particular Barking in East London and Addenbrookes in Cambridge

27–For a history of NUPE see B. Dix and S. Williams, *Building the Union, Serving the Public*, Lawrence & Wishart, 1987

28–See TUC Congress Report, Brighton, 1986

29–Quoted in Philip Bassett, *Strike Free*, Macmillan, 1986

30–Keith Middlemas, *Politics in Industrial Society: The Experience of British Society Since 1911*, André Deutsch, 1979

31–*The Economy, the Government, and Trade Union Responsibility: A Joint Statement by the TUC and the Government*. HMSO, London, February 1979. For a useful analysis of corporatism in Britain and its consequences for working-class politics, see also Leo Panitch, *Working Class Politics in Crisis*, Verso, 1986.

32–Quoted in Philip Basset, *op. cit.*

33–For details of this evidence and an interview with Arthur Scargill on nuclear energy see *A Nuclear Future*, Socialist Society, 1986

34–Len Murray put it to the *Guardian* on September 5, 1981 like this: 'We are homing pigeons. We home in on power wherever it is, with governments, with employers, with international organisations.'

35–All three approaches are anticipated in a general way by James Prior, Tony Benn and Lionel Murray in the Granada Guildhall Lectures on *The Role of the Trade Unions*, Granada, 1980.

36–Pendulum or 'final offer' arbitration is a system by which the arbitrator is presented with the employer's final offer and the workers' final demand and must simply choose one or the other.

37–*T&GWU Record*, March 1987. See also Bea Campbell, *Marxism Today*, April 1987

38–In *The Miners' Strike*, Routledge & Kegan Paul, 1986.

39–Mark Hollingsworth's notes of his interview

40–Mark Hollingsworth, *Tribune*, January 23, 1987

41–Francis Pym, *The Politics of Consent*, quoted in Bill Schwartz, 'Let Them Eat Coal: The Conservative Party and the Strike' in Huw Beynon (ed), *Digging Deeper*, Verso, 1985

42–John Savile, 'An Open Conspiracy: Conservative Politics and the Miners' Strike 1984–85, in R. Miliband, Leo Panitch, J. Savile, *Socialist Register*, 1985.

43–For a summary description see Doreen Massey and Hilary Wainwright, 'Beyond the Coalfields' in Huw Beynon, *op. cit.* For a more detailed document- ation and analysis see Barbara Bloomfield, Guy Boanes and Raphael Samuel (eds), *The Enemy Within*, Routledge & Kegan Paul, 1987

44–I am grateful to David Miliband for being able to read his excellent BA thesis on the miners' strike (available from the Bodleian Library, Oxford).

45–See John Kelly, *Labour and the Unions*, Verso 1987

46–Peter Jenkins in the *Independent*, April 1, 1987; Peter Kellner, *New States- man*, March 20, 1987

47–The resilience of union organisation even under Thatcherism is documented in *British Workplace Industrial Relations 1980–84* (Surveys by the Department of Employment, the Economic and Social Research Council, the Policy Studies Institute and ACAS), Gower, 1986.

Chapter 6   A Party in Waiting?

1–A statement made in the television series *The Writing on the Wall*, Brook Productions, 1985

2–For reports on the organisation of the campaign, see issues of *Mobilise for*

Labour Democracy 1980–81. For a sense of its impact outside the Labour Party, see Paul Foot, *Letters to a Comrade*, Bookmarx, 1981.

3– Some on the left, for instance Eric Heffer, now consider that the electoral college might be the wrong way to elect the Leader, and that with reselection the PLP would be more democratic. This was a view put forward at the time of the debate on constitutional reforms by an independent left-winger from the north-east in the AEUW delegation in 1979 and 1980, Jim Murray.

4– See Ann Philips, *Hidden Hands*, Virago, 1984, for a useful summary of the debate among socialist feminists about economic strategy. See Raymond Williams, *Towards 2000*, Chatto & Windus, 1983, for a summary of the ecological and green influences on modern socialism. See Mary Kaldor, *The Baroque Arsenal*, André Deutsch, 1981, for the influence of the peace movement on thinking about economic strategy. See the GLC's *Industrial Strategy* for an illustration of all these and other influences at work.

5– See the West Midlands Design Collective, *Nice Work if You Can Get it*, Spokesman, 1985, and the publications of the Centre for Alternative Industrial and Technological Systems (CAITS), North London Polytechnic, London N7

6– See the *Health Hazards Bulletin* produced by the British Society for Responsibility in Science; *Stress at Work*, T&GWU 9/12 Branch, March 1981; Maureen Mackintosh on the implications of one-person-operated buses in 'People's Jobs, People's Lives', Mackintosh and Wainwright *op. cit.*; Issues 1–16 of *Jobs For a Change*, the paper of the GLC's Industry and Employment Branch; Lesley Doyal with Imogent Pennel, *The Politics of Health*, Pluto Press, 1979; David Widgery, *Health in Danger*, Macmillan, 1979.

7– On the division of labour, see Cynthia Cockburn, *Brother*, Pluto Press, 1983, and *Machinery of Dominance*, Pluto Press, 1986; Anne Philips and Barbara Taylor, 'Sex Skill: Notes Towards a Feminist Economics', *Feminist Review* 79–80 (1980); Michele Barrett, *Women's Oppression Today: Problems in Marxist Feminist Analysis*, London, 1980; Peter Fryer, *Staying Power, The History of Black People in Britain*, Pluto Press, 1984; Mike Cooley, *Architect or Bee?* Chatto & Windus, 1987.
On the connections between work and the community see A. Curno *et al*, *Women in Collective Action*, Association of Community Workers in the UK, 1982. Writing on the community involvement in the 1984–85 miners' strike, for instance North Yorkshire Women Against Pit Closures, *Strike 84–85*, Norma Dolby, *Norma Dolby's Diary*, Verso, 1986, Jean McCrindle and Sheila Rowbotham, 'More than Just a Memory', *Feminist Review* 23; Suzanne Mackenzie, 'Women's Responses to Economic Restructuring: Changing Gender, Changing Space', in Roberta Hamilton and Michele Barrett (eds), *The Politics of Diversity*, Verso, 1986.

8– Robin Murray 'Withering Heights', *New Socialist* No 48, April 1987

9– See Andrew Glyn, 'The Economic Case Against Pit Closures', NUM, 1984, *Tribune*, July 10, 17 and 24, and Teresa Hayter, 'Industrial Democracy and GLEB' in Mackintosh and Wainwright, *op. cit.*

10– See Hilary Wainwright and Dave Elliott, *The Lucas Plan: A New Trade Unionism in the Making*, Allison and Busby, 1982. The GLC's Industry and Employment Committee *Report of the Fords Inquiry*

11– Alec Nove's book *The Feasibility of Practical Socialism* provides a stimulating

critique of bureaucratic planning, but in my view does not explore sufficiently
the practicalities of democratic planning.

See also *Market Socialism*, Fabian Society, 1986. The models of market
socialism held up, Yugoslavia, the Mondragon area in the Basque country,
are not wholly relevant, because they are economies which have never faced
such a problem; they moved from petty commodity production to socialism–
co-operativism. Those who generalise from either of these models underestimate the monopolistic character of the modern capitalist economy and the
vast amount of undemocratic planning which goes on within. If this is borne
in mind, there are still important lessons to be learnt both from the Yugoslav
experience and, differently, from Mondragon.

12–See GLEB, *Turning the Tables*, 1984, and FTAT and the GLC's Popular
Planning Unit, *Beneath the Veneer*, 1986

13–This is (or was when I visited Mondragon in 1982) the arrangement among
the Mondragon co-operatives, which are actually more planned – co-operation
between the co-operatives – than some of their more market-oriented advocates
imply. See an essay on the right to work in Mike Rustin, *For a Socialist
Pluralism* Verso, 1985.

14–See Dave Spooner, 'The GLC and Transnationals', in Maureen Macintosh
and Hilary Wainwright, *A Taste of Power*, Verso, 1987. Also, *International
Reports* contains regular reports of such international organisation.

15–Paul Hirst in the *New Statesman* issue on 'The Future of Socialism', in which
he describes, interestingly but rather abstractly, how an economy of democratic
associations might run itself, but says nothing about the historical and struc-
tural conditions for its achievement. Yet these would significantly affect the
character of its political institutions.

16–For an analysis of the historic roots of Labour's attitude to Europe, see John
Palmer, *Crisis in Atlanticism*, Oxford University Press, 1987

17–For a detailed analysis, see Leo Panitch, *op. cit.*

18–Bernard Shaw, Letter to W. P. Johnson, April 24, 1893 in Dan H. Laurence
(ed), *G. B. Shaw: Collected Letters, 1874–1894*, Reinhardt, 1965, p. 389,
quoted in Stephen Yeo, 'Three Socialisms; Statism, Collectivism, Association-
ism' in which is a fascinating discussion of some of the hidden historical roots
of the kind of socialism I am describing in this chapter.

19–Labour Research Department Survey of support for the miners. The results
are summarised in *Solidarity with the Miners*, Labour Research Department,
1985.

20–See Raphael Samuel's introduction to R. Samuel, Barbara Bloomfield, Guy
Boanes, *The Enemy Within*, Routledge & Kegan Paul, 1987

21–Red Wedge was formed in 1986. It is an organisation started by artists,
musicians, young actors and writers to create, through the world of the arts,
a 'fresh and direct approach to politics'. Red Wedge believes that 'everyone
is a star. It's time we started treating each other like one.'

22–*Financial Times*, February 9 1987

23–In recent German elections the Green Party obtained up to 13% of the vote
in some areas. Recent opinion polls in Denmark give the radical People's
Socialist Party 16% of the vote. And in Holland, Finland and Italy radical
socialist and green parties have made considerable advances.

24 – For arguments from the left against proportional representation see Peter Hain, *Proportional Misrepresentation*, Wildwood House, 1987, and arguments for see Arthur Scargill in *New Left Review* 1986, Dave Cook 'Proportional Representation – Threat or Opportunity', *Marxism Today*, Mike Rustin, *op. cit.*

25 – The shift to the right in party policy over the last year or so is not an indication of a similar move in the constituencies. It is more a reflection of the increased centralisation of the policy-making process. There has however been a surge of loyalty to the leadership in the last year (1986–87), an expression of the overriding desire for a Labour government.

Chapter 7   After 1987: Just an Electoral Machine?

1 – There were criticisms of the lack of democracy under the old system, but as Eric Robinson, Director of Preston Polytechnic and a member of the previous NEC Education Committee put it in a letter to the General Secretary, 'Geoff Bish's circular, [sent to all sacked members of the old committees] implies the use of specialist expertise in future on a more informal and even less democratic basis than in the past.'

2 – See report of MORI poll, *Sunday Times*, May 17, 1987

3 – See R. Bhaskar, *Scientific Realism and Human Emancipation*, Verso, 1986, Chapter 2, Section 2, for a fuller discussion of the philosophical underpinnings. Also his *The Possibility of Naturalism*, Harvester Press, 1979, Chapter 2, Sections 2–4.

4 – Much of this mainly back-bench opposition comes from members of the Campaign Group of MPs, although individual members of the Tribune Group have scored notable propaganda successes – for instance Robin Cook on the City and Zircon. The Campaign Group was formed in 1982 as an attempt to organise the links – established during the campaign for constitutional reforms and for Tony Benn as Deputy Leader – between left MPs and the left outside Parliament. The new 1987 MPs have significantly expanded the Group's base to include a strong group of women (for example Dawn Primarolo from Bristol, Audrey Wise from Preston, Mildred Gordon from Tower Hamlets, and Joan Ruddock, ex-chairwoman of CND, from Deptford), four black MPs, and men from the radical left such as Ken Livingstone, or from campaigning working-class CLPs such as Pat Wall from Bradford North. Some of these are also members of the Tribune Group. Media labels give the impression of a cohesive, disciplined group, the epitome of their image of the 'hard left'. But in fact, like most of what the press and Labour leaders brand in this way, it is a complex combination of socialists, with a variety of backgrounds, either in Labour Party politics, the trade unions, community, feminist, black and peace movements, or in some combination of them all. As a parliamentary force, the Group can tend to be sectarian in its approach – an understandable protection against the compromising pressures of Westminster. However, in the Shadow Cabinet election in June 1987 it was the right wing of the Tribune Group who proved to be the sectarians by refusing to agree to a joint slate. Moreover, in its work with wider struggles and movements, the Campaign Group appears increasingly open to and supportive of the new ideas and debates emerging in reaction to the failures of Labourism.

Acknowledgements

At first I was anxious at the prospect of writing a book on my own. In the past I have always worked with someone else, usually as part of some political or trade-union project. However, one way or another the writing of this book has involved just as many people as the previous books, even if, in the end, it is I alone who must take the flak.

It took a deep breath to embark on it and my first thanks must go to Anthony Barnett, as editor of the Tigerstripe series, for encouraging to me to plunge in and for cheering me on as I went. When the first draft was ready he read it through and together with several others gave me comments which made me more confident in my arguments and enabled me to improve it. I am especially thankful to him. Other people who helped in this way were Doreen Massey, Ralph Miliband, Jim Mortimer, Leo Panitch and Mike Rustin. I am grateful to them all for reading a weighty unpruned manuscript at speed and providing very useful comments and criticisms. Peter Hain managed a quick read in the middle of his election campaign and gave me helpful comments. Anthony Arblaster and Reg Race gave it a last-minute read which led me to make what I hope are some final improvements.

Several others gave me invaluable comments, corrections or encouragement on particular sections. Tony and Caroline Benn, John Bennington, Robin Blackburn, John Bohanna, Phil Bradbury, Ian Brown, Kevin Davey, Bill Gilby, Slim Hallett, Mark Hollingsworth, Fran Holmwood, John Kelly, Jane Kenrick, Nick Lewis, Anne McDermid, Andy McSmith, Pat Masters, Narendra Makenji, Chris Mullin, Jill Page, John Palmer, Sarah Perrigo, Anne Philips, Anita Pollock, Sheila Rowbotham, Tom Sawyer, Lynne Segal, Geoff Sheridan, Steve Stevenson, Graham Stringer, Tessa Wainwright, and Patrick Wintour. Some of these, like Tony Benn, Ian Brown, Narendra Makenji, Jill Page, Tom Sawyer, Graham Stringer and Steve Stevenson were people whom I interviewed in the course of my research. They went far beyond the call of the duty of an interviewee in digging out further material, reading the relevant section and putting me in touch with others to interview. I really felt at times quite taken aback by their helpfulness to a time-consuming nosyparker like me. I hope when they read the book that this will not turn out to have been a complete waste of time, even where they disagree. And I nominate Tony Benn and his secretary, Kathy Ludbrook archivists of the year.

This book had to be done at some speed. Two people in particular made this possible: Gordon Donald and Peter Bleyer, by helping in their spare time to follow up references, track down library books and file six filing drawers full of material. They and their friends also helped me to carry out a survey of 60 randomly chosen constituency party delegates at the 1986 conference. Thanks to all of them and to the willing interviewees as well. I am also grateful to several others who helped with information: Bill Bush, Jane Thomas at the *New Statesman*, Pat Francis and her colleagues at the Labour Party Library, Moira Williamson, Philip Whitehead and Lucy Needham at *A Week in Politics*, Brian Gorschuck at MORI, staff at *Weekend World*, Tariq Ali at *Bandung File*, Sally Keble and Joy Copley at GMB, Harold Frayman at *Labour Weekly*, Vera and Vladimir Dierer of the Campaign for Labour Party Democracy, and Nick Richmond and my brother Martin Wainwright at the *Guardian*.

I list all those who I interviewed below and I owe them a special thanks for being willing to spend so long and in most cases to be so frank when they had no control over my use of what they said. I hope none of them feel abused, and that where they disagree with my analysis they will at least understand my point of view as I hope I understand theirs. There are several people who went out of their way to give advice, hospitality and in some instances to suggest and help arrange further interviews. For this I am especially grateful to Huw Beynon, Jim and Debbie Coulter, Bob Fryer, Hilary Knight, Geoff Green, Ray Challinor, Kenny Bell, Joyce Keane, Bob Davis, Jean Mackenzie, Tony Mainwaring, Tom Nairn, George Kerevan, Patrick Seyd, Mike Ward, Stuart Weir, Johnathan Upton and Stephen Yeo. Karen Miller and her colleagues at The Typing Pool typed many of the tapes and did so with great patience and intelligence. I could not have written the book without them.

In addition, I must thank the Open University for providing me with some funds at a crucial stage, especially for the research involved in Chapter 3 on the more innovative of Labour local authorities. Especial thanks to Alan Cochrane, Dean of the Social Sciences Faculty for arranging this.

In the final, and psychologically most difficult stages of writing this book I was helped enormously by the personal support and editing skill of Chatto's editor Jenny Uglow, and the immensely patient skilled teamwork of Jane Turner, Robert Lacey, and others at Chatto. In spite of all this help it can be an isolating task writing a book. Sheila Rowbotham kept up a constant flow of intriguing gossip and ideas, Kevin Davey and others in the *Socialist Society* provided a regular sounding board, and John and Joan Bohanna, shop stewards at Fords and Glaxo sent me constant encouragement and criticism from the front line. Above all the person who kept me sane even if my work at times drove him crazy was Roy Bhaskar. He put up with everything and read everything and I am eternally grateful.

People interviewed for this book

Hassan Ahmed (Chair of the Nottingham East Black Section)
Ragib Ahsan (Birmingham Labour Party, Textile Low Pay Unit).
Graham Allen (Now MP for Nottingham North)
Jane Andrews (Islington North Labour Party)
Sharon Atkin (Selected Prospective Candidate for Nottingham East, suspended as PPC by the National Executive Committee)
Anne Ayre (Unemployed Women's Action Group, Glasgow)
Hector Barlow (Member of EETPU Executive from Scotland)

Roger Barton (Sheffield Councillor, Secretary of Sheffield Trades Council and Sheffield District Party)

John Bailey (ex-Sun NGA member)

Jeremy Beecham (Leader Newcastle Council)

Tony Benn (MP for Chesterfield)

Meg Beresford (General Secretary CND)

Phil Blayer (Trade Union Liaison Officer at the West Midlands Enterprise Board)

David Blunkett (Now MP for Sheffield Brightside)

Phil Bradbury (GMC Delegate and past officer Newham North East CLP)

John Bohanna (Senior T&GWU steward, Fords Halewood)

Ben Bousquet (Founder member black sections)

Roland Boyes (MP for Houghton and Washington)

Ian Brown (*Flashlight*, EETPU)

Nick Burden (TASS Official and North London co-ordinator of Trade Unions for Labour).

Tom Burlison (Regional Secretary of the Northern Region of the GMB)

Bill Bush (Ex-Head of the Labour Members' secretariat at the GLC, now works for ILEA)

Barry Camfield (T&GWU South East Organiser)

Pete Carter (Communist Party Industrial Organiser)

Barbara Castle (Cabinet minister in three Labour governments now MEP for Greater Manchester West)

Cathy Chaplin (Keresley Miners' Wives)

Campbell Christie (General Secretary of the STUC)

Bob Clay (MP for Sunderland North)

Mike Conerty (Stirling Council and Scottish Labour Co-ordinating Committee)

Robin Cook (MP for Livingston)

Jeremy Corbyn (MP for Islington North)

Jim Coulter (Barnsley Labour Party and NUM)

David Cowling (Polling expert and previously assistant to Peter Shore)

Michael Crick (Author of two books on Militant)

Walter Cunningham (T&GWU Convener, Hull Docks)

Anna-Joy David (Political Co-ordinator Red Wedge)

Teresa Davies (Birmingham Women's Section)

Vladimir Dierer (CLPD)

Bill Dodds (Newcastle Councillor; Newcastle East CLP)

John Edmonds (General Secretary of the GMB)

David Edwardes (Coventry Councillor)

Murray Elder (Research Officer for the Scottish Labour Party)

Mike Elliott (Chair Sheffield District Party – at the time of interview)

Chris Farrands (Nottingham East CLP)

Jean Ferguson (NUPE Branch Secretary Newcastle Royal Infirmary)

Paul Field (Coventry Workshop – a trade-union and community resource centre)

John Foster (Branch Organiser North Tyneside NALGO)

John Foster (Scottish Marxist historian)

Cath Fry (Secretary, Manchester District Labour Party)

William Gannom (member EETPU Executive from the South-west Region.)

John Golding (Previously MP for Newcastle Under Lyme and member of the NEC, now General Secretary of the NCU)

Evelyn Gorham (Doncaster Women's Section)

Bryan Gould (Election Campaign Organiser, now shadow minister for Trade and Industry)

Bernie Grant (MP for Haringey, founder member black sections)

Judy Green (Officer, Newcastle Council, North Tyneside Labour Party)

Roy Green (Researcher on economic and industrial policy, Walworth Rd)

Walter Greendale (Ex-Chair T&GWU)

Karen Greenwood (GC delegate Islington North Labour Party)

Peter Hain (Member of the Labour Co-ordinating Committee and author of several books on the new Labour left)

Carol Haslan (Harlow Labour Party)

Billy Hayes (UCW Broad left)

Peter Heathfield (General Secretary of the NUM)

Eric Heffer (MP for Liverpool Walton)

Fred Higgs (T&GWU officer South East Region)

Keith Hodgson (Education Officer Northern Division of NUPE)

Sarah Hodgson (Party Womens' Officer in Bradford)

Phil Holt (NCU Broad left and secretary of the Broad left mobilising committee)

Fran Homewood (Sheffield Council)

Tony Hood (Liverpool Councillor 1983–86)

George Hope (Ex-Regional Organiser for AUEW–TASS in Coventry)

Ann Howard (Sheffield District Labour Party)

Lucy Huberman (Steering Committee, Red Wedge)

Helen Jackson (Chair of the Employment Committee, Sheffield Council)

Tony Jennings (Ex-Merseyside County Councillor, Liverpool Councillor 1986–87)

Doreen Lartey (Secretary Bentink Tennants Association, Newcastle)

Mark Lazarowicz (Leader Edinburgh Council and leading member of Scottish LCC)

Phil Lenton (NUPE Organiser, Northern Region)

Colin Lindsay (Coventry Trades Council)

Ken Livingstone (MP for Brent North)

Tommy Lyons (EETPU Convener Port Talbot Steel Works)

Mary Kaldor (Labour Party defence advisor; editor of END Journal)

John Kirby (NALGO, Sheffield Council)

Roger Kline (Birmingham Trade Union Resource Centre)

Cathy Maines (Newcastle Councillor; Newcastle Central Constituency)

Jack McConnell (Stirling Council and Scottish Labour Co-ordinating Committee)

Willie McElvey (MP for Kilmarnock and Loudon)

Alex McFadden (Newcastle Trades Council Centre for the Unemployed)

Tina Mackay (Birmingham Trade Union Resource Centre)

Ellen McLaughlan (Women's Section, Glasgow Maryhill CLP)

Walter Mclellan (Strathclyde Councillor)

Ken Macmillan (NUPE organiser Scotland)

Jock MacQuinn (AUEW Broad left)

Narendra Makenji (Haringey and national black sections)

Val Manchee (Newcastle Women's Section)

Peter Mandelson (Head of Labour Party Communications)

Michael Meadowcroft (Previously Liberal MP for Leeds West; Member of CND Council)

Alan Milburn (Trade Union Information and Studies Unit, and Newcastle Central CLP)

David Morgan (Sheffield Councillor)

Jim Mortimer (General Secretary Labour Party 1982–85)

Jane Morris (Ex-Islington Councillor; Islington North Constituency)

Chris Mullin (Editor of *Tribune* 1982–84, now MP for Sunderland South)

Robin Murray (Secretary Sheffield Attercliffe CLP)

Mo O'Toole (Newcastle Councillor; Newcastle Central Constituency)

George Nicholson (Ex-Chair of GLC's Planning Committee, member of Labour Party Joint Policy Committee)

Jill Page (Leeds Women's Council, member of National Women's Advisory Council.)

Judith Parsons (Women's Section, Glasgow Maryhill CLP)

Ann Pettifer (Women's Action Committee)

Liz Philipson (ASTMS delegate to Labour Party Conference, member of ASTMS London Regional Council)

Dick Pickering (President of the GMB at the time of interview)

Steve Pickering (GMB official and East Midlands Co-ordinator of Trade Unions for Labour)

Anita Pollock (Newham North East Labour Party)

Mike Power (Campaign for Press and Broadcasting Freedom)

John Prescott (At the time of interview Shadow minister for Employment, and now Shadow minister for Energy)

Dawn Primarolo (MP for Bristol South)

Pauline Purnell (Birmingham Women's Section)

John Rentoul (Branch Delegate to the Stepney Labour Party)

Jo Richardson (Front-bench spokesperson on Women; MP for Barking)

Steve Riley (T&GWU Branch Secretary Fords Dagenham)

George Robertson (MP for Hamilton)

Sarah Roeloff (Women's Action Committee)

Tom Sawyer (Deputy General Secretary of NUPE)

Victor Schonfield (CLPD)

John Shiers (Ex-Chair Manchester District Party)

Kevin Scally (Expelled from Birmingham Sparkbrook CLP for revealing mass applications to join the party, but later reinstated by the NEC)

Maureen Shevlin (Coventry Women's Section)

Bill Spiers (Chair of the Scottish Labour Party)

Nigel Stanley (Member of the Labour Co-ordinating Committee)

Steve Stevenson (*Flashlight*, EETPU)

Teresa Stewart (Ex-Chair of Birmingham Social Services Committee)

Val Stevens (Manchester Councillor)

Isabel Stone (Sheffield Positive Action Project)

Gavin Strang (MP for Edinburgh East)

Graham Stringer (Manchester District Councillor)

Ann Suddick (Durham Miners' Support Groups, now Links)
Ken Ternent (Trade Union Information and Studies Unit, Newcastle)
John Tidball (Ex-South Yorkshire County Councillor, Barnsley Labour Party)
John Tocher (Secretary Manchester AEU District Committee)
Nigel Todd (Newcastle Councillor)
Mark Wadsworth (Press Officer Black Sections)
Steve Walmsley (NUPE Branch Secretary Sheffield Council)
David Warburton (GMB Political Liaison Officer)
Mike Ward (Ex-Chair of GLC's Industry and Employment Committee, now Director of the Centre for Local Economic Studies)
Nigel Williamson (Editor of Tribune at the time of interview, currently Editor of New Socialist)
Joyce Wilson (NUPE Shop Steward, Newcastle Royal Infirmary)
Audrey Wise (Member the National Executive Committee, now MP for Preston)
Valerie Wise (Ex-Chair of GLC Women's Committee)
Heather Woods (Easington Labour Party)
Alex Woods (Edinburgh Councillor, previously Leader of the Council)
Anna Wyatt (Chief Executive, Sheffield Council)

I also interviewed several others who would prefer not to be named and had several group discussions in Sheffield, Glasgow, Newcastle, Birmingham, Coventry, Harlow, Manchester and London which included party members not listed here.

Thanks also to the NUPE delegation at the Women's TUC and several members of the UCATT delegation at the TUC.

Index

330 LABOUR: A TALE OF TWO PARTIES